BARRON'S
FOREIGN LANGUAGES

201
MANDARIN
CHINESE
VERBS

SECOND EDITION

Compounds and Phrases for Everyday Usage

Eugene and Nora Ching
The Ohio State University

Ling Yan
Columbia University

Civic Center

BARRON'S

Dedicated to our father,
Professor Tieh-han Chao,
a devoted teacher and scholar

© Copyright 2007, 1977 by Barron's Educational Series, Inc.

All inquiries should be address to:
Barron's Educational Series, Inc.
250 Wireless Blvd.
Hauppauge, New York 11788
www.barronseduc.com

Library of Congress Catalog Card No. 2007002593

ISBN-13: 978-0-7641-3761-7
ISBN-10: 0-7641-3761-1

Library of Congress Cataloging in Publication Data
Ching, Eugene, 1921–
   201 Mandarin Chinese verbs : compounds and phrases for everyday usage / Eugene and Nora Ching,
Ling Yan. — 2nd ed.
      p. cm
  English and Chinese.
  Includes bibliographical references.
  ISBN-13: 978-0-7641-3761-7 (alk. paper)
  ISBN-10: 0-7641-3761-1 (alk. paper)
  1. Chinese language—Verb. 2. Chinese language—Terms and phrases. I. Ching, Nora C.,
1937–   II. Yan, Ling. III. Title.
  PL1235.C5 2007
  495.1 '5—dc22   2007002593

PRINTED IN THE UNITED STATES OF AMERICA
9 8 7 6 5 4 3 2 1

CONTENTS

PREFACE

Since Chinese is an uninflected language, the format of this book is unique. Instead of the neat conjugation tables, which the verbs of other languages have, for each of the 201 monosyllabic verbs selected, the most useful compounds, phrases, and idioms containing the verb are listed. Although most of them remain verbs in these contexts, some of them may not. To show the differences, grammatical labels are used. It is hoped that students who became familiar with the characteristics of these classifications will be able to use the entries as an active part of their knowledge of Chinese. Considering the items listed under the 201 monosyllabic verbs, we could have called this book *201 Mandarin Chinese Verbs*.

In the preparation of this book, the first problem is a matter of selection. In principle, only free forms should have been selected. However, a few bound forms are included because of the useful constructions in which they are components. Some free forms are omitted not because of they are rarely used but because of the paucity of the constructions in which they are components. Entries under each verb have been selected also for their frequency and usefulness. For verbs with few entries, some items not so frequently used may be included as well as more examples. For verbs with abundant expressions, the problem becomes a painful process of elimination. Nevertheless, we have tried to exclude those lexical terms which are easily found in a dictionary and those combinations which are synthesizable or endocentric. In other words, special emphasis is given to items of which the real meaning or grammatical function can not be readily figured out just by examining the components. Although items with the monosyllabic verb as the initial component are the overwhelming majority of the entries, items in which it occupies other positions may also be listed after the former, both alphabetically.

The second problem we face is the labeling of the entries. For many of them labeling is not difficult. For some, we have to leave them unanalyzed and unclassified. For verbal constructions, we have to limit our labels to V (for verb) and SV (for status verbs, including quality verbs). Beyond those, we urge our readers to consult *A Grammar of Spoken Chinese* if our introduction in this book cannot help. Adj (for adjective) is used to indicate an item which is primarily used as a nominal modifier, unlike a status verb which may also be used as a predicate. The labels are usually in this order: analysis of construction/classification of form class. Classification of form class may be omitted whenever it is obvious. For example, when a V-O (verb-object) is in its usual role as a verbal, only V-O is given. However, when a V-O functions as a noun or transitive verb, N or TV will follow: V-O/N or V-O/TV. In order to take care of the ionization problem of a verb-object construction, VO is for solid verb-object, V-O for limited separability, and VO for phrases. Although the labels are given last for each entry, they are for the entries themselves rather than for the examples.

Wherever possible, English translations follow this order: literal translation precedes an approximate equivalent separated by a slant (/). A comma or semicolon instead of a slant would mean that the item may be used both literally and figuratively. For example, *zǒu mǎ kàn huā* means literally "to view the flowers on horseback" while it is used for "going over things quickly." *Chī dòufu* means both "to eat bean curd" and "to flirt."

These two items are listed as follows:

zǒu mǎ kàn huā	走馬看花	to view the flowers on horseback/to go over things quickly
chī dòufu	吃豆腐	to eat bean curd, to flirt

One other problem lies in the treatment of verbs with different pronunciations and/or different ideographic written forms. Some have been treated as different verbs listed on separate pages, such as *dǎo* 倒 and *dào* 倒, *zuò* 作 and *zuò* 做. Many have been put together with the differences marked, such as *dāng* 當 and *dàng* 當, *diào* 調 and *tiáo* 調, and *qìngjia* under *qīn* 親. *Yóu* 遊 and *yóu* 游 are treated as one word. The romanization system used in the book is the one known as *pinyin*, officially adopted by the People's Republic of China in 1957. Other systems which are commonly used in this country are presented in the appended contrastive table. Chinese characters for the entries are those of the regular forms. A table to show the difference between the regular and simplified forms is also appended in the back of the book.

To prepare a book of this nature, we have consulted many dictionaries and vocabulary lists. The ones we depend upon heavily are Lin Yutang's *Chinese-English Dictionary of Modern Usage*, Wang Yi's *Kuo Yu Tz'u Tien*, Matthews' *Chinese-English Dictionary*, He Jung's *Kuoyu Jihpao Tz'u Tien*. Appendix II, "From Regular to Simplified Characters" is taken from *Jianhuazi Zongbiao Jianzi*, published by Wenzi Gaige Chubanshe with the asterisks and footnote reference numbers removed. It is hardly necessary to say that we owe Professor Y. R. Chao more than anybody else for drawing freely from his monumental work *A Grammar of Spoken Chinese*. If anything has been left unexplained, answers will be found from his book. Our gratitude is due to some of our students who, after using some of our trial pages, enthusiastically endorsed this project. James R. Moore and Josephine Matthews participated in the final stages of the project. In this connection we wish to thank the federally supported work-study program for making it possible for them to work for us. Our thanks are also due to Mr. Charles Lin, who did the calligraphical work, and to Mrs. Gloria Corrigan for putting our manuscript in a form which is ready for the camera. To Professor Fang-yu Wang who read the manuscript and offered valuable suggestions we wish to express our sincere thanks also. It goes without saying, all the mistakes remain our own.

INTRODUCTION

This introduction discusses the major differences between the Chinese verb and the English verb, gives a brief description of the Chinese verb, particularly in relation with aspect markers, adverbs of degree, reduplication, and compounds, and provides examples in which Chinese verbs are used. Since there are not any neat conjugation tables to begin with, this introduction may offer a kind of framework in which the question how Chinese verbs function may in a very modest way be answered.

THE DIFFERENCE BETWEEN THE CHINESE VERB
AND THE ENGLISH VERB

As Chinese is not an inflective language, it is not possible to construct a Chinese conjugation. We must adopt a different approach for *201 Mandarin Chinese Verbs*. Let us begin by discussing some unique qualities of Chinese verbs.

First, Chinese verbs do not indicate tense. Whether they are used in the past, present, or future, the form of the verb remains the same. For example, the verb *chī* "to eat" is always *chī* in each of the following sentences:

Cóngqián wǒ chī Zhōngguó fàn.	"Formerly I ate Chinese food."
Xiànzài wǒ chī Zhōngguó fàn.	"Now I eat Chinese food."
Jiānglái wǒ chī Zhōngguó fàn.	"In the future I shall eat Chinese food."

Note that in each of the above examples, the tense of the Chinese sentence is expressed by such time words as *cóngqián*, *xiànzài*, etc. while the tense of the English sentence has to be indicated by the verb itself.

Second, Chinese verbs do not indicate person or number. Whether the subject is in first, second, or third person, singular or plural, the form of the verb is always the same. For example:

Wǒ chī Zhōngguó fàn.	"I eat Chinese food."
Nǐ chī Zhōngguó fàn.	"You eat Chinese food."
Tā chī Zhōngguó fàn.	"He (or she) eats Chinese food."

In the above sentences, if any of the subjects had been in plural number, the verb would still have been *chī*.

Third, Chinese verbs, particularly the dissyllabic ones, may be used as nouns without changing their morphological forms. For example, *dàibiǎo* may be "to represent" or "a representative"; *xuǎnjǔ*, "to elect" or "an election." Of course, English has verbs like "walk," "work," "vote," etc., which may all be used as nouns; but this kind of class overlap is more common in Chinese.

Fourth, Chinese verbs include adjectives. *Gāo* "tall," for example, may be used attributively in *gāo lóu* "a tall building," or predicatively without the verb "to be" as in *Tā gāo* "He is tall."

Fifth, English prepositional expressions are verbal expressions in Chinese. "In New York" would be *zài Niǔyuē*; "work for me," *gěi wo zuòshì*; "eat with chopsticks," *yòng kuàizi chī.*

Sixth, unlike English, Chinese verbs have no voice distinction. The forms for both active and passive voices are the same. Only the context can give some clue to the direction of the action. For example, in *Wǒ xiǎng chī fàn* "I would like to eat," and in *Fàn hái méi chī ne* "The food has not been eaten yet," without any change, *chī* is in the active voice in the former sentence while it is in the passive in the latter. *Yú hái méi chī ne* may mean the active voice "The fish has not eaten yet." or the passive voice "The fish has not been eaten yet." Only the context makes the intended meaning clear.

Naturally, this increased reliance on context for clarity has, in turn, led to preferred syntactical patterns. The topic-comment pattern is very common in Chinese. In English a topic is usually introduced by a preposition, while in Chinese a topic can take the position of the subject, even though it may not be the beginning point of the action. Using the same examples given to illustrate the lack of voice distinction of verbs in Chinese, we can say that in *Fàn hái méi chī ne* and *Yú hái méi chī ne*, both *fàn* and *yú* may be considered the topic of the sentence; *hái méi chī ne* is the comment that can be another sentence with the subject omitted.

Fàn (wǒ) hái méi chī ne.	"So far as the food is concerned, (I) have not eaten it yet."
Yú (wǒ) hái méi chī ne.	"So far as the fish is concerned, (I) have not eaten it yet."

From the translations we can see that in English, we have to introduce these topics with "so far as . . . is concerned," "concerning . . . ," "talking about . . . ," etc.

While verbal sentences are preferred in English, adjectival sentences are often preferred in Chinese. For example:

"He eats a lot."	*Tā chīde hěn duō.*	(Literally, what he eats is very much.)
"He walks very fast."	*Tā zǒude hěn kuài.*	(Literally, his walking is very fast.)

With this understanding, a student of Chinese as a foreign language should avoid the following mistake:

Although *Wo bùshuō Zhōngguó huà hěn hǎo* means "It is very good that I don't speak Chinese," an English speaker may mistakenly use it for "I don't speak Chinese very well," which has to be the adjectival sentence *Wǒde Zhōngguó huà shuōde bùhǎo* (literally, "So far as my Chinese is concerned, the speaking is not good."). This point has been reinforced by Professor Y. R. Chao in A *Grammar of Spoken Chinese*, in which he says that Chinese adjectives are used predominantly in the predicative positions.[1] The example he gives is *Wǒmen rén duō, cháwǎn shǎo, chá gòule wǎn búgòu.* Literally, it means "So far as we are concerned, people are many, teacups are few, tea is enough but cups are not enough." Idiomatic English would be "There are many of us but few teacups; we have enough tea, but not enough cups."[2]

Aside from purely grammatical considerations, other differences, like unequal ranges of meaning with lexical items and different cultural settings for usage often appear when we compare Chinese and English. *Wánr* for example, means "play." However, one cannot but feel uncomfortable when one translates *Yǒu kòngr qǐng dào wǒ jiā lái wánr* into "When you have time, please come to my house to play." Conversely, "He plays an important role in this matter" can hardly be translated into *Tā duì zhèi jiàn shì wánr zhòngyàode rènwù.* "Visit" would probably be a better translation for *wánr*, even though the Chinese version for "visit" is usually *bàifǎng. Zhàn zhòngyàode wèizhi* (literally, "occupy an important location") probably should be used for "play an important role." Cultural differences usually dictate different responses to similar stimuli under similar situations. An American accepts a compliment with "Thanks," while a Chinese, at least in appearance, tries hard to deny it by saying *Náli Náli*, literally, "Where, where?"[3]

WHAT IS A CHINESE VERB?

A Chinese verb has been defined as "A syntactic word which can be modified by the adverb *bù* (except for the verb *yǒu* "to have," which takes *méi*) and can be followed by the phrase suffix *le*."[4] These are the two common characteristics shared by all verbs in Chinese. Without going into the finer divisions of the Chinese verb, the following major types may be recognized:[5]

(1) **Action verbs**: intransitive verbs like *lái* "to come," *qù* "to go," *zuò* "to sit," etc; transitive verbs like *kàn (xì)* "to see (a play)," *chī (fàn)* "to eat (food)," *shā (rén)* "to kill (people)," etc.
(2) **Quality verbs**: intransitive verbs or adjectives like *dà* "big," *hǎo* "good," *xíng* "all right," etc.; transitive verbs like *ài (cái)* "to love (wealth)," *xìn (jiào)* "religious," *yǒu (qián)* "to have (money), rich," etc.
(3) **Stative verbs**: *bìng* "to be sick," *zuì* "to be drunk," *è* "to be hungry."
(4) **Classificatory verbs**: *xìng (Lǐ)* "to have the family name of (*Lǐ*)," *zuò (guān)* "to serve as (an official)," *dāng (bīng)* "to serve as (a soldier)," etc.

1. Y. R. Chao, *A Grammar of Spoken Chinese*, Berkeley, California, University of California Press, 1968, p. 679.
2. *Ibid.*
3. Eugene Ching, "Cultural Implications in the Teaching of Chinese," *Papers of the CIC Far Eastern Language Institute, University of Michigan, 1963*, edited by Joseph K. Yamagiwa, Ann Arbor, Michigan, 1964.
4. Y. R. Chao, *Mandarin Primer*, Cambridge, Mass., Harvard University Press, 1947, p. 47.
5. In the body of the book, verbs are not even classified in this manner. As has been mentioned in the Preface, only (V) and (SV) are used as labels to denote their functions. Examples are given wherever possible to show the usage.

(5) **Auxiliary verbs**: *huì* (*fēi*) "can (fly)," *xiǎng* (*shuì*) "would like to (sleep)," *kěn* (*zuò*) "willing to (do it)," etc.
(6) **Shì and yǒu**: *shì* (*rén*) "is a person," *yǒu* (*shū*) "to have (a book)," etc.

Verbs may be discussed in terms of their behavior with **aspect markers -*le*, -*guo*, -*zhe*, etc.**, **adverbs of degree *hěn*, *gèng*, etc., reduplication, compounds**.

ASPECT MARKERS

-*Le* as a word suffix should be distinguished from .*le* as a phrase suffix. Although all verbs may be followed by .*le*, only transitive verbs of Types (1) and (2) may be followed by -*le* without any restrictions. Intransitive verbs take the suffix -*le* only before cognate objects or quantified objects, as in *bìngle sāntiān* "sick for three days."[6] The two *le*'s are used primarily for complete action and new situations, often the two sides of the same thing: a new situation takes place after something has been completed.[7] It is wrong to assume that completed action is the same past tense as in English. Let's examine the following sentences:·

(1)	*Wǒ zuòle.*	"I did it."
(2)	*Wǒ zuòle cái néng zǒu.*	"I cannot leave until I have done it."
(3)	*Wo zuòle cái zǒu de.*	"I didn't leave until I had done it."
(4)	*Zuòle zài shuō, hǎo ma?*	"Talk about it after it's done, O.K.?"

In the above sentences, *zuòle* has been used in each case without any formal change. It is interesting to note that the negative versions of the sentences reveal the nature of the verb even more clearly. Compare those four sentences with their negative versions.

(1)	*Wǒ méizuò.*	"I didn't do it."
(2)	*Wǒ búzuò jiù bùnéng zǒu.*	"I can't leave if I don't do it."
(3)	*Wǒ méizuò jiù zǒu le.*	"I left before I had done it."
(4)	*Méizuò bié shuō, hǎo ma?*	"Don't talk about it if it's not done, O.K.?"

The negative version of sentence (2) clearly shows that the completed action is not the same as the English past tense. While the affirmative uses -*le* in the verb *zuòle*, the negative uses *bù*-, usually considered the present negative, instead of *méi*-, usually considered the past negative. The affirmative (4) is definitely referring to the future perfect tense, while the negative refers to the present status of the work. Sometimes, the completed action is the same as the past tense, as in sentence (1). Very often, the completed action -*le* is used in a dependent clause that begins with "after" in English, while the literal Chinese equivalent, *yǐhòu*, is optional:

Nǐ chīle fàn. (yǐhòu) zǒu.   "You leave after eating."

Meanwhile the negative form of completed action is often used in a dependent clause that begins with "before" in English, and the literal Chinese equivalent, *yǐqián*, is also optional.

Tā méichīfàn (yǐqián) jiù zǒu le.   "He left before eating."
Tā méichīfàn (yǐqián) wǒ jiù zǒu le.   "I left before he ate."

For the use of *méi*- in the *yǐqián* clause, there is a positive alternate form: *Tā chīfàn yǐqián wǒ jiù zǒu le.* "I left before he ate." The reason why an *yǐqián* clause in Chinese may take either the affirmative or the negative form lies in the difference between the two versions of the *yǐqián* clause. With the negative form, *yǐqián* is optional as well as redundant, while in the positive form *yǐqián* is obligatory.

.*le* for a new situation is usually connected with adjectives (intransitive quality verbs), intransitive status verbs, and auxiliary verbal phrases. For example:

---

6. Chao, *Mandarin Primer*, p. 48.
7. *Ibid*, pp. 193–195.

(1)	*Tā hǎo le.*	"He is well now."
(2)	*Tā bìng le.*	"He is sick now."
(3)	*Tā huì zǒu le.*	"He knows how to walk now."

Without *.le*, these sentences mean (1) He is well, (2) He is sick, and (3) He knows how to walk, without considering how he was before. With *.le*, they imply (1) He has not been well, (2) He has been well, and (3) He did not know how to walk before.

-Guo as a verbal suffix means "to have the experience of doing something at least once up to a certain point of time." For example, *Tā chīguo Zhōngguo fàn.* "He has had the experience of eating Chinese food." When *-guo* and *-le* are used together, the *-guo* is actually redundant. *Tā chīguole fàn le.* is not really much different from *Tā chīle fàn le.* "He has eaten." Again, we may use the negative forms to prove it. In *Tā méichīguo Zhōngguo fàn.* "He has not had the experience of eating Chinese food." both *mei-* and *-guo* are used; while in *Tā méichīfàn.* "He didn't eat." *-guo* cannot be used. With *-guo* it would mean "He has not had the experience of eating rice."

-Guo may be used with adjectives or stative verbs to mean that one has or has not had the experience of being such and such. For example, *Tā cónglái méibìngguo.* "He has never been sick."

-Guo as a suffix is unstressed, while *guò* as a verb-complement ending is generally stressed. In *Ta méiguòguo hǎorìzi.* "He has never had a good day." the first *guò* is a verb, while the second is a suffix. In *Nǐ dǎdeguò ta ma?* " Can you beat him (in a fight)?" *guò* is a verb-complement (VC) compound ending.

Zhe is usually translated as the "-ing" of English. However, one may get into trouble if one always tries to use *-zhe* in Chinese the way one uses *-ing* in English. When one wants to say that an action is in the midst of taking place, *-zhe* is suffixed to the verb. For example, *Wǒ chīzhe fàn ne.* "I am eating." A *-zhe* phrase may be used as a setting for another action: In *Wǒ chīzhe fàn kàn bào.* "I read the paper while eating." *chīzhe fàn* "eating" is the setting for *kàn bào* "reading paper." In *Kànzhe tiān yào hēi le.* "Soon it will be dark." *kànzhe* "looking" is used here as an adverb, as if to mean "As one is looking at the sky, it is getting dark." The English gerund should not be translated into the Chinese verb + *-zhe*. "His acting is good" should not be translated as *Tāde yǎnzhe hǎo.* Instead, it should be *Tā yǎnde hǎo.*

ADVERBS OF DEGREE

We will use *hěn* "very" for illustration. It is usually used as a tester for adjectives. Although most adjectives can be modified by *hěn*, items which can be so modified are not always adjectives. Let's examine the following sentences:

(1)	*Tā hěn hǎo.*	"He is very good."
	(*Hǎo* is an adjective.)	
(2)	*Tā hěn huì shuōhuà.*	"He knows how to talk very well."
	(*Huì shuōhuà* is a verbal phrase with an auxiliary verb.)	
(3)	*Tā hěn chīle jǐwǎn fàn.*	"He ate quite a few bowls of rice."
	(*Chīle jǐwǎn fàn* is a verbal phrase without an auxiliary verb, but with a quantified object.)[8]	
(4)	*Tā hěn zhīdao téng nǐ.*	"He knows how to care about you very much."
	(*Zhīdao téng nǐ* is a verbal phrase without either an auxiliary verb or a quantified object. Verbs that involve mental activity or physical action may have something to do with this.)	

This proves one thing: in the above sentences, the constructions after *hěn* have been used as adverbs. Even (3), without *hěn*, means "He ate quite a few bowls of rice." However, with *hěn*, the sentence shifts its emphasis from how much he actually ate to the fact that he is a big eater.

Similarly, a Chinese sentence wihout an aspect marker is usually a description or a statement of truth or prinicple. Only when the center of attention is shifted to the verb itself do we need the aspect markers to show whether the action has or has not been completed, whether the action is in the midst of taking place, or whether one has or has not had the experience of doing something. In one Chinese reader, in connection with a professor's conducting a class, a student is quoted, "*Gāo Xiānsheng zěnme bùjiǎng kè ne?*"[9] "How come Mr. Gao did not give lectures?" Since it was said after the class

---

8. Rao Jiting, "Hen Plus Verbal Constructions," *Zhongguo Yuwen* (Chinese Language), No. 107, 1961.
9. Richard Chang, *Read Chinese Book Two*, New Haven, Far Eastern Publications, 1966, p. 68.

(as a matter of fact the first one), a past tense is definitely required. In Chinese, however, the sentence describes how Mr. Kao conducts his class, rather than whether or not he gave any lecture in the first class; *bù*, instead of *méi* is used. In *"Tāmen kànjiàn yǒu hěn duō xuésheng zài nàr niànshū."*[10] "They saw there were many students reading there." the absence of the aspect marker *-le* shows the sentence stresses what they saw not whether they actually saw it or not. If we change the sentence around a little bit, it will be easier to see the difference: *Yǒu hěn duō xuésheng zài nàr niànshū, tāmen kànjiànle ma?* "There were many students reading there, did they see?" As the center of attention in this sentence has been shifted from what they saw to whether or not they saw, the aspect marker *-le* must be used.

REDUPLICATION

Reduplication is an important morphological process in Chinese.[11] Verbs are generally reduplicated in the following forms:

Vv	*chī.chi*
Vlev	*chī.lechi*
Vyiv	*chī.yichi*
Vle. yiv	*chīle.yichi*

If there is an object, it follows the reduplicated verb. Two-syllable verbs are reduplicated in an ABAB fashion with the reduplicated portion unstressed as the one-syllable verb. For the two syllable verbs, however, there is no AB*yi*AB form. Sometimes it is possible to reduplicate a two-syllable verb as if it were two one-syllable verbs. For example, the two-syllable verb *qīngsuàn* "to liquidate" may be reduplicated normally *qīngsuànqingsuan*, or for special effect, *qīngyiqing suànyisuan*. But there is no *qīngsuànyiqingsuan*.

Adjectives are reduplicated somewhat differently: the reduplicated part is changed to a high level tone if the original is not, and is suffixed with a retroflex *-er*. Examples in all four tones are given below:

1st Tone:	*gāo*	"tall"	*gāogāor (de)*
2nd Tone:	*hóng*	"red"	*hónghōngr (de)*
3rd Tone:	*hǎo*	"good"	*hǎohāor (de)*
4th Tone:	*màn*	"slow"	*mànmānr (de)*

Two-syllable adjectives are generally reduplicated in AABB fashion.

Rènào	"exciting"	*rèrenaonāorde*
Qīngchu	"clear"	*qīngqingchūchurde*

Most AABB reduplication of two-syllable adjectives occurs, however, with coordinative compounds. Other kinds of compounds are either not reduplicable or reduplicated differently. *Hǎokàn* "good-looking," a subordinative compound, cannot be reduplicated. *Xuěbái* "white as snow" is, however, reduplicated in the manner of a two-syllable verb.

A verb may be reduplicated in AABB fashion to be used as an adjective, while an adjective which is usually reduplicated in AABB fashion may be reduplicated in ABAB fashion to be used as a verb. *Shānglaing* "to discuss" may be reduplicated *shāngliangshangliang* (ABAB), "to discuss a little," or *shāngshanglianglāngde* (AABB), "to be indecisive." *Rènào* "to be exciting" as an adjective is usually reduplicated *rèrenaonāorde*; but may be reduplicated *rènaorenao* "to have some excitement" to become a verb. A very interesting example is found in the compound noun *yìsi* "idea." It is reduplicated *yìyisisīde* (AABB) "hesitant" and *yìsiyisi* (ABAB) "to show friendship, to give something as a token of friendship."

The functions of reduplication for verbs are trial, casualness, duration of time, and quantity of object; and primarily for adjectives, vividness. The following examples illustrate these points.

Trial: *Nǐ zěnme bújìde le? Zài xiǎngxiang kàn.* "How can it be that you don't remember it? *Try to think* and see whether or not you can remember."

10. *Ibid,* p. 59.
11. Eugene Ching, "Reduplication in Chinese," *Papers of the CIC Far Eastern Language Institute, Indiana University, 1964,* Ann Arbor, Michigan, 1965.

Casualness: *Tā búguò shuōshuo bale, nǐ hébi rènzhēn ne?* "He was *just talking*, why should you take it so seriously?"

Duration of time: *Nǐ búhui shuō zhèijù huà, liànxilianxi jiu huì le.* "If you don't know how to say this, *practice a little* and you will."

Quantity of the object: *Shuō liǎngjù hǎo huà, dàodaoqiàn, bújiu wánle ma?* "Say a few nice words, *apologize a little*, and won't it be all right?" It is worth noting that in this sentence, *shuō liangju hǎo huà* may be replaced with *shuōshuo hǎo huà*, and *dàodaoqiàn* may be replaced by *dào (yi) ge qiàn* without changing the meaning.

Vividness: *Tāmen gāogaoxīngxingrde jìnlai le.* "They came in *in high spirits* (very happily)."

There is a variant reduplicated form for adjectives, A*li*AB, which carries a pejorative connotation. *Húdu*, "muddle-headed," is obviously a word with pejorative meaning. However, *húhududū* may be used to describe a person that the speaker is fond of, while *húlihudū* definitely conveys the speaker's displeasure.[12]

COMPOUNDS

Chinese morphemes are primarily monosyllabic except for a few like *pútao* "grapes," *wúgong* "centipede," ect.[13] Since there are only four hundred syllables (without considering the tones) in modern Mandarin Chinese, compounding becomes one of the most important devices for word construction. Generally speaking, there are five basic kinds of compounds; that is, coordinate compounds (CC), subordinative compounds (SC), verb-object compounds (VO), verb-complement compounds (VC), and subject-predicate compounds (SP). Some examples are listed in the following:

CC:	*xǐhuān*	"joy and happy/to like"
	mǎnzú	"full and sufficient/to satisfy"
	zhāohu	"beckon and call/to greet, to take care of"
	qíguài	"strange and odd/strange"
SC:	*qiángdiào*	"strong accent/to emphasize"
	bùxíng	"footstep-go/go on foot"
	rèxīn	"hot heart/enthusiastic; to devote oneself to"
	xiǎokàn	"small look upon/to despise"
VO:	*bǎoxiǎn*	"to insure; to be reliable"
	dézuì	"get offense/to offend"
	chūbǎn	"issue an edition/to publish"
VC:	*kànjiàn*	"look see/to see"
	chībǎo	"to eat full"
	dǎdǎo	"to knock down"
	shuìzháo	"to fall asleep"
SP:	*tóuteng*	"headache"
	dìzhèn	"the earth quakes"
	dǎnxiǎo	"spleen-small/timid"
	mìngkǔ	"luck-hard"

Without going into the details of the characteristic behaviors of these compounds, which by itself would need more space than this introduction, a brief statement on the general behavior of the Chinese verb seems necessary.[14]

As a rule, Chinese verbs may take an auxiliary verb to indicate potentiality or an aspect marker such as *le* to indicate actuality. In their original forms, they are used to state habits, principles, and state of being. For example, *néng chī* means "can eat, able to eat"; *chīle*, "ate (the eating has been done)"; *chī*, "eat (one usually eats such and such, one would eat, as a rule one eats, etc.)." Verb-complement compounds have, in addition, two infixes for the potential forms; *-de-* for positive potentiality, *-bu-* for negative potentiality. For example, *chīdebǎo* "can eat to satisfaction," and

---

12. Chao, *Grammar*, pp. 205–210.
13. Eugene Ching, "Dissyllabicity of Modern Mandarin," *Chinese Culture Quarterly*, Dec. 1969, pp. 88–104 and George A. Kennedy, "The Monosyllabic Myth," *Selected Works of George A Kennedy*, edited by Tien-yi Li, New Haven, Far Eastern Publications, 1964, pp. 104–118.
14. For the most authoritative treatment on the subject, see Chao, *Grammar*, Chapters 6 and 8.

chībubǎo "cannot eat to satisfaction." The following sentences which use all of these forms may be helpful:

Tā chī Zhōngguó fàn.	"He eats Chinese food (When Chinese food is served, he will eat)."
Tā néng chī Zhōngguó fàn.	"He can (is able to) eat Chinese food."
Tā chīle fàn le.	"He has eaten."
Tā chīzhe fàn ne.	"He is in the midst of eating."
Tā chīguo Zhōngguó fàn.	"He has had the experience of eating Chinese food."
Tā néng chīzhe fàn shuōhuà.	"He can talk while eating."
Tā děi chībǎo.	"He must eat his fill."
Tā chī Zhōngguó fàn chībubǎo.	"He can't eat to his satisfaction when he eats Chinese food."
Tā chī Zhōngguó fàn chīdebǎo.	"He can eat to his satisfaction when he eats Chinese food."
Tā chībǎole.	"He ate his fill."
Tā méichībǎo.	"He didn't eat his fill."
Tā chībǎole cái zǒu de.	"He left after he had eaten his fill."
Nǐ chībǎole zài zǒu.	"Don't leave until you have eaten your fill."

Chinese verbs may be used together without changing them into gerunds, participles, or infinitives. However, they may appear in different relationships.

Coordinate relationship: *Tā chōuyān hējiǔ dōu huì.* "He can smoke and drink." Monosyllabic verbs, particularly bound ones, are used together in more or less fixed orders; for example, *chī-hē-piáo-dǔ* "eat, drink, visit prostitutes, and gamble"; *shēng-lǎo-bìng-sǐ* "to be born, to get old, to be sick, and to die"; *chuī-pāi-piàn* "boast, flatter, and cheat."

Subordinative relationship: *Yòng kuàizi chīfàn* "to eat with chopsticks"; *Chīle fàn dào xuéxiào qù* "to go to school after eating."

Sequential relationship: *Yí kànjiàn ta jiù shēngqì* "get mad immediately upon seeing him"; *Shuō gei wo tīng* "say it so that I can hear"; *Jiào ta qǐng yíge rén lai gěi wo zuò fàn* "tell him to get somebody to cook for me."

Verb-object relationship: *Wǒ tīng shuō tā zǒu le* "I heard it said that he left."

PRONUNCIATION

A typical Chinese syllable consists of a consonantal initial and a final with a vowel nucleus. The final may be further analyzed into a medial, a main vowel (or the vowel nucleus), and an ending. The main vowel being the obligatory element, a Chinese syllable may be any of the following: a vowel (such as *a*); an initial and a vowel (such as *la*); an initial, a medial, and a vowel (such as *lia*); and an initial, a medial, a vowel, and an ending (such as *lian* with consonantal ending and *liao* with vowel ending). Suffix *er* is added to a syllable simply by affixing *r* to its end without considering the phonological change involved (such as *wanr*). Tone marks are put over the main vowel as follows: first tone ā, second tone á, third tone ǎ, fourth tone à, neutral or unstressed tone a (no tone mark).

INITIALS

b	as in English buy, but without voicing like English p in spy, *bài* "to worship"
c	like the ts in English its with the initial i left off, but with a stronger puff of breath, *cài* "vegetable"
ch	a cross between the initial sounds of true and choose as though we said chrue instead of true, *chū* "exit"
d	as in English die, but without voicing like English t in sty, *dài* "to put on"
f	as in English father, *fǎ* "law"
g	as in English guy, but without voicing like k in English sky, *gài* "to cover"
h	like the English h in how but with friction at the back of the mouth, *hǎo* "good"
j	Like Chinese q but without puff of breath, *jì* "remember"
k	as in English kite, but with a stronger puff of breath, *kāi* "to open"
l	as in English law, *lǎo* "old"
m	as in English mother, *mā* "mother"
n	as in English now, *nào* "to annoy"
p	as in English pie, but with a stronger puff of breath, *pài* "to appoint"
q	much as ch in English cheat, but with the tip of the tongue held down behind the lower front teeth, *qì* "air"
r	as in English run, but without rounding of the lips, *rén* "person"
s	as in English sign, *sài* "to compete"
t	as in English tie, but with a stronger puff of breath, *tài* "too"
w	as in English way, *wèi* "to feed"
x	much as sh in English she, but with the tip of the tongue held down behind the lower front teeth, and without any rounding of the lips, *xī* "west"
y	as in English yeah, *yá* "tooth"
z	like the ds in English adds with the initial a left off, *zài* "again"
zh	like Chinese ch but without puff of breath, *zhū* "pig"

MEDIALS

Medials are main vowels when no other vowel follows them.

i	like the English i in machine except as main vowel after z, c, s, zh, ch, sh, r, *liá* "two"
u	like the English u in suave, *luàn* "mess"
u	like the French u in nuance, with umlaut after l, n, only, *nǔ* "female," *qù* "to go"

MAIN VOWELS

a	(1) like the English a in father, *mǎ* "horse," (2) between i or y and n, like the English a in hand, *liǎn* "face," *yān* "smoke"; (3) between u and n, like the English a in bat, *yuàn* "courtyard"; (4) between u or w and ng, like (1) or the English o in long, *huáng* "yellow"
ai	like the English ai in aisle, *ài* "love"

ao	like the English au in umlaut, *lǎo* "old"
e	(1) about like the English u in but or huh, *hē* "to drink"; (2) after i and *ü*, like the English e in met, *yě* "also," *yuè* "moon"
ei	like the English ei in reign, *lèi* "tired"
i	(1) final in the syllable except (3) and (4), like the English ee in see, *xǐ* "to wash," (2) not final in the syllable, like the English i in pin, *pín* "poor"; (3) after z, c, and s, like the English oo in look without rounding the lips, *zì* "character," *cì* "jab," *sì* "four;" (4) after zh, ch, sh, r, like the middle-western American English ir in shirt, or ur in hurt, *chī* "to eat," *zhī* "to know," *shì* "yes," *rì* "sun"
o	like the English u in urn, *wǒ* "I"
ou	like the English ow in know, *hòu* "behind"
u	(1) final and not after j, q, x, y, like the English oo in moon, *wù* "fog"; (2) after j, q, x, y, like the French u in nuance or the Chinese ü, *yǔ* "rain"
ü	like the French u in nuance, or the English oo in moon and the ee in see pronounced simultaneously: while, pronouncing ee, round your lips without other changes, *lǘ* "donkey"

ENDINGS

Vowel endings are pronounced as described above. The following consonants occur as endings:

n	like the English n in tan, *tán* "to talk"
ng	like the English ng in sing or singer, but not like the ng in finger, *xíng* "O.K."
r	(1) like the English r in bar, fur, *wánr* (pronounced wár) "to play"; (2) after ng, the vowel is strongly nasalized, r as (1), *héngr* "horizontal stroke"

Everybody knows that nobody can learn the pronunciation of a foreign language by reading the description of its sounds only. It is of utmost importance that one should get the assistance of a native speaker. Ask him to read the Chinese words in which a particular sound is found. After one has more or less mastered the sound system, he should go on to learn to read the expressions, phrases, and sentences, still with a native speaker as the model. Unless he is a trained linguist, the native speaker should not be asked to explain how a sound is pronounced and why a certain expression or group of words is spoken in such a way. Just imitate him, repeat after him again and again until you have learned it. Although recording is no substitute for a native speaker, it could be used when a native speaker is not available.

ABBREVIATIONS USED IN THE TEXT

Adj	Adjective
Adv	Adverbs
Budd.	Buddhist
CC	Coordinate Construction
Conj	Conjunction
Col. pron.	Colloquial pronunciation
esp.	especially
fig.	figuratively
LC	Literary Chinese
lit.	literally
math.	mathematics
N	Noun
PRC	People's Republic of China
SC	Subordinative Construction
SP	Subject-predicate Constructions
SV	Stative Verb
Transli.	Transliteration
TV	Transitive Verb
TW	Time Word
V	Verb
VC	Verb-complement Construction
VO	Verb-object Construction (solid)
V-O	Verb-object Construction (with limited separability)
V O	Verb-object Construction (free components)

àicái	愛財	to love money, to be covetous [VO/SV]
àidài	愛戴	love and endearment; reverence; popular support: 他深受愛戴。[N] *Tā shēn shòu àidài.* He was deeply loved (by people.)
àiguó	愛國	to love one's country, to be patriotic: 愛國心 *àiguóxīn*, patriotism [V-O/SV]
àihào	愛好	to be fond of (dress, gambling, etc.) [CC/V] 愛好游泳 *ài hào yóu yǒng*, fond of swimming
àihǎo(r)	愛好兒	to desire to be good; to be particular about being good [VO/SV]
àihù	愛護	to cherish, support, and protect (country, children, reputation, etc.): 要是一個人愛護他的名譽，他決不會做出這種見不得人的事的。*Yàoshi yíge rén àihù tāde míngyù, tā jué búhuì zuòchū zhèizhǒng jiànbude rén de shi de.* If one cares about his reputation, he definitely cannot do this kind of shameful thing. [CC/V]
àilián	愛憐	to love, to show tenderness towards (an orphan, a young widow, etc.) [CC/V]
ài měi	愛美	to love beauty, to be esthetic: 愛美的觀念，*àiměide guānniàn*, esthetic sense [V O]
àimiànzi	愛面子	to care about "face" [VO/SV]
àimù	愛慕	to love, to adore (lover, a great author, etc.) [CC/V]
àiqíng	愛情	love, especially romantic love between man and woman [SC/N]
ài qù búqù	愛去不去	Go if you want, stay if you don't.
àiren	愛人	lover, sweetheart, spouse (PRC) [SC/N]; to love others: 愛人如己 *ài rén rú jǐ*, to love one's neighbors as oneself [V O]
àishang	愛上	to fall in love with: 你怎麼會愛上她? *Nǐ zěnme huì àishang tā?* How could it be possible for you to fall in love with her? [VC]
ài wū jí wū	愛屋及烏	to love the house to love the crow on the roof/"love me, love my dog"
àixi	愛惜	to love and cherish [CC/V]
ài (zhàn) xiǎo piányi	愛佔小便宜	to love trifling advantages, to be keen on petty profits
ài zhòng	愛重	admire [N] 他為人正直，故受到了大家的愛重。*Tā wéi rén zhèngzhí, gù shòudàole dàjiā de ài zhòng.* He is frank and direct. Therefore he is admired by people.

ānchā	安插	to place (friend, etc.) in organization, to find a job for (a person): 請你給他安插一個職位。 *Qǐng nǐ gěi tā ānchā yíge zhíwèi.* Please arrange a position for him. [CC/V]
ān diànhuà	安電話	to install a telephone
āndìng	安定	to settle down: 等他安定一下再說吧。 *Děng tā āndìng yíxia zài shuō ba.* Wait until he has settled down a bit and then talk about it. [CC/V]; to be peaceful and secure: 住在這兒很安定。 *Zhùzai zhèr hěn āndìng.* It is very peaceful to live here. [SV]
ānfèn	安分	to be law-abiding: 安分守己 *ānfèn shǒu jǐ* [VO/SV]
ānhǎo	安好	to install well [VC]; to be well, in good health [CC/SV]
ānjiā	安家	to settle down a family: 安家費 *ānjiā fèi*, allowance for setting up a family [V-O]
ān jiǎn	安檢	safety inspection: 安全檢查 *ānquán jiǎn chá*
ānjìng	安靜	peaceful and quiet (place, person) [CC/SV]
ān jū lè yè	安居樂業	to make a good living and be contented, each in his station
ānlèwō	安樂窩	a happy retreat
ānpái	安排	to arrange (things), to provide (meals, jobs, etc.) [CC/V]
ānquán	安全	to be safe [CC/SV]; safety, security
ānrán	安然	to be calm [SV]; calmly: 他安然渡過難關。 *Tā ānrán dùguò nánguān.* He calmly went through the difficulties. [Adv]
ānshén	安神	to calm down nerves, to relax one's mind [V-O]
ān zhěn wú yōu	安枕無憂	to be free of worries
ānzhì	安置	to place a person (= *ānchā*), to install (= *ānzhuāng*)
ānzhuāng	安裝	to install: 電話已經安裝好了。 *Diànhuà yǐjing ānzhuānghǎole.* The telephone has been installed.
bùān hǎo xīn	不安好心	to be malicious, with bad intentions: 他這樣對你顯然是不安好心。 *Tā zhèiyang duì nǐ xiǎnrán shì bùān hǎo xīn.* That he treats you this way shows clearly his bad intentions.
xīnli bùān	心裏不安	to feel uneasy

bàn'àn	辦案	(of judge, official) to take charge of a case [V-O]
bànbào	辦報	to run a newspaper [V O]
bànbudào	辦不到	impossible to do it: 這個辦不到 *Zhèige bànbudào*. It is impossible to do this.
bàndedào	辦得到	possible to do it: 這件事辦得到 (*Zhèi jiànshì bàndedao*.) This is doable.
bàngōng	辦公	to handle official business 辦理公事 *bànlǐ gōngshì* [V O]
bàn hòushì	辦後事	to make preparations for a funeral
bàn huo	辦貨	to purchase supplies [V O]
bàn jiǔxí	辦酒席	to prepare a banquet
bànlǐ	辦理	to take charge of (affairs): 這件事由我辦理。 *Zhèijian shì yóu wǒ bànlǐ.* Let me take charge of this matter. [CC/V]
bàn sāngshì	辦喪事	to make preparations for a funeral
bàn shì	辦事	to handle administrative affairs, to do things: 他很會辦事。 *Tā hěn huì bàn shì.* He knows how to handle things. [V O]
bàn shòu	辦壽	to make preparations for a birthday celebration (for elders) [V O]
chábàn	查辦	to investigate charges [CC/V]
chuàngbàn	創辦	to establish (schools, hospitals, etc.), to found: 這個學校是甚麼時候創辦的? *Zhèige xuéxiào shì shénme shíhou chuàngbàn de?* When was this school founded? [CC/V]
dūbàn	督辦	commissioner [CC/N]
fǎbàn	法辦	deal with according to law; bring to justice 他被(依)法(懲)辦了。 *Tā bèi(yī) fǎ(chéng)bànle.* He was punished according to the law. [V]
kāibàn	開辦	= 創辦 *chuàngbàn* [CC/V]
mǎibàn	買辦	compradore [CC/N]
méibànfa	沒辦法	There is no way out: 沒辦法做。 *Méibànfa zuò.* Cannot be done.
méifázi bàn	沒法子辦	no way to do it
zhàobàn	照辦	to do accordingly (official documents), will do as you wish: 只要你說出來，我一定照辦。 *Zhǐyào nǐ shuōchulai, wǒ yídìng zhàobàn.* If you will only tell me, I will do as you say. [CC/V]

3

bāobàn	包辦	to take full responsibility for an assignment: 這事由我包辦。 *Zhè shì yóu wǒ bāobàn.* I will be solely responsible for this matter.
bāobì	包庇	to shelter someone for wrongdoing [CC/V]
bāochāo	包抄	to outflank and attack (enemy) [CC/V]
bāofēng	包封	to seal (package) [CC/V]
bāofu	包袱	wrapping cloth (for travel); burden of past habits of thinking [SC/N]
bāofu dǐr	包袱底兒	the bottom of the wrapping cloth/secrets, the most precious possessions, best act in performance: 透露包袱底兒 *dǒulou bāofu dǐr.* Show one's best act (usually reserved for the last).
bāoguǎn	包管	to guarantee, to assure: 包管沒錯。 *Bāoguǎn méicuò.* I guarantee it is all right. [CC/V]
bāogōng	包工	contract for labor [V-O/N]: 包工頭 *bāogōng tóu,* person who gets labor-work with contract
bāoguǒ	包裹	parcel [CC/N]; to wrap [V]
bāohán	包含	to include, to contain: 這句話包含的意思很多。 *Zhèijù huà bāohánde yìsi hěn duō.* This sentence means more than is apparent. [CC/V]
bāokuò	包括	to include [CC/V]
bāoluó wànxiàng	包羅萬象	to cover and contain everything: 那本小說兒真是包羅萬象，甚麼都有。 *Nèiběn xiǎoshuōr zhēn shì bāoluó wànxiàng, shénme dōu yǒu.* That novel covers everything.
bāopéi	包賠	to guarantee to pay compensation [V]
bāoqilai	包起來	to wrap up [VC]
bāoróng	包容	to forgive, to pardon [CC/V]
bāowéi	包圍	to surround [CC/V]
bāoxiāng	包廂	box at theater [SC/N]
bāozhā	包扎	to tie up (bundle) to bandage [CC/V]
bāozhuāng	包裝	to pack; package 包裝不好。 *Bāozhuāng bùhǎo.* The package is not good. [V/N]

bǎoān jīguān	保安機關	security organization
bǎobiāo	保鏢	bodyguard [VO/N]
bǎobúzhù	保不住	cannot guarantee [VC]
bǎochí	保持	to maintain (road condition, temperature, liaison, etc.) [CC/V]
bǎocún	保存	to preserve [CC/V]
bǎodān	保單	certificate of guarantee; insurance policy [SC/N]
bǎoguǎn	保管	to be in charge of (jewelry, property, etc.): 保管人 *bǎoguǎnrén*, custodian [CC/V]
bǎohù	保護	to protect [CC/V]; protection: 保護國土 *bǎohù guótǔ*, to protect one's territory; 保護色 *bǎohù sè*, protective coloration
bǎoliú	保留	to reserve (rights, etc.) [CC/V]; reservation
bǎomì	保密	to keep something secret 請給我保密。 *Qǐng gěi wǒ bǎomì.* Please keep it a secret for me. [VO]
bǎomǔ	保姆	nurse-maid (also written 保母) [SC/N]
bǎoquán	保全	to protect (reputation, life, property, etc.) [VC]
bǎorén	保人	guarantor [SC/N]
bǎoshǒu	保守	to be conservative [CC/SV]
bǎoxiǎn	保險	to insure [V-O]; insurance; dependable [SV]: 那個保險公司不保險。 *Nèige bǎoxiǎn gōngsī bùbǎoxiǎn.* That insurance company is not dependable.
bǎozhàng	保障	to protect (civil rights, life, property, etc.) [CC/V]; protection: 人權的保障 *Rénquánde bǎozhàng*, protection of human rights
bǎozhèng	保證	guarantee [CC/V, N]: 保證人 *bǎozhèngrén*, guarantor; 保證書 *bǎozhèng shū*, certificate of guarantee
bǎozhòng	保重	to take good care of (oneself): 請好好兒保重身體。 *Qǐng hǎohāor bǎozhòng shēntǐ.* Please take very good care of your health. [CC/V]
bǎozhǔnr	保准兒	I guarantee: 保准兒沒事。 *bǎozhǔnr méishì.* I guarantee nothing will happen to you. [VC]
nánbǎo	難保	It is hard to say that: 難保他不會生氣。 *Nánbǎo tā búhuì shēngqì.* It's hard to say that he will not be mad. [SC/ADV]

bàoàn	報案	to register complaints at court, to submit official report on case [V-O]
bàochóu	報仇	to revenge for grudge [V-O]
bàodá	報答	to pay back debt of gratitude [CC/V]
bàodào	報到	to report arrival, to report for duty [V-O]
bàodào	報導	to report (news, intelligence, etc.) [CC/V]; report: 新聞報導 *xīnwén bàodào*, news report
bàoēn	報恩	to recompense for kindness: 報父母養育之恩。 *bào fùmǔ yǎngyù zhī ēn*, to make oneself worthy of parents' care and upbringing [V-O]
bàofèi	報廢	to invalidate, to be declared worthless: 這部車子報廢了。 *Zhèibù chēzi bàofèi le.* This car has been junked. [VO]
bàogào	報告	report [CC/V, N]
bàogōng	報功	to report achievement (victory, etc.), to claim credit [V-O]
bàoguān	報關	to pay custom duties [V-O]
bàoguó	報國	to serve the country worthily: 立志報國 *lì zhì bào guó*, to make a resolution to serve the country [V-O]
bàokǎo	報考	to register for examination [V-O]
bào kǔqióngr	報苦窮兒	to pretend poverty
bàomíng	報名	to register (for school, entrance examination, etc.) [V-O]
bàomìng	報命	to respond to an order or command: 無以報命 *wú yǐ bào mìng*, without anything to respond to an order [VO]
bào shuì	報稅	to pay tax [V O]
bàosāng	報喪	to announce death [V-O]
bàoxǐ	報喜	to announce joyful events (wedding, birth, etc.): 報喜不報憂 *bàoxǐ búbàoyōu*, to report joyful vents but not saddening news [V-O]
bàoxìn	報信	to report news [V-O]
bàoxiè	報謝	to pay back debt of gratitude, to show gratitude [CC/V]

bèibǔ	被捕	to be arrested [V]
bèidòng	被動	passive (opposite of 主動 *zhǔdòng*, active)
bèigào	被告	to be accused; the defendant (opposite to 原告 *yuángào*, the plaintiff)
bèihài	被害	to be murdered, to be harmed
bèihuǐ	被毀	to be destroyed 這座城市被毀了。 *Zhèi zuò chéngshì bèi huǐle.* This city was destroyed. [V]
bèilèi	被累	to be implicated
bèinàn	被難	to be killed in an uprising (martyr): 這次起義被難的烈士很多。 *Zhèicì qǐyì bèinànde lièshi hěn duō.* In this uprising many were killed.
bèipiàn	被騙	to be cheated
bèiqī	被欺	to be humiliated
bèiqiǎng	被搶	to be robbed
bèiqǐng	被請	to be invited: 怎麼你沒被請? *Zěnme nǐ méi bèiqǐng?* How come you've not been invited?
bèiqū	被屈	to be wronged
bèi rén tīngjian	被人聽見	to be heard, overheard by others: 你說這話不怕被人聽見? *Nǐ shuō zhè huà búpà bèi rén tīngjian?* Aren't you afraid that somebody may overhear what you have said?
bèishā	被殺	to be killed
bèi tā názǒule	被他拿走了	was taken away by him
bèi xuǎn	被選	to be elected
bèixuǎnquán	被選權	the right to be elected
bèizhuā	被抓	to be arrested: 賊被抓住了。 *Zéi bèi zhuāzhule.* The thief has been caught.

bèi
to prepare, to provide, to furnish

備

bèiàn	備案	to register for the record [V-O]
bèibàn	備辦	to prepare (luggage, banquet, etc.) [CC/V]
bèichá	備查	to keep for future reference or investigation
bèichē	備車	to provide with cars, to get the car ready [V-O]
bèi ér búyòng	備而不用	to prepare for future needs
bèikè	備課	to prepare for teaching 這位教師備課很仔細。 *Zhèi wèi jiào shī bèi kè hěn zǐxì.* This teacher prepares teaching very carefully.
bèikǎo	備考	to keep for future investigation; an appendix for reference
bèiqǔ	備取	alternates for admission (college, office, etc.)
bèiwànglù	備忘錄	memorandum
bèi wèi chōng shù	備位充數	just to fill a post (self-depreciatory)
bèiwén	備文	to prepare a document [V O]
bèiyòng	備用	to provide for use
bèizhàn	備戰	to prepare for war [V-O]
bèizhù	備註	a note for future investigation
chóubèi	籌備	to plan and provide (funds, proposals, etc.) [CC/V]
fángbèi	防備	to provide against: 我們得時時防備敵人的襲擊。 *Wǒmen děi shíshí fángbèi dírende xíjī.* We must be prepared to deal with enemy attack all the time. [CC/V]
jièbèi	戒備	to be on the alert: 在敵佔區，我們必須時時戒備。 *Zài dí zhàn qū, wǒmen bìxū shíshí jièbèi.* In enemy territory, we must be on the alert at all times. [CC/V]
jūnbèi	軍備	armament, military preparedness [SC/N]
yǒu bèi wú huàn	有備無患	with all the preparations, there is nothing to worry about.
yùbèi	預備	to prepare [SC/V]
zhànbèi	戰備	military preparedness [SC/N]
zhǔnbèi	準備	to prepare, to be prepared

bǐbúshàng	比不上	to be inferior to: 我比不上他。 *Wǒ bǐbúshàng tā.* I am not as good as he is. [VC]
bǐfāng	比方	for instance; a supposition, an illustration by example: 比方說 *bǐfāng shuō*, for example; 打個比方 *dǎ ge bǐfāng*, to give an example
bǐfēn	比分	score 比分不差上下。 *Bǐfēn búchà shàngxià.* The score is very close/tight. (N)
bíhuà	比畫	to make hand gestures, to demonstrate with gestures [CC/V]
bǐjiān zuòzhàn	比肩作戰	to fight shoulder to shoulder = 並肩作戰 *bìng jiān zuò zhàn*
bǐjiào	比較	to compare; comparatively, relatively: 比較好 *bǐjiào hǎo*, relatively better; comparative: 比較語言學 *bǐjiào yǔyán xué*, comparative linguistics [CC/V, Adv]
bǐrú	比如	for example
bǐsài	比賽	to have a contest: 比賽講故事 *bǐsài jiǎng gùshi*, to have a contest in story telling [CC/V]; contest: 講演比賽 *jiǎngyǎn bǐsài* speech contest
bǐ shàng bùzú, bǐ xià yǒu yú	比上不足 比下有餘	worse off than some, better off than many (formula for contentment)
bǐ shì	比試	to compete; to have a competition 我們比試一下，好不好? *wǒmen bǐ shì yíxià, hǎobùhǎo?* Let's compete. [V]
bǐ shǒu huà jiǎo	比手畫腳	to make lively gestures while talking = 指手畫腳 *zhǐ shǒu huà jiǎo*
bǐ wǔ bǐsàiwǔyì	比武 = 比賽武藝	demonstration of and competition in military or martial art skills 他喜歡與人比(賽)武(藝)。 *Tā xǐ huan yǔ rén bǐ (sài) wǔ (yì).* He likes to compete with others in martial art skills. [VO/N]
bǐyì	比翼	to be side by side 比翼齊飛 *bǐyìqífēi* to fly side by side. [V]
bǐyù	比喻	a parable, a metaphor, an allegory [CC/N]
bǐzhòng	比重	specific weight or gravity [SC/N]
bǐzuò	比作	to compare someone as: 你把他比作甚麼? *Nǐ bǎ tā bǐzuò shénme?* What do you compare him to be? [CC/V]
rén bǐ rén, qìsǐ rén	人比人 氣死人	One may be upset to death if he compares himself with those who are more successful.
tā bǐ wǒ gāo	他比我高	He is taller than I.
yòng shǒu bǐhuà	用手比畫	to describe with hands

biānchéngxù	編程序	to write/design a program 他在一家計算機公司編程序。 *Tā zài yì jiā jìsuànjī gōngsī biān chéngxù.* He is writing programs in a computer company. [V O]
biāndìng	編訂	to edit (book) with the idea of restoring the correct version to establish (correct list of names, numbers, etc.) [CC/V]
biānduì	編隊	to organize troop units, to form groups [V-O]
biānhào(r)	編號兒	to assign a number (to a list of persons or things) [V-O]
biānhù	編戶	to register residents (for police record) [V-O]
biānjí	編輯	to edit (paper, magazine, etc.) [CC/V]; editor
biānjié	編結	to tie, to weave [CC/V]
biānjù	編劇	to write plays [V-O]; script writer
biānlèi	編類	to classify [V-O]; classification
biānlù	編錄	to extract and edit [V]
biān míngcè	編名冊	to make a roster
biānnián(shǐ)	編年(史)	form of history arranged by years and months, chronicles
biānpái	編排	to arrange in order, to write and to direct [CC/V]; writing and directing of a play
biānshěn	編審	to examine and approve, to pass judgement on books, publications [CC/V]; person who examines and approves
biānshū	編書	to compile a book [V O]
biānxiě	編寫	to compile 編寫教材 *biānxiě jiàocái* to compile a textbook; [V] to write/compose 編寫一部書 *biānxiě yíbùshū.* to write a book. [V]
biānxuǎn	編選	to select and edit = 編輯選定 *biānjíxuǎndìng* 編選課本 *biānxuǎn kèběn* to select and edit a textbook [V]
biānyì	編譯	to edit and to translate [CC/V]; editor and translator
biānzào	編造	to fabricate: 編造謠言 *biānzào yáoyán*, to fabricate rumors [CC/V]
biānzhī	編織	to knit [CC/V]
biānzhì	編制	to organize [CC/V]; organization, chain of command
biānzhù	編著	to compile [CC/V]; compilation, compiler
biān zìdiǎn	編字典	to compile a dictionary

biàndòng	變動	to change [CC/V]: drastic change: 變動很大 *Biàndòng hěn dà*. The change is great.
biànfǎ	變法	to reform [V-O]; political reform; ways to change
biàngé	變革	change for the new (in system, policy) [CC/N]
biàngēng	變更	change of course, of action [CC/N]
biàngù	變故	any untold change or turn of events [SC/N]
biànhǎo	變好	to grow better: 這孩子變好了。 *Zhè háizi biànhǎole*. This child becomes better. [VC]
biànhuà	變化	to change in form or character [CC/V]; change: 千變萬化 *qiān biàn wàn huà*, unending changes
biànhuáng	變黃	to become yellow [VC]
biànjié	變節	to switch loyalty; to remarry [V-O]
biànliǎn	變臉	to change countenance (when mad) [V-O]
biànmài	變賣	to sell (estate, store, etc.) [CC/V]
biànqiān	變遷	change in trend, conditions [CC/V]
biànsè	變色	to change color; to change countenance [V-O]
biàntài	變態	change of attitude, abnormal: 變態心理 *biàntài xīnlǐ*, abnormal psychology [SC]
biàntiān	變天	(weather) to turn overcast: 變天了，別忘了帶傘。 *Biàntiān le, bié wàngle dài sǎn*. The weather has changed. Don't forget to bring your umbrella. [V-O]
biàntōng	變通	to use another method to : 變通辦理 *biàntōng bànlǐ*, to do it by circumventing the rules [VC]
biànxiàng	變相	change in appearance: 變相賣淫 *biànxiàng màiyín*, prostitution in a different form [VO]
biàn xìfǎ	變戲法	to perform magic, to play tricks
biànxīn	變心	to change heart/to change mind (about love, etc.):她已經變了心，你就別再死心眼兒了。 *Tā yǐjing biànle xīn, Nǐ jiù bié zài sǐ xīnyǎnr le*. She has already changed her mind. You shouldn't be so obstinate (about her). [V-O]

cānbài	參拜	to pay respect to (high officials), to worship (gods) [CC/V]
cāndìng	參訂	to revise text [CC/V]
cānguān	參觀	to visit as a tourist, to observe [CC/V]
cānjiā	參加	to take part in, to join [CC/V]
cānjiàn	參見	to see (superior) [CC/V]
cānjūn	參軍	to join the army 他是去年參的軍。 *Tā shì qùnián cān de jūn.* He joined the army last year. [V O]
cānkàn	參看	to compare [CC/V]
cānkǎo	參考	to use as a reference: 寫文章你得參考很多書。 *Xiě wénzhāng nǐ děi cānkǎo hěn duō shū.* Writing a paper, you must use many books as references. [CC/V]; reference materials: 給你作個參考。 *Gěi nǐ zuò ge cānkǎo,* give you as a reference
cānmóu	參謀	staff officer [CC/N] to offer advice [V]
cānsài	參賽	to take part in a match = 參加比賽 *cānjiā bǐsài* 我們收到了幾百件參賽的作品。 *Wǒmen shōudàole jǐ bǎi jiàn cānsài de zuòpǐn.* We have received several hundred pieces of articles (paintings) for the competition. [V]
cāntiān	參天	to be tall enough to reach to the sky; very tall 參天大樹 *cān tiān dà shù* [Adj/SV]
cāntòu	參透	to penetrate, to understand (mysteries, profundities) [CC/V]
cānwù	參悟	to understand (mystery from meditation) [CC/V]
cānyàn	參驗	to verify (truth by personal experience): to personally inspect [CC/V]
cānyì	參議	to partake in deliberations of policy [CC/V]; a senator
cānyù	參與	to take part in (discussion, plan): 從昨天起， 我參與了他們的討論。 *Cóng zuótian qǐ, wǒ cānyúle tāmende tǎolùn.* Starting yesterday, I've taken part in their discussion. [CC/V]
cānzá	參雜	to mix [V]
cānzàn	參贊	to act as advisor on project [CC/V]; a counsellor
cānzhàn	參戰	to participate in the war [V-O]
cānzhào	參照	to consult; to refer to = 參考仿照 *cānkǎo fǎngzhào* 這個句子必須參照上下文來理解。 *Zhèige jùzi bìxū cānzhào shàngxiàwén lái lǐjiě.* This sentence can only be understood via the context. [V]
cānzhèng	參政	to participate in government [V-O]

chábān	查班	to inspect class [V-O]
chábàn	查辦	to investigate and prosecute (case, person) [CC/V]
cháchāo	查抄	to take inventory/to confiscate (property) [CC/V]
chádiǎn	查點	to check item by item [CC/V]
chá duì wú é	查對無訛	After checking, no error was found. (formula for okaying accounts)
cháfēng	查封	to confiscate and seal up (property, goods) [CC/V]
cháhé	查核	to examine (accounts) [CC/V]
chá hùkǒu	查戶口	to check residents, to take census
chájìn	查禁	to search and ban (smuggled goods, etc.) [CC/V]
chájīng	查經	to study the Bible: 查經班 *chájīngbān*, Bible study class [V-O]
chájiū	查究	to investigate and follow up (a case) [CC/V]
chákàn	查勘	to investigate on the spot [CC/V]
chámíng	查明	to find out: 查明真相 *chámíng zhēnxiàng*, to find out the true facts [VC]
cháqīng	查清	to clear up by an investigation [VC]
cháshào	查哨	to serve as a sentry [V-O]
cháshōu	查收	(letter writing) please receive: 隨信寄給你相片三張。 請查收。 *Suí xìn jì gei nǐ xiàngpiàn sānzhāng. Qǐng cháshōu.* I am enclosing in the letter three photographs. Please receive. [CC/V]
cháyuè	查閱	to read (report, correspondence) [CC/V]
cházhàng	查賬	to audit accounts [V-O]
cházhào	查照	(in official documents) to submit for your attention: 請查照辦理。 *Qǐng cházhào bànlǐ.* Please consider and act accordingly. [CC/V]
chá zìdiǎn	查字典	to look up in a dictionary: 你要是有不認識的字， 就查字典。 *Nǐ yàoshi yǒu búrènshide zì, jiù chá zìdiǎn.* If there are words that you don't know, look them up in a dictionary.

chá'àn	察案	to investigate a case
chábàn	察辦	to investigate and take measures [CC/V]
cháchū	察出	to find out [VC]
cháfǎng	察訪	to go about to find out (conditions, rumors) [CC/V]
cháhé	察核	(official document) please use your discerning judgment [CC/V]
chájué	察覺	to scent, to read [CC/V]
chákàn	察看	to look into, to inspect [CC/V]
chákān	察勘	to examine (place of robbery, landmarks, etc.) on the spot [CC/V]
chámíng	察明	to ascertain clearly: 察明責任。 *chámíng zérèn*, to ascertain clearly who is responsible [VC]
cháshōu	察收	to examine and receive [CC/V]
cháwèn	察問	to inquire into [CC/V]
chá yán guān sè	察言觀色	to pay attention to what is said and to how it is said; to check what one says against what he does; to observe the words and gestures of sb. 他很擅於察言觀色。 *Tā hěn shànyu cháyán guān sè.* He is good at observing others. [V O]
cházhào	察照	to take notice and do accordingly [CC/V]
dūchá	督察	to supervise, to watch over [CC/V]
guānchá	觀察	to observe [CC/V]
jiānchá	監察	to supervise, to watch over [CC/V]
jǐngchá	警察	police [CC/N]
jiūchá	糾察	to investigate (a case) [CC/V]
kǎochá	考察	to investigate; to visit for the purpose of learning 他一共出國考察過三次。 *Tā yígòng chūguó kǎochá guò sāncì.* He went abroad to visit three times altogether. [V]
shìchá	視察	to inspect [CC/V]; inspector
xìchá	細察	to observe carefully: 細察來意。 *xìchá lái yì*, to judge the motive of his coming [SC/V]

產

chǎndì	產地	origin of products [SC/N]
chǎn'é	產額	rate of volume of production [SC/N]
chǎnfáng	產房	maternity ward [SC/N]
chǎnfù	產婦	lying-in woman (woman in maternity) [SC/N]
chǎnhòurè	產後熱	puerperal fever
chǎnkē	產科	obstertrics, maternity department [SC/N]
chǎnliàng	產量	capacity or volume of production [SC/N]
chǎnpǐn	產品	products [SC/N]
chǎnpó	產婆	midwife [SC/N]
chǎnshēng	產生	to produce (fish, grapes, etc.); to create (misunderstanding, trouble, etc.) [CC/V]
chǎnwù	產物	products of land [SC/N]
chǎnyè	產業	property, industry [CC/N]
cáichǎn	財產	property [CC/N]
dòngchǎn	動產	movable effects: 不動產 *búdòngchǎn*, realty [SC/N]
fángchǎn	房產	realty [CC/N]
Gòngchǎndǎng	共產黨	Communist Party
jiāchǎn	家產	family property [SC/N]
nánchǎn	難產	difficult labor (maternity) [SC/N]
pòchǎn	破產	to go into bankruptcy [V-O]
shuǐchǎn	水產	marine products (fish, etc.) [SC/N]
sīchǎn	私產	private property [SC/N]
tǔchǎn	土產	local products [SC/N]
xiǎochǎn	小產	to give premature birth [SC/V]
yíchǎn	遺產	inherited property [SC/N]
zhèr chǎn mǐ	這兒產米	This place produces rice.

chàngběn(r)	唱本(兒)	song text [SC/N]
chàng gāodiàor	唱高調兒	to use high-flown words; to brag without actual deeds: 他就會唱高調兒。別指望他做出甚麼來。 *Tā jiù huì chàng gāodiàor. Bié zhǐwàng tā zuòchu shénme lai.* He just talks. Don't expect him to do anything. [V O]
chàng gēr	唱歌兒	to sing a song [V O]
chànghǎo	唱好	to sing well [VC]; to give cheers as audience [V-O]
chànghé	唱和	to write (poem) in reply
chàng hēitóu	唱黑頭	to sing the role of a painted face (Chinese opera)
chàngjī	唱機	a singing machine/record player (also, 留聲機 *liúshēngjī*) [SC/N]
chàngjiào	唱叫	to yell and scream [CC/V]
chànglǐ	唱禮	(Buddhist) prayer at end of mass with "five forgivenesses" and "five wishes" [SC/N]
chàngmíng	唱名	to make roll call [V-O]
chàngpiàn(r)	唱片(兒)	singing disc/records [SC/N]
chàng piào	唱票	to call votes [V O]
chàng shī	唱詩	to chant, to sing hymns [V O]
chàngxì	唱戲	to hold, have, or sing an opera: 今天晚上城裏唱戲。 *Jīntian wǎnshang chéngli chàngxì.* Tonight, there is an opera in the city.
dúchàng	獨唱	to perform a solo [SC/V]
fū chàng fù suí	夫唱婦隨	husband sings and wife follows/to have a harmonious married life
héchàng	合唱	to sing in chorus [SC/V]
mài chàng	賣唱	to sell singing/to sing as minstrel at restaurants, streets [V O]
qīngchàng	清唱	to sing without accompaniment or stage makeup [SC/V]

chēngbà	稱霸	to assume hegemony, to declare oneself as superpower [V-O]
chēngbìng	稱病	to plead illness 他稱病不出。 *Tā chēngbìng bùchū.* He stayed home with the excuse of being sick. [V]
chēngdài	稱貸	to borrow money [VO]
chēngdào	稱道	to praise, to declare: 稱道不絕。 *chēngdào bùjué,* to praise unceasingly [CC/V]
chēng gū dào guǎ	稱孤道寡	to call oneself king
chēnghào	稱號	title [SV/N]
chēnghè	稱賀	to congratulate [VO]
chēnghu	稱呼	to address [CC/V]; way by which one is addressed
chèngshēn	稱身	to fit well: 這件衣裳很稱身。 *Zhèijian yīshang hěn chèngshēn.* This dress fits well. [VO]
chēngshù	稱述	to state; to narrate [V]
chēngsòng	稱頌	to praise, to adore [CC/V]
chēngwángchēngbà	稱王稱霸	to domineer; to lord it over [VO]
chēngwèi	稱謂	way of addressing a person [CC/N]
chēngxiàn = *sòngyáng xiànmù*	稱羨 = 頌揚羨慕	to praise and admire [V]
chēngxióng	稱雄	to declare oneself as leader, to be considered as leader [V-O]
chēng xiōng dào dì	稱兄道弟	to address each other in great familiarity
chēngxǔ	稱許	to praise, to show approval (especially by a superior) [CC/V]
chēngzàn	稱讚	to praise [CC/V]
chènzhí	稱職	to be competent [VO/SV]
chènxīn	稱心	to have as one wishes [VO/SV]
chènyì	稱意	to be satisfactory, to be satisfied [VO]
chèngyuàn	稱願	to go as one desires; to have as one wishes [V-O]

chéngbài	成敗	success and failure/result: 不計成敗 *bújì chéngbài*, don't care about what the result will be [CC/N]
chéngběn	成本	capital: 成本太高的生意不好做。 *Chéngběn tài gāo de shēngyi bùhǎo zuò.* Business requiring high capital is not easy to do. [SC/N]
chénggōng	成功	to be successful [VO/SV]
chénghūn	成婚	to get married [V-O]
chéngjī	成績	achievement, results [SC/N]
chéngjiā	成家	to establish family/to get married [V-O]
chéngjiàn	成見	set views/prejudice [SC/N]
chéngjiāo	成交	to complete the business deal [V-O]
chéngjiù	成就	accomplishment, achievement [CC/N]
chéngle shénme le	成了甚麼了	What has it (one) become to?
chénglì	成立	to establish [CC/V]
chéngmíng	成名	to become famous [V-O]
chéngnián	成年	to become adult, to have grown up [SC/V]; the whole year [TW]
chéngqīn	成親	to become relatives/to get married [V-O]
chéngquán	成全	to help complete: 我這樣做還不是想成全他那一片孝心。 *Wǒ zhèyang zuò háibúshì xiǎng chéngquán tā nà yípiàn xiàoxīn.* I do this to help him fulfill his filial obligation. [CC/V]
chéngshú	成熟	to be mature [CC/SV]
chéngtiān	成天	the whole day [TW]
chéngwéi	成為	to become [CC/V]
chéngxiào	成效	effect, result [SC/N]
chéngxīn	成心	intentionally: 他成心氣他媽媽。 *Tā chéngxīn qì ta māma.* He intentionally angers his mother. [VO]
chéngyǔ	成語	established sayings/proverbs [SC/N]
chéngzhǎng	成長	to grow [CC/V]

乘

chéngbiàn	乘便	to do something at one's convenience: 請乘便把他帶回去。 *Qǐng chéngbiàn bǎ ta dài huí qu.* Please take him home at your convenience (since you are going that way). [V-O]
chéngchú	乘除	multiplication and division [CC/N]
chéngfǎ	乘法	(method of) multiplication [SV/N]
chéngfāng	乘方	(mathematics) square, cube, power of nth degree
chéng fēng pò làng	乘風破浪	to ride the wind and waves/to have a smooth and swift trip
chéngjī	乘機	to take the chance and . . . : 乘機脫逃, *chéngjī tuōtáo,* to take the chance and escape; to ride a plane [V-O]
chéng jī	乘機	to take advantage of the opportunity
chéngjǐng	乘警	police officer who works on trains [N]
chéngkè	乘客	passenger [SC/N]
chéngkòng(r)	乘空(兒)	to take advantage of a free moment or unguarded situation: 你現在沒事,還不乘空兒把那封信寫完? *Nǐ xiànzài méishì, hái bù chéng kòngr bǎ nèifeng xìn xiěwán?* Since you are not busy now, why don't you finish that letter? [V-O]
chéngliáng	乘涼	to enjoy cool air [V-O]
chéng rén bú bèi	乘人不備	to take advantage of other's unpreparedness
chéngshí	乘時	to take advantage of an opportune time [VO]
chéngshì	乘勢	to avail oneself of the opportunity, to strike while the iron is hot [VO]
chéngshù	乘數	a multiple [SC/N]
chéngxìng	乘興	to do something on impulse to enjoy: 乘興多畫幾張吧。 *Chéngxìng duō huà jǐzhāng ba.* You'd better paint a few more while you are enjoying it. [VO]
chéngxū	乘虛	to do something when the opponent is weak [VO]
sān chéng sān dé jiǔ	三乘三得九	Three multiplied by three is nine.

chī cù	吃醋	to eat vinegar, to be jealous
chī dà guō fàn	吃大鍋飯	to eat rice cooked in a big pot (institutional food)
chī dòufu	吃豆腐	to eat bean curd, to flirt (with opposite sex), to make fun of (person of the same sex)
chī ěrguāng	吃耳光	to be slapped on the face
chī fàngguǎnr	吃飯館兒	to eat at a restaurant
chījǐn	吃緊	to be tense: 時局很吃緊。 *Shíjú hěn chījǐn.* The situation is very tense. [VO/SV]
chījìn	吃勁	to be hard, to try: 這件事很吃勁。 *Zhèijiàn shì hěn chījìn.* This is hard. 你得吃勁拉。 *Nǐ děi chījìn lā.* You have to pull hard.
chījīng	吃驚	to be frightened: 大吃一驚 *dà chī yìjīng*, to be greatly frightened [V-O]
chīkǔ	吃苦	to suffer hardship [V-O]
chīkuī	吃虧	to suffer loss; to be disadvantageous [V-O]
chīlì	吃力	to be difficult, requiring strength [VO/SV]
chī ruǎn bù chī yìng	吃軟不吃硬	to bully the weak but yield to the strong
chī ruǎn fàn	吃軟飯	to eat soft rice, to live on one's wife (or woman)
chīshuǐ	吃水	to be absorbent: 這種紙不太吃水。 *Zhèizhǒng zhǐ bútài chīshuǐ.* This kind of paper is not too absorbent. [VO/SV]
chīsù	吃素	to abstain from eating meat [V-O]
chītòu	吃透	to have a thorough grasp 吃透課本 *chītòu kèběn* to be very familiar with the content of the textbook [V]
chī xián fàn	吃閒飯	to eat leisure food/to be a loafer or sponger
chīxiāng	吃香	to be popular: 他現在很吃香。 *Tā xiànzài hěn chīxiāng.* He is now very popular. [VO/SV]
chī yādàn	吃鴨蛋	to eat a duck egg, to fail to win any points

chí bǐ	持筆	to hold a pen/to write [V-O]
chífǎ	持法	to maintain the law: 持法森嚴 *chífǎ sēnyán*, to administer sharp justice [VO]
chíjiā	持家	to run a household, to maintain family fortune and status [VO]
chíjiǔ	持久	to hold out long, to last: 持久戰 *chíjiǔ zhàn*, protracted warfare [VC]
chípíng	持平	to keep balance: 收支持平 *shōu zhī chípíng*; to hold unbiased views; to hold just views: *chípíng zhī lùn*, a balanced view [VO]
chíshēn	持身	to conduct oneself [VO]
chíxíng	持行	(Budd.) conduct [VO]
chíxù	持續	to carry on, to last [CC]
chíyǎng	持養	to take good care (of health), to cultivate spiritual regimen [VO]
chíyǒu	持有	to hold ... 持有博士學位 *chíyǒu bóshì xuéwèi* to hold a doctorate diploma [V]
chízhèng	持正	to support what is right [VO]
chízhòng	持重	to act with gravity (not frivolous): 老成持重 *lǎochéng chízhòng*, experienced and steady [VO/SV]
chízhīyǐhéng	持之以恒	to preserve; to keep doing
chízhīyǒugù	持之有故	have sufficient grounds for one's views
bǎchí	把持	to monopolize (power, position) [CC/V]
bǎochí	保持	to maintain (status, distance): 跟他還是保持點兒距離好些。 *Gēn tā háishi bǎochí diǎnr jùlí hǎo xie*. It is better to keep a distance from him.
fúchí	扶持	to support [CC/V]
zhīchí	支持	to support, to sustain (person to stand up, tottering regime, etc.) [CC/V]
zhǔchí	主持	to be in charge [SC/V]

chūbǎn	出版	to publish: 出版一本書 *chūbǎn yìběn shū*, to publish a book [V-O/TV]
chūchāi	出差	to be sent on a business trip [V-O]
chūchǎn	出產	to produce [CC/V]; products, natural products
chūchàr	出岔兒	to go wrong: 要是出個岔兒，誰負責? *Yàoshi chū ge chàr, shéi fùzé?* If anything goes wrong, who is going to take the responsibility? [V-O]
chū fēngtou	出風頭	to enjoy publicity
chūjiā	出家	to get out of home/to become a monk [V-O]
chūkǒu	出口	export, exit [SC]; to speak [V-O]
chūlù	出路	future, employment prospect: 學音樂，出路不太好。 *Xué yīnyuè, chūlù bútài hǎo.* If one studies music, the employment prospects aren't too good. [SC/N]
chūménr	出門兒	to go out of the door, to be out of town [V-O]
chū mǐ	出米	to produce rice [V O]
chūmiàn	出面	to appear: 這件事，由我出面接洽。 *Zhèi jiàn shì, yóu wǒ chūmiàn jiēqia.* Let me go to deal with this matter. [V-O]
chūmíng	出名	to become famous [V-O]
chūqì	出氣	to vent the spleen [V-O]
chūqián	出錢	to pay: 買汽車，誰出錢? *Mǎi qìchē, shéi chūqián?* Buy a car? Who is going to pay? [V-O]
chūqu	出去	to go out [VC], also used as complement to other verbs
chūrù	出入	difference, discrepancies [CC/N]
chūsè	出色	to be superior [VO/SV]
chūshēn	出身	background: 他是做買賣出身。 *Tā shi zuò mǎimai chūshēn.* He has a business background. [VO/N]
chūshén	出神	to be completely absorbed by something, to be absent minded. [V-O]
chūshì	出事	to have an accident [V-O]
chūtóu	出頭	to become prominent in one's field: 你好好做，總有出頭的一天。 *Nǐ hǎohāor zuò, zǒng yǒu chūtóude yìtiān.* If you work hard, one day you will get ahead. [V-O]
chūxi	出息	ability, promise: 這孩子，真沒出息。 *Zhè háizi zhēn méi chūxi.* This child has no ability (or future). [SC/N]
chūyáng	出洋	to go abroad [V-O]
chū yángxiàng	出洋相	to make fun of (oneself or sombody else)

chú bào ān liáng	除暴安良	to drive out the rascals and protect good people
chúcǎo	除草	to weed; to root out or remove (a weed or weeds), as from a garden; to weed out crab grass from a lawn. 夏天，我每個星期都得除草。 *Xiàtiān, wǒ měige xīngqī dōu děi chúcǎo.* In the summer time, I have to weed each week.
chúchóng	除蟲	to exterminate insects [V-O]
chúdiào	除掉	to remove [VC]
chúfǎ	除法	(math.) division [SC/N]
chúfēi	除非	unless, except: 除非你去不行。 *Chúfēi nǐ qù bùxíng.* It won't do unless you go. [Conj]
chúgēn	除根	to uproot: 斬草除根 *zhǎn cǎo chú gēn*, to get rid of grass, it must be uprooted [V-O]
chúhài	除害	to suppress the evil: 政府應當替老百姓除害。 *Zhèngfǔ yīngdāng tì lǎobǎixìng chúhài.* Governments ought to suppress the evil on behalf of the people. [V-O]
chúhào	除號	(math.) sign of division "÷"
chúkāi	除開	to count off, to take away [VC]
chúle	除了	Besides: 除了你(以外)，沒有別人會。 *Chúle nǐ (yǐwài) méiyou bié ren huì.* Besides you, there are no others who can. 除了你(以外)，還有別人去。 *Chúle nǐ (yǐwài) hái yǒu biéren qù.* In addition to you there are others who also go.
chúmíng	除名	to dismiss, to expel (to remove from list of names): 他常常逃學，所以被學校除名了。 *Tā chángcháng táoxué, suóyi bèi xuéxiào chúmíng le.* He was expelled from school because he was often truant. [V-O]
chúqù	除去	to remove [VC]
chúshù	除數	(math.) the divisor; 被除數 *bèichúshù*, the dividend
chúwài	除外	not to be counted, to be excluded: 星期日除外。 *Xīngqīrì chúwài.* Sundays are excepted.
chúxī	除夕	New Year's Eve
fèichú	廢除	to abolish: 廢除不平等條約。 *fèichú bùpíngděng tiáoyuē*, to abolish unequal treaties [CC/V]
kāichú	開除	see 除名 *chúmíng* [CC/V]
pòchú	破除	to abolish: 破除迷信 *pòchú míxìn*, to abolish superstition [CC/V]
sān chú liù dé èr	三除六得二	Six divided by three is two.

chǔbùlái	處不來	cannot get along: 我跟他處不來。 *Wǒ gēn tā chǔbùlái.* I can't get along with him. [VC]
chǔduàn	處斷	to decide [CC/V]
chǔfá	處罰	to punish [CC/V]
chǔfāng	處方	to prescribe [V-O]; prescription
chǔfèn	處分	to punish
chǔjìng	處境	circumstances [SC/N]
chǔjué	處決	to execute (criminal), to decide [CC/V]
chǔlǐ	處理	to dispose of, to arrange, to settle: 這件事真不好處理。 *Zhèjiàn shì zhēn bùhǎo chǔlǐ.* This matter is really hard to deal with. [CC/V]
chǔnǚ	處女	maiden; virgin [N]
chǔshì	處士	a retired scholar [SC/N]
chǔshì	處世	to deal with the world: 他不會待人處世，所以常常得罪人。 *Tā búhuì dài rén chǔshì, suǒyǐ chángcháng dézuì rén.* He offends people often because he doesn't know how to deal with people. 處世之道 *chǔshì zhī dào*, a way of life [V-O]
chǔsǐ	處死	to sentence to death [VO]
chǔ xīn jī lù	處心積慮	to brood over a matter for a long time
chǔxíng	處刑	to punish: 處極刑 *chǔ jíxíng*, sentence to death [V-O]
chǔ yú sǐ dì	處於死地	to send somebody to his doom
chǔjíxíng	處極刑	to execute (criminal) [CC/V]
chǔzhì	處治	to punish [CC/V]
chǔzhì	處置	= 處理 *chǔlǐ* [CC/V]
xiāngchǔ	相處	to get along with each other: 他們兩個相處得很好。 *Tāmen liǎngge xiāngchǔde hěn hǎo.* The two of them get along fine. [SC/V]

chuán'àn	傳案	to summon to court [V-O]
chuánbō	傳播	to spread (news, ideas, disease, etc.) [CC/V]
chuánbù	傳佈	to spread, to publicize [CC/V]
chuándá	傳達	to communicate (thoughts, ideas); to transmit (order from above); 傳達命令 *chuándá mìnglìng* [CC/V]
chuándān	傳單	a handbill, a publicity circular or flyer [SC/N]
chuándì	傳遞	to pass around (letter, message) [CC/V]
chuán'gei ta	傳給他	to pass on to him
chuánguān	傳觀	to circulate for people to see [CC/V]
chuánjiā	傳家	to bequeath to the family: 傳家之寶 *chuánjiā zhī bǎo*, art object kept as heirloom [VO]
chuánjiào	傳教	to preach: 傳教士 *chuánjiàoshì*, a missionary [V-O]
chuánpiào	傳票	a court summons, subpoena; (accounting) a voucher [SC/N]
chuánrǎn	傳染	to infect: 傳染病 *chuánrǎn bìng*, communicable disease [CC/V]
chuán rè	傳熱	to transmit heat [V O]
chuánshén	傳神	to be vivid, to give lively expression (of portraiture) [VO/SV]
chuánshěn	傳審	to summon for trial [CC/V]
chuánshòu	傳授	to teach [CC/V]
chuánsòng	傳送	to deliver (message, news) [CC/V]
chuánshuō	傳說	folktale [CC/N]
chuánwén	傳聞	It is reported that: 傳聞敵人佔領王庄。 *Chuánwén díren zhànlǐng Wáng Zhuāng.* It is reported that the enemy occupied Wang Zhuang. [CC]
chuánxìn	傳信	to deliver letters, to communicate (tradition, belief); 傳信兒 *chuán xìnr*, to deliver a message [V-O]
chuányáng	傳揚	to spread (teaching, etc.) [CC/V]
chuányuè	傳閱	to pass around for people to read [CC/V]

dá'àn	答案	answer, solution of mathematical problem [SC/N]
dábài	答拜	to pay a return call
dábiàn	答辯	to argue back [CC/V]
dábushanglai	答不上來	can't answer [VC]
dáchár	答碴兒	to make an answer to question, to strike up conversation [V-O]
dácí	答詞	a response (to an address of congratulation): 現在請王博士致答詞。 *Xiànzài qǐng Wáng Bóshì zhì dácí.* Now we ask Dr. Wang to say a word (as a response). [SC/N]
dáduì	答對	to answer, to respond [CC/V]; to answer correctly [VC]
dáfu	答覆	to reply [CC/V]; a reply
dáhuà	答話	to answer [V-O]
dálǐ	答禮	to respond to a salutation [V-O]; a gift in return [SC/N]
dápìn	答聘	to reply on acceptance of appointment [VO]; formal acknowledgement of betrothal gift
dáshù	答數	correct number in mathematical solutions [SC/N]
dáxiè	答謝	to return a courtesy call; a letter to thank someone
dāying	答應	to consent, to promise [CC/V]; 不答應 *bùdāying,* to disapprove, to take offense at: 你亂花錢，爸爸不答應。 *Nǐ luàn huā qián, Bàba bùdāying.* Dad will not approve your careless spending.
dáyǔ	答語	reply, words of reply [SC/N]
bàodá	報答	to repay person for kindness or favor [CC/V]
duì dá rú liú	對答如流	answer like flowing water/to answer quickly
huídá	回答	to answer [CC/V]; a reply
jiědá	解答	to explain [CC/V]; an explanation
suǒ dá fēi suǒ wèn	所答非所問	What was answered was not what was questioned/answer evades the question
wèndá	問答	question and answer: 問答題 *wèndá tí,* question and answer topics in an examination [CC/N]

dǎ bǎizi	打擺子	to have an attack of malaria [V-O]
dǎbāo	打包	to make a doggy bag [V O]
dǎ biāngǔ	打邊鼓	to beat the side drum/to spread or circulate praise of actor, etc.
dǎchéng yípiàn	打成一片	to become one piece/to become a harmonious whole
dǎchū shǒur	打出手兒	(Chinese opera) to throw weapons back and forth on the stage
dǎ dànzi	打彈子	to play billiards [V O]
dǎ dìpù	打地鋪	to sleep on floor (due to lack of accommodation)
dǎ dìtānr	打地攤兒	to fall down flat on ground
dǎ dǐzi	打底子	to make a draft [V O]
dǎ diànhuà	打電話	to make a phone call
dǎgōng	打工	to have a temporary job (of students doing summer work) [V-O]
dǎ guānqiāng	打官腔	to put person off by talking formalities as excuse
dǎhāha	打哈哈	to laugh out loud, to make fun [V-O]
dǎjià	打架	to fight, to engage in a brawl [V-O]
dǎ jiāodao	打交道	to have dealings with
dǎ máoyī	打毛衣	to knit a sweater
dǎ qíng mà qiào	打情罵俏	to flirt
dǎshǒu	打手	professional rioters [SC/N]; to beat the hand [V O]
dǎtāi	打胎	to have an abortion [V-O]
dǎtīng	打聽	to find out [CC/V]
dǎ yájì	打牙祭	to have a good meal
dǎzá(r)	打雜兒	to do odd jobs as handyman [V-O]
dǎ zhāohu	打招呼	to say "hello"

dài
to carry, to lead, to bring up
帶

dài'àn	帶案	to subpoena [VO]
dài biǎo	帶錶	to wear a watch [V O]
dài bīng	帶兵	to lead troops [V O]
dàicìr	帶刺兒	to be sarcastic 他常常話中帶刺兒。 *Tā chángcháng huàzhōng dài cìr.* He is often very sarcastic. [V O]
dàidǎ	帶打	to rain fisticuffs; show of combat in Chinese opera [VO]
dàidào	帶道	to lead the way, to serve as guide [V-O]
dàifēnshu	帶分數	mixed fraction (mathematics)
dàigōu	帶鈎	best buckle [SC/N]
dài hǎo(r)	帶好兒	to carry greetings to: 請替我給你父母帶個好兒。 *Qǐng tì wǒ gěi nǐ fùmǔ dài ge hǎor.* Please remember me to your parents. [V O]
dài kǒuyīn	帶口音	to speak with an accent: 說話帶口音。 *shuōhuà dài kǒuyīn*
dàilei	帶累	to involve someone in trouble or expense [CC/V]
dàilǐng	帶領	to lead, to be in charge of (troops) [CC/V]
dàilù	帶路	= 帶道 *dàidào*
dài qián	帶錢	to carry money [V O]
dàishang mén	帶上門	to close the door [V O]
dài shēnzi	帶身子	to be pregnant [V O]
dàitóu(r)	帶頭(兒)	to lead [V-O]
dàixiào	帶孝	to wear mourning [V-O]
dà xiǎoháir	帶小孩兒	to bring up children: 別把小孩兒帶壞了。 *Bié bǎ xiǎoháir dàihuàile.* Don't spoil the child.
dài xiāoxi	帶消息	to take message
dài xǐsè	帶喜色	to wear a pleased expression
lián dǎ dài mà	連打帶罵	to beat and scold at the same time
lián tī dài dǎ	連踢帶打	to mix kicks with hand blows

dāngbīng	當兵	to be a soldier [V-O]
dāngchāi	當差	to run errand, to work for (someone) [V-O]; a servant
dāngdài	當代	the present age, that period [VO/TW]
dāng jī lì duàn	當機立斷	to decide on the spot or moment, to make quick decision
dāngjiā	當家	to be the head of, to oversee [V-O]
dāngjú	當局	the authorities [VO/N]
dāngmiàn	當面	face to face: 你當面對他講。 *Nǐ dāngmiàn duì tā jiǎng.* You talk to him face to face. [VO/Adv]
dāngquán	當權	to be in power: 當權派 *dāngquánpài*, faction in power [VO]
dāngrán	當然	naturally [Adv]
dāng rén bú ràng	當仁不讓	in good causes, don't lag behind
dāngshí	當時	at that very moment, that time [VO/TW]
dāngshìrén	當事人	person in charge, parties to a quarrel or lawsuit
dāngtóu	當頭	right overhead: 當頭棒喝 *dāng tóu bàng hè*, to give sharp advice for one to make up from error [VO/Adv]
dāngxīn	當心	to take care, to be careful [V-O]
dāngxuǎn	當選	to be elected [V-O]
dāng zhī wú kuì	當之無愧	to merit the credit, to be deserving
dāngzhòng	當眾	in the presence of all: 當眾宣佈 *dāngzhòng xuānbù*, to announce publicly [VO/Adv]
cháiláng dàng dào	豺狼當道	wolf stands astride the road/bad person in power
mén dàng hù duì	門當戶對	(of betrothal) two families match in social status
shàngdàng	上當	to go to pawnshop/to be cheated [V-O]
dàng ěrbiān fēng	當耳邊風	to take advice as passing wind
dàngzhēn	當真	really: 他當真不會。 *Tā dàngzhēn búhuì.* He really cannot. [VO/Adv]
ná ta dàng péngyou	拿他當朋友	to treat him as a friend

dǎobānr	倒班兒	to take turns [V-O]
dǎobāo	倒包	to substitute one thing for another [V-O]
dǎobì	倒閉	to go bankrupt: 好幾家銀行倒閉了。 *Hǎo jǐjiā yínháng dǎobì le.* Quite a few banks went bankrupt. [CC/V]
dǎobuguòlái	倒不過來	= *dǎobùkāi* 倒不開 [VC]
dǎobukāi	倒不開	cannot meet the turnover in business [VC]
dǎodàn	倒蛋	to make trouble, to create mischief (also 搗蛋) [V-O]
dǎo fèng diān luán	倒鳳顛鸞	to have sexual intercourse
dǎogé	倒戈	to turn around weapon/to change sides (of warlords) [V-O]
dǎohuàn	倒換	to replace [CC/V]
dǎojià	倒價	selling-out price [SC/N]
dǎosǎng	倒嗓	to have a hoarse voice (of opera singers) [V-O]
dǎotā	倒塌	to tumble down [CC/V]
dǎoteng	倒騰	to turn upside down
dǎotì	倒替	to substitute, to replace [CC/V]
dǎotóu	倒頭	to lay down one's head to sleep, to die: 倒頭紙 *dǎotóu zhǐ*, paper money burned at death [V-O]
dǎowèikou	倒胃口	to lose one's appetite [V O]
dǎoyùn	倒運	to have bad luck [V-O]; bad luck: 走倒運 *zǒu dǎoyùn*
dǎozhàng	倒帳	to go bankrupt because of deficit, to fail to collect debts
dǎozìr	倒字兒	to mispronounce (in Peking opera) [V-O]
biàndǎo	辯倒	to defeat by arguing [VC]
dǎdǎo	打倒	to knock down, down with . . . !
tuīdǎo	推倒	to push down [VC]
zāidǎo	栽倒	to fall down [VC]

dàocǎi	倒彩	false applause: 喝倒彩 *hè dàocǎi*, to hiss a speaker or actor [SC/N]
dào chē	倒車	to back up a car [V O]
dào dǎ luór	倒打鑼兒	to beat the gong upside down/everything is upside down
dàoguà	倒掛	to hang upside down [SC/V]
dàoguolai	倒過來	to put in reverse
dàohǎor	倒好兒	false applause: 叫個倒好兒 *jiào ge dàohǎor*, to hiss at performance (= *dàocǎi*) [SC/N]
dàoliú	倒流	to flow back [SC/V]
dàoqì	倒氣	to gasp [V-O]
dàoqiàn	倒欠	to owe instead of gaining: 他原來欠我很多錢。 後來我倒欠他。 *Tā yuánlái qiàn wǒ hěn duō qián. Hòulai wǒ dàoqiàn tā.* He owed me a lot of money originally. Later I owed him instead. [SC/V]
dàoshǔ	倒數	to count backward: 他是倒數第一。 *Tā shì dàoshǔ dìyī.* He is No. 1 counted backward. [SC/V]
dàotiē(r)	倒貼(兒)	to lose in bargain, to sell below cost; to pay her paramour instead of being paid [SC/V]
dàotuì	倒退	to fall back [SC/V]
dào xíng nì shī	倒行逆施	to govern or manage in opposition to right principles
dàoxuán	倒懸	to hang upside down, tyrannical treatment [SC/V]
dàoyǐng(r)	倒影(兒)	inverted image, reflection in water [SC/N]
dàozāicōng	倒栽蔥	to plant the onion upside down/to fall headfirst
dàozhì	倒置	to set up wrong: 因果倒置 *yīn guǒ dàozhì*, cause and result are set up wrong/to put the carriage before the horse [SC/V]
dàozhuàn	倒轉	to turn in reverse [SC/V]
guàdàole	掛倒了	to hang something upside down [VC]

dàochāi	到差	to arrive at post, to appear for duty [V-O]
dàochù	到處	everywhere: 到處是水。 *Dàochù shì shuǐ.* Water is everywhere. [VO/Adv]
dào cǐ wéi zhǐ	到此為止	to stop here
dàodá	到達	to reach: 今天動身的話，甚麼時候可以到達? *Jīntian dòngshēn dehua, shénme shíhou kéyi dàodá?* If you leave today, when can you arrive? [CC/V]
dàodǐ	到底	after all, to the bottom of the matter: 這到底是怎麼回事? *Zhè dàodǐ shì zěnme huí shì?* What is the matter after all; to the end: *kàngzhàn dào dǐ*, to fight to the end
dàoguo	到過	to have been somewhere: 我到過紐約。 *Wǒ dàoguo Niǔ Yuē.* I have been to New York.
dàojiār	到家兒	to be proficient: 他的畫兒可畫得到家兒了。 *Tāde huàr kě huàde dàojiār le.* His painting is really good [VO/SV] (cf. *dào jiā*, to reach home)
dào mòliǎor	到末了兒	to the end, finally, at last
dàoqī	到期	due time: 八月一號到期。 *Báyuè yíhào dàoqī.* It is due August 1. 你借的書到期了嗎? *Nǐ jiè de shū dàoqīle ma?* Is the book you borrowed due today? [VO]
dào rújīn	到如今	until now
dàoshǒu	到手	to succeed in getting: 那些錢甚麼時候才能到手? *Nèixie qián shénme shíhou cái néng dàoshǒu?* When can I get that money? [V-O]
dàotóulai	到頭來	in the end: 到頭來全丟了。 *Dàotóulai quán diūle.* In the end everything was lost. [VO/Adv]
bái tóu dào lǎo	白頭到老	to reach old age with white hair/to live together for an entire lifetime (husband and wife)
mǎ dào gōng chéng	馬到功成	horse gets there and job is done/to succeed without delay
niàn dào dìsānkè	念到第三課	study to Lesson 3
xiǎngdào	想到	to think of (something, someone): 想到這件事就頭痛。 *Xiǎngdào zhèijiàn shì jiù tóuténg.* I get a headache whenever I think of this matter. [VC]
zhǎodào	找到	to be found: 我的帽子找到了。 *Wǒde màozi zhǎodàole.* I have found my hat. [VC]
zhōudào	週到	to be considerate: 他做事很週到，從來不得罪人。 *Tā zuòshì hěn zhōudào, cónglái bùdézuì rén.* Being considerate in his dealings, he never offends people. [CC/SV]

diǎnbīng	點兵	to muster soldiers [V-O]
diǎn cài	點菜	to select dishes from a menu [V O]
diǎnchuān	點穿	to point out the secret [VC]
diǎn huǒ	點火	to light a fire [V O]
diǎnjiǎo(r)	點腳(兒)	to walk lamely [V-O]
diǎnmíng	點名	to make roll call [V-O]
diǎnmíng	點明	to point out (importance, meaning); to make a clear account [VC]
diǎnpíng	點評	to check one by one and comment [V]
diǎnpò	點破	to expose (lie, falsehood) [VC]
diǎnrán	點燃	to light up; to kindle; to ignite [V]
diǎnshù	點數	to count heads check the number [V]
diǎn shū	點書	to punctuate a book [V O]
diǎn tóu	點頭	give a nod: 點頭朋友 *diǎntóu péngyou*, friends who don't know each other very well [V-O]
diǎn xì	點戲	to select play from repertoire offered [V O]
diǎnxīn	點心	a snack, pastry [VO/N]
diǎnxǐng	點醒	to remind gently [VC]
diǎnxuè	點穴	to hit at selected points (of Chinese kungfu, capable of causing internal bleeding) [VO]
diǎn yǎn	點眼	to apply eyedrop into the eye; to secure a point of anchorage in Chinese chess [V O]
diǎn yǎnyào	點眼藥	to apply eyedrop [V O]; 點眼藥 *diǎnyǎn yào*, eyedrop [SC/N]
diǎnzhuì	點綴	to decorate; to add a lively detail on painting, writing, or furniture in a room [CC/V]
dǎdiǎn	打點	to put in order (baggage): 打點行李 *dǎdiǎn xíngli*
qīngtíng diǎn shuǐ	蜻蜓點水	dragonfly skims water surface/to use a light touch in writing, to travel around with short stopovers
zhǐdiǎn	指點	to point out, to show [CC/V]

dìngguī	定規	to set up rules [V-O]
dìnghūn	定婚	to be engaged to marry [V-O]
dìnghuò	定貨	to order goods [V-O]
dìngjì	定計	to decide, to set a plan [V-O]; a fixed plan [SC/N]
dìngjià	定價	to set the price [V-O]; fixed price, list price [SC/N]
dìngjū	定居	to settle down (in a town) [CC/V]
dìngjú	定局	a settled situation [SC/N]
dìnglǐ	定理	a maxim, theorem [SC/N]
dìnglǜ	定律	laws (moral, physical) [SC/N]
dìnglùn	定論	accepted opinion [SC/N]
dìngqī	定期	to set a time [V-O]
dìngqian	定錢	earnest money, deposit [SC/N]
dìngqíng	定情	to pledge love between lovers [V-O]
dìngshén	定神	to calm down [V-O]
dìng tiānxià	定天下	to bring peace and stability to country
dìngxīnwán(r)	定心丸(兒)	tranquillizer, hence, anything that soothes the nerves or helps make up one's mind
dìngyì	定義	definition: 下定義 *xià dìngyì*, to define [SC/N]
dìng zhǔyì	定主意	to make a decision
dìngzuì	定罪	to convict, to sentence [C-O]
dìngzuò	定做	to have it custom-made [CC/V]
dìngzuòr	定座兒	to book seats, to make reservations [V-O]
shuōbudìng	說不定	cannot say for sure: 說不定他會來 *Shuōbúdìng tā huì lái*. He may come. Who knows? [VC]
shuōdìng	說定	to settle after talking: 我們說定了明天一塊兒走。 *Wǒmen shuōdìngle míngtian yíkuàir zǒu*. We have decided to leave together tomorrow. [VC]
nádìng zhúyì	拿定主意	to make up one's mind

dòngbīng	動兵	to move the soldier/to start a war [V-O]
dòngbudong	動不動	very often, do something for no reason at all, for nothing: 這孩子動不動就哭。 *Zhè háizi dòngbudong jiù kū.* This child cries for nothing. [Adv]
dòngcí	動詞	verb [SC/N]
dònggōng	動工	to commence work (on construction, building) [V-O]
dònghuǒ(r)	動火(兒)	to start fire/to feel angry [V-O]
dòng nǎojin	動腦筋	to move the brain/do a lot of thinking
dòng niàntou	動念頭	to think of a plan, to plot
dòngqì	動氣	to get angry [V-O]
dòngrén	動人	to be moving, touching, attractive [VO/SV]
dòngshēn	動身	to set out, to depart [V-O]
dòngshǒu	動手	to raise hand to fight, to start (work), to begin: 我動手慢了。 *Wǒ dòngshǒu mànle.* I started late.
dòng shǒu dòng jiǎo	動手動腳	to be fresh with girls
dòngtīng	動聽	(speech) to be moving, persuasive [SV/VO]
dòngtǔ	動土	to move dirt/to break ground [V-O]
dòngxīn	動心	to be moved (by attractive offer) [V-O]
dòngxiōng	動兇	to resort to violence [V-O]
dòngyòng	動用	to touch, to draw upon (funds): 動用公款 *dòngyòng gōngkuǎn*, to draw upon public funds [CC/V]
dòngyuán	動員	to move personnel/to mobilize: 動員民眾 *dòngyuán mínzhòng*, to mobilize the people [VO/TV]
bié dòng	別動	Don't move!
bù wéi suǒ dòng	不為所動	not to be swayed (by speech) or attracted (by beauty)
nábúdòng	拿不動	cannot carry (too heavy) [VC]
wú dòng yú zhōng	無動於衷	to be completely indifferent
xīndòng	心動	to be moved, to begin considering [SP/V]
yùndòng	運動	to do exercise [CC/V]; exercise, movement: 五四運動 *Wǔsì Yùndòng*, that May Fourth Movement
zhèige qián bùnéng dòng	這個錢不能動	This money cannot be touched.

dúbào	讀報	to read newspaper [V O]
dúběn	讀本	a reader, a school text [SC/N]; 漢語讀本 *Hànyǔ Dúběn*, Chinese Reader
dú dàxué	讀大學	to go to college or university
dúfǎ	讀法	way of pronouncing [SC/N]
dújīng	讀經	to read the Scripture, to read classics [V-O]
dúshū	讀書	to read a book: 讀書人 *dúshūrén*, a scholar, a literate person [V-O]
dú sǐshū	讀死書	to read dead books/to read without digesting
dú wàiwén	讀外文	to study foreign languages
dúwù	讀物	reading material [SC/N]
dú yèxiào	讀夜校	to go to night school
dúyīn	讀音	to pronounce [V O]; pronunciation, literary pronunciation [SC/N]
dúzhě	讀者	a reader, one who reads: 讀者文摘 *Dúzhě Wénzhāi*, Reader's Digest [SC/N]
dú Zhōngwén xì	讀中文系	to study in the Chinese department, to major in Chinese
dúzǒule yīn	讀走了音	to pronounce incorrectly
jìdú	寄讀	to study as a boarding student
lǎngdú	朗讀	to read aloud [SC/V]
mòdú	默讀	to read silently [SC/V]
zǒudú	走讀	to attend school while living at home

duò dé liàng lì	度德量力	to estimate one's virtue and measure one's strength/to assess one's ability before launching something
dùliàng	度量	capacity to tolerate: 度量大 *dùliang dà*, can tolerate a lot
dùmìyuè	度蜜月	to celebrate one's honeymoon [V O]
dù niánguān	度年關	to pass the New Year by paying all one's debts
duòzhī	度支	to estimate expenditures [VO]
duòliàng	度量	to consider, to measure [CC/V]
dùrì	度日	to pass the day, to live [VO]
dù rì rú nián	度日如年	to spend a day like one year/the days are long (with waiting), to have a miserable life
chuǎiduò	揣度	= *cǔnduò*
chuǎi qíng duò lǐ	揣情度理	to make an intelligent appraisal
cǔnduò	忖度	to conjecture, imagine (another's attitude)
guòdù	過度	excessively, beyond measure; 過度小心 *guòdù xiǎoxīn*, excessively careful [VO/Adv].
nián huá xū dù	年華虛度	one's years spent for nothing/to waste one's live (especially for young women)
yǐ jǐ duò rén	以己度人	to place oneself in another's position
yǐ xiǎorén zhī xīn duò jūnzi zhī fù	以小人之心度君子之腹	to estimate a gentleman's mind with a hypocrite's way of thinking
zhì zhī duò wài	置之度外	to disregard entirely

fābiǎo	發表	to publish, to express: 發表意見 *fābiǎo yìjian*, to express ideas [CC/V]
fācái	發財	to get rich [V-O]
fāchóu	發愁	to be worried, sad [V-O]
fādāi	發呆	to be dazed [V-O]
fādòng	發動	to promote, initiate (movement, campaign, an engine): 發動機 *fādòngjī*, dynamo, an electric motor [CC/V]
fāfēng	發瘋	to grow crazy: 你發瘋了。 *Nǐ fāfēng le.* You are out of your mind. [V-O]
fāfú	發福	to grow fat (a compliment in Chinese) [V-O]
fāhěn	發狠	to work with angry determination [V-O]; diligently [Adv]
fāhéng	發橫	to become obstinate, violent [V-O]
fāhuāng	發慌	to panic [V-O]
fāhuǒ	發火	to become angry [V-O]
fākuáng	發狂	to become mad, to grow crazy [V-O]
fālèng	發愣	to be stunned [V-O]
fāmáo	發毛	to be afraid (to enter a diserted house), to be covered with goose pimples [V-O]
fāmíng	發明	to invent
fā píqi	發脾氣	to get mad
fāshāo	發燒	to have fever [V-O]
fāshēng	發生	to arise, to cause to happen: 發生誤會 *fāshēng wùhui*, to cause misunderstanding [CC/V]
fāshì	發誓	to take an oath, to swear, also 發咒 *fāzhòu* [V-O]
fāxiàn	發現	to discover [CC/V]
fāxiè	發洩	to blow off steam, anger [CC/V]
fāzǐ	發紫	to emit purple glow/to be extremely popular: 紅得發紫 *hóngde fāzǐ*, so popular (red), that one turns purple

fǎnbó	反駁	to reply to criticism
fǎncháng	反常	to be abnormal [VO/SV]
fǎnchuàn	反串	(of actor) to play a different role: 反串老生 *fǎnchuàn lǎoshēng*, to play the male character (female character being the customary role)
fǎndào	反倒	to the contrary [CC/Adv]
fǎndòng	反動	to be reactionary: 反動派 *fǎndòngpài*, the reactionaries [SC/SV]
fǎnduì	反對	to oppose: 反對派 *fǎnduìpài*, the political opposition [CC/V]
fǎnfù	反覆	again and again: 反覆解釋 *fǎnfù jiěshì*, to explain again and again; 反覆無常 *fǎnfù wúcháng*, to change one's mind constantly (can't be trusted) [CC/Adv]
fǎngǎn	反感	reaction, bad reaction: 引起反感 *yǐnqǐ fǎngǎn*, to cause a bad reaction [SC/N]
fǎngémìng	反革命	counter-revolutionary
fǎngōng	反攻	to counterattack [SC/V]
fǎngòng	反共	to oppose Communism [V-O]; [SV] as in 他非常反共。 *Tā fēicháng fǎngòng.* He is very anti-Communist.
fǎnhuǐ	反悔	to repent
fánjī	反擊	to fight back, to counterattack [SC/V]
fǎnkàng	反抗	to resist [CC/V]; resistance
fǎn Kǒng	反孔	to oppose Confucius [V-O]
fǎnmù	反目	to fall out (esp. between husband and wife) [V O]
fǎnpàn	反叛	to rebel [CC/V]; rebellion
chuānfǎnle	穿反了	to wear it inside out (or in some other wrong way) [VC]
zàofǎn	造反	to rebel [V-O]

fēibái	飛白	a style of Chinese calligraphy with dry brush showing hollow lines [SC/N]
fēibēn	飛奔	to dash (away) [SC/V]
fēidàn	飛彈	flying bullet/a stray bullet, missle, rocket [SC/N]
fēidié	飛碟	flying saucer [SC/N]
fēi duǎn liú cháng	飛短流長	to spread rumors
fēi'é	飛蛾	moth [SC/N]
fēi huáng téng dá	飛黃騰達	to get rapid promotions or series of successes in politics or business
fēijī	飛機	a flying machine/airplane [SC/N]
fēijiǎo	飛腳	a flying foot/a flying kick [SC/N]
fēi lái zhī huò	飛來之禍	unexpected trouble
fēimáotuǐ	飛毛腿	a fast walker [SC/N]
fēipǎo	飛跑	to run as if flying/to run very fast [SC/V]
fēipù	飛瀑	(flying) waterfalls [SC/N]
fēiqiáo	飛橋	a flying bridge/a very high bridge [SC/N]
fēiténg	飛騰	to go up (to the sky) [CC/V]
fēiwěn	飛吻	to fly a kiss [V-O]; a flying kiss
fēixíng	飛行	to fly, to go by plane: 飛行員 *fēixíngyuán*, airplane pilot [CC/V]
fēiyáng	飛揚	to float in the sky [CC/V]
fēiyáng báhù	飛揚跋扈	to become powerful and intransigent
fēiyǎnr	飛眼兒	to give a darting glance [V-O]
fēiyīng zǒu gǒu	飛鷹走狗	flying hawks and running hounds/underlings
fēiyuè	飛越	to fly over: 飛越長城 *fēiyuè chángchéng*, to fly over the Great Wall [V]
fēizhǎng	飛漲	to go up like flying/(of price) sudden and rapid increase [SC/V]

gǎibiān	改編	to reorganize: 改編軍隊 *Gǎibiān jūnduì*, to regroup troops; to revise and rewrite [CC/V]
gǎibiàn	改變	to change: 把那些不好的習慣改變過來。 *Bǎ nèixie bùhǎode xíguàn gǎibiàn guolai.* Change over those bad habits. [CC/V]
gǎigé	改革	to reform [CC/V]; reform
gǎiguān	改觀	to present a new look [V-O]
gǎiguò	改過	to repent: 改過自新 *gǎiguò zì xīn*, to repent and reform [V-O]
gǎiháng	改行	to change one's occupation [V-O]
gǎihuàn	改換	to exchange or substitute one for another, to make changes in (words, titles, etc.) [CC/V]
gǎijià	改嫁	to remarry [V-O]
gǎijìn	改進	to improve [CC/V]; improvement
gǎikǒu	改口	to give a different story or affidavit; also 改嘴 *gǎizuǐ* [V-O]
gǎiliáng	改良	to improve, to reform [SC/V]
gǎiqī	改期	to change date [V-O]
gǎirì	改日	to change a date/later: 改日再談 *gǎirì zài tán*, to talk about it later; also 改天 *gǎitiān* [VO/Adv]
gǎishàn	改善	to improve (treatment, method, etc.) [VC/V]
gǎi tóu huàn miàn	改頭換面	to change the head and face/to make superficial changes
gǎixuǎn	改選	to hold a new election [V-O]
gǎiyàng	改樣	to refashion, remodel (room), to change manner (of person) [V-O]
gǎizào	改造	to remodel (building), to reform [CC/V]
gǎizhèng	改正	to correct errors: 改正錯誤 *gǎizhèng cuòwu* [CC/V]
gǎizhuāng	改裝	to change into another kind of dress, to disguise, to remodel (a building), to put in new containers [VO]
gǎizuòyè	改作業	to correct a student's homework

gàobái	告白	public notice [CC/N]
gàobié	告別	to take leave, to say goodbye [V-O]
gàochéng	告成	to announce the completion of some important project: 大功告成 *Dà gōng gàochéng*. The great task has been completed.
gàocí	告辭	to bid goodbye, to take leave [V-O]
gàodài	告貸	to make a request for a loan, to borrow money [V-O]
gàofā	告發	to formally inform court of a crime, to lodge a complaint [CC/V]
gàojí	告急	to make an emergency request for help [VO]
gàojià	告假	to ask for leave of absence: 告病假 *gào bìngjià*, to ask for sick leave [V-O]
gàojié	告捷	to announce victory [V-O]
gàojiè	告誡	to warn, to admonish [CC/V]
gàomì	告密	to give secret information against someone [V-O]
gàoshi	告示	a public announcement [CC/N]
gàosu	告訴	to tell; (law) to bring suit against someone [CC/V]
gào yíduànluo	告一段落	to consider one phase of a project completed
gàozhī	告知	to tell, to notify [CC/V]
gàozhuàng	告狀	to sue at court [V-O]
gàozuì	告罪	(courtesy) please excuse me for an unintentional offense: 告罪! 告罪! *Gàozuì! Gàozuì!* [V-O]
bùkě gào rén zhī shì	不可告人之事	an affair that is not mentionable
guǎnggào	廣告	advertisement [SC/N]
tōnggào	通告	public notice [CC/N]
wǒ gào ni	我告你	I will sue you.
zì gào fèn yǒng	自告奮勇	to volunteer one's service

géchú	革除	to expel, to dismiss [CC/V]
géchū	革出	to excommunicate sb. [V]
gé gù dǐng xīn	革故鼎新	to discard the old ways of life in favor of the new
gélǚ	革履	leather shoes [N]
gé miàn xǐ xīn	革面洗心	to start life anew
gémìng	革命	to revolt, to overthrow the established authorities [V-O]; revolution: 國民革命 *guómín gémìng*, people's revolution
géxīn	革心	to change one's mind [V-O]
géxīn	革新	to reform, to innovate
gézhí	革職	to dismiss, to be dismissed from office: 她先生被革了職。 *Tā xiānsheng bèi géle zhí.* Her husband was fired. [V-O]
gézhìpǐn	革制品	leather goods [N]
biàngé	變革	to replace the old with the new [CC/V]
gǎigé	改革	to reform [CC/V]
kāigé	開革	to dismiss (= *géchú*) [CC/V]

gěifù	給付	to make payment [CC/V]
gěijià	給假	to grant leave of absence: 給了三天假 *gěile sāntiān jià*, granted three days' leave of absence [V-O]
gěiliǎn	給臉	to show courtesy to someone who does not really deserve it, to save someone's face: 給臉不要臉 *gěiliǎn búyào liǎn*, to show courtesy to one, but he is not worthy of it [V-O]
gěi rén dǎ le	給人打了	was beaten by somebody (= 被人打了 *bèi rén dǎle*)
gěi tā zuò fàn	給他做飯	to cook for him
jǐyǎng	給養	Provisions, allowance [CC/N]
jǐyǔ	給予	to present as a gift or favor [CC/V]
bǎ fànwǎnr gěi zá le	把飯碗兒給砸了	to have the rice bowl smashed, to have lost one's job
gōngjǐ	供給	to supply with things [CC/V]
jiā jǐ hù zú	家給戶足	to be abundantly provided
jiāogěi	交給	to hand over to: 請你把這張畫兒交給他。 *Qǐng nǐ bǎ zhèizhāng huàr jiāogei tā.* Please hand over this painting to him. [CC/V]
màigei ta	賣給他	to sell something to him. Sell it to him.
pèijǐ	配給	to ration [CC/V]
ràng rén gěi dǎ le	讓人給打了	= 給人打了 *gèi rén dǎ le*
sònggei ta	送給他	to give something to him as a gift
zì jǐ zì zú	自給自足	to be self-sufficient

gēnbanr(de)	跟班兒(的)	servant of an official, entourage [VO/N]
gēnbāo (de)	跟包(的)	= *gēnbānr* [VO/N]
gēn nǐ xuéxí	跟你學習	to learn from you
gēn pái	跟牌	(of card game) to follow suit [V O]
gēnqian	跟前	place nearby: 講台跟前 *jiǎngtái gēnqian*, near the platform; 你跟前有沒有小孩兒? *Nǐ gēnqian yǒu méiyou xiǎoháir?* Do you have children with you? [SC/N]
gēnshang	跟上	to catch up with 快點，跟上來。 *Kuàidiǎn, gēnshanglai.* Hurry and catch up with us. [V]
gēnshǒur	跟手兒	immediately, smoothly: 跟手兒去做 *gēnshǒur qù zuò*, to do it at once [VO/Adv]
gēnsuí	跟隨	to follow someone [CC/V]; follower
gēn ta bànshì	跟他辦事	to work with him; to handle things with him
gēn tā jiéhūn	跟他(她)結婚	to get married with him (or her)
gēn tā liáotiānr	跟他聊天	to chat with him
gēn tā yào qián	跟他要錢	to ask him for money
gēntàngr	跟趟兒	(colloquial) = 來得及 *láidejí* there is still time to do something; to keep up with; [V]
gēntou	跟頭	a fall: 栽跟頭 *zāi gēntou*, to have a fall; a somersault: 翻跟頭 *fān gēntou*, to do a somersault
gēnzhe	跟着	in the wake of, right away: 跟着就來了 *gēnzhe jiù lái le*, came over right away; to follow: 你跟着他。 *Nǐ gēnzhe ta.* You follow him.
gēnzōng	跟蹤	to follow in the track of, to shadow (someone) [V-O]
Tā gēn Lǎo Lǐ shì lǎo péngyou.	他跟老李是老朋友	He and Old Li are good friends.

gòngchǎn	共產	to share property: 共產黨 *gòngchǎndǎng*, Communist Party [V-O]
gòngcún gòngróng	共存共榮	co-existance and co-prosperity
gòngfàn	共犯	accomplice [SC/N]
gòngguǎn	共管	to manage together: 國際共管 *guójì gòngguǎn*, controlled internationally [SC/V]
gònghé dǎng	共和黨	Republican Party
gònghé zhèngtǐ	共和政體	republican form of government
gòngjì	共計	to sum up, altogether: 共計多少錢? *gòngjì duōshao qián?* How much altogether? [SC/Adv]
gòngmíng	共鳴	sympathy, sympathetic understanding [SC/N]
gòngmóu	共謀	to plan together [SC/V]
gòngshì	共事	to work together: 你跟他共過事嗎? *Nǐ gēn tā gòngguo shì ma?* Have you ever worked with him? [V-O]
gòngsù	共宿	to lodge in the same place [VO]
gòng xiāng shèng jǔ	共襄盛舉	to offer help to a great cause together
gòngyíng	共營	to manage jointly: 公私共營 *gōngsī gòngyíng*, managed by both public and private concerns [SC/V]
gòngyǒu	共有	to possess together: 這些東西為我們所共有。 *Zhèxie dōngxi wéi wǒmen suǒ gòngyǒu.* These things are for our mutual possession. [SV/V]
gòngzǒng	共總	altogether (= *gòngjì*) [CC/Adv]
búgòng dài tiān	不共戴天	will not live under the same sky as the man who slew his father/ inveterate hatred
zǒnggòng	總共	= 共總 *gòngzǒng* [CC/Adv]

guān'ài	關愛	關心 guānxīn, be concerned, and 愛護 àihù, love/to express solicitude for the well-being of (someone) [CC/V]
guānbì	關閉	to close 關閉學校。 Guānbì xuéxiào. The schools were closed. [V]
guāndēng	關燈	to close the lamp/to turn off the lights [V-O]
guāndiàn	關電	to close the electricity/to turn off the electricity [V-O]
guān diànmén	關電門	= 關電 guāndiàn
guāngù	關顧	to show loving care for sb. 公務繁忙，疏於照顧。 Gōngwù fánmáng, shūyú guāngù. I have been too busy with my work to take care of you. [V]
guānhuái	關懷	關心 guānxīn, to be concerned, and 懷念 huáiniàn, to think of / to be concerned about, for, show interest in [CC/V]; solicitude
guānlián	關連	relations, connections: 這件事跟那件事沒有甚麼關連。 Zhèijiàn shì gēn nèijiàn shì méiyou shénme guānlián. This matter has no connection with that one. [CC/N]
guānmén	關門	to close the door [V-O]; (Chinese medicine) the kidneys
guānqiè	關切	to be concerned about (someone), to be intimately related, connected [CC/SV]
guānshang	關上	to close (door, window, etc.) [VC]
guānxi	關係	他跟她有沒有關係沒關係。 to be related to one another [CC/V]; relationship, consequences: Tā gēn tā yǒu méi you guānxi méi guānxi. It is not important whether he and she have had any relationship. (CC/V)
guānxīn	關心	to be concerned about (someone) or for (something): 他很關心你。 Tā hěn guānxīn nǐ. He is very concerned about you. 關心國事 guānxīn guóshì, to show interest in national affairs [VO/SV]
guānyu	關於	regarding, concerning, about: 關於這件事，我一點兒都不知道。 Guānyu zhèijiàn shì, wǒ yìdiǎnr dōu bùzhīdao. I know nothing about this matter. [Preposition]
guānzhào	關照	guānxīn and zhàoying, to take care of/to notify: 有事，請關照一聲。 Yǒu shì, qǐng guānzhào yìshēng. If anything comes up, please notify me. to take care of: 請你多多關照。 Qǐng nǐ duōduō guānzhào. Please take good care of (him). [CC/V]
guānzhù	關注	關心 guānxīn and 注意 zhùyi, to pay attention to/to pay close attention to, to be intensely concerned about, for [CC/V]
kāiguān	開關	to open and to close/to turn on and off; switch [CC/N]
shì bù guān jǐ	事不關己	The matter doesn't concern one personally.

guāncè	觀測	to prognosticate through observation [CC/V]
guānchá	觀察	to look into, to observe [CC/V]; observation
guāndiǎn	觀點	point of view, standpoint: 各人有個人的觀點。 *Gèren yǒu gèrende guāndiǎn.* Each has his own viewpoint. [SC/N]
guānfēng	觀風	to look for an opportunity to do something, to stand watch for something expected to happen: 你們進去，我在外邊兒觀風。 *Nǐmen jìnqu, wǒ zài wàibianr guānfēng.* You go in and I'll keep watch outside for you. [VO]
guāngǎn	觀感	to observe and to react/observations and comments [CC/N]
guānguāng	觀光	to visit as a tourist, to take a tour: 觀光客 *guānguāngkè*, tourist; 觀光行業 *guānguāng hángyè*, the tourist business [V-O]
guānkàn	觀看	to take a look at, to see [CC/V]
guānmó	觀摩	to study and fondle (works of art), to study by visiting other institutions [CC/V]
guānniàn	觀念	concept, idea, notion: 新觀念 *xīn guānniàn*, new concepts [CC/N]
guānshǎng	觀賞	觀看 *guānkàn*, to see, and 欣賞 *xīnshǎng*, to appreciate/to enjoy by sight (art, flower, view, etc.) [CC/V]
guānwàng	觀望	to take a wait-and-see attitude: 持觀望態度 *(chí) guānwàng tàidù*; 觀望不前 *guānwàng bùqián*, to wait and see without taking any action [CC/V]
guānzhān	觀瞻	(of things) outward appearance: 有礙觀瞻 *yǒu ài guānzhān*, will adversely affect the outward appearance [CC/N]
guānzhòng	觀衆	the audience, spectators [SC/N]
bēiguān	悲觀	to be pessimistic [SC/SV]
cānguān	參觀	to visit (school, hospital, etc.) [CC/V]
kèguān	客觀	objective [SC/SV]; objectivity
lèguān	樂觀	to be optimistic [SC/SV]
míng ruò guān huǒ	明若觀火	as clear as viewing a fire/very clear
pángguān	旁觀	to look on: 袖手旁觀 *xiù shǒu pángguān*, to look on with folded arms [SC/V]
zhǔguān	主觀	subjective [SC/SV]; subjective

guǎnbǎo	管保	to guarantee, to be sure: 我管保他不來。 *Wǒ guǎnbǎo tā bùlái.* I'm sure he will not come. [CC/V]
guǎn bǎo	管飽	to guarantee adequate food [V O]
guǎnbuliǎo	管不了	cannot manage: 這件事我可管不了。 *Zhèijiàn shì wǒ kě guǎnbuliǎo.* It is really beyond my power to manage this affair. [VC]
guǎn chī guǎn zhù	管吃管住	to provide food and lodging
guǎn fàn	管飯	to provide food, to include board [V O]
guǎnjiā	管家	to be in charge of domestic affairs [V-O]; person in charge of domestic affairs, also 管家的 *guǎnjiāde*, a butler
guǎnjiào	管教	to take care of and discipline (children): 管教小孩兒 *guǎnjiào xiǎoháir*; to make or cause (someone) to do something: 管教他給你說好話。 *Guǎnjiào tā gěi nǐ shuō hǎo huà.* I will see to it that he apologizes to you. [CC/V]
guǎnjiāpó	管家婆	a housewife, a woman who likes to interfere
guǎnlǐ	管理	to manage [CC/V]
guǎnménde	管門的	a doorkeeper
guǎnshì	管事	to be in charge of: 這兒誰管事? *Zhèr shéi guǎnshì?* Who is in charge here? [V-O]; person in charge, also 管事的 *guǎnshìde*
guǎnshù	管束	管理 *guǎnlǐ*, to manage, and 約束 *yuēshù*, to control/supervise (children, students, etc.) [CC/V]
guǎnxiá	管轄	to exercise control over [CC/V]
guǎn xiánshì	管閒事	to poke one's nose into another's business
guǎnyòng	管用	to be efficacious; to be of use; to be effective [V]
guǎnzhàng	管賬	to do bookkeeping [V-O]; 管賬的 *guǎnzhàngde*, bookkeeper, person in charge of accounts
guǎnzhì	管制	管理 *guǎnlǐ*, to manage, and 節制 *jiézhì*, to regulate/to administer, to control [CC/V]
bùguǎn	不管	don't care, no matter . . .
dàiguǎn	代管	manage on behalf of (someone)
zhǔguǎn	主管	to be responsible for [SC/V]; head of an office

hàibìng	害病	to be ill: 害了兩天病。 *hàile liǎngtiān bìng*, to be ill for two days [V-O]
hài háizi	害孩子	= 害喜 *hàixǐ*
hài guó yāng mín	害國秧民	to harm the country and the people
hàikǒu	害口	= 害喜 (of pregnant woman) to show appetite for certain foods [V-O]
hàipà	害怕	to fear, to be afraid of [VO]
hài qún zhī mǎ	害群之馬	horse that harms the group/person who gives the group a bad name
hài rén	害人	to harm people: 害人不淺, *hái rén bùqiǎn*, to do someone a lot of harm [V O]
hài rén fǎn hài jǐ	害人反害己	a plot to harm others boomeranged
hàisào	害臊	to blush, to feel shy [VO]
hài shāyǎn	害沙眼	to contract trachoma
hàisǐ	害死	to murder, to harm severely: 你害死我了。 *Nǐ hàisǐ wǒ le.* You are killing me. [VC]
hàixǐ	害喜	to have morning sickness [V-O]
hàixiū	害羞	to feel shy, to feel ashamed [VO]
cánhài	殘害	to do severe injury [CC/V]
lìhài	利害	利益 *lìyì*, advantage, and 害處 *hàichu*, disadvantage [CC/N]
lìhai	厲害	to be severe: 厲害得很 *lìhaide hěn*, very severe; 病得很厲害。 *bìngde hěn lìhai*, severely ill [CC/SV]
móu cái hài mìng	謀財害命	to kill for money
móuhài	謀害	to conspire [CC/V]
pòhài	迫害	壓迫 *yāpò*, to oppress, to harm [CC/V]
shāhài	殺害	to kill [CC/V]
shānghài	傷害	to injure [CC/V]
xiànhài	陷害	to trap and harm/to betray [CC/V]

hébàn	合辦	to cooperate; to set up a company, school, factory by cooperation. [V]
hébìng	合併	to unite, to annex [CC/V]
héchàng	合唱	to sing together [SC/V]; a chorus
héchéng	合成	to complete by bringing together [VC]
hé duōshao měijīn	合多少美金	How much U.S. money does it correspond to?
héfǎ	合法	to be legal, in accordance with the law [VC/SV]
hégé	合格	to be up to standard, qualified [VO/SV]
héhu	合乎	to be in accordance with: 合乎道理 *héhu dàoli*, to be in accordance with reason
héhuǒ(r)	合夥(兒)	to go into partnership [VO]
héjì	合計	to count together [SC/V]
hélǐ	合理	to be reasonable, right, in accordance with reason [VO/SV]
héqún	合群	to be gregarious, to go along with the group [VO/SV]
héshēn	合身	to fit; to suit; to be well-fitting 這條褲子很合身。 *Zhèi tiáo kùzi hěn héshēn.* This pair of pants fit you well. [V O]
héshang	合上	to close (books, etc.) [VC]
héshí	合時	to be fashionable, to be timely [VO/SV]
héshi	合適	to be suitable [CC/SV]
hésuàn	合算	to be worthwhile, reasonable in price [SC/SV]
hétong	合同	contract: 定合同 *dìng hétong*, to have a contract [CC/N]
héyì	合意	to be agreeable, in accordance with one's ideas [VO/SV]
hézhù	合住	to close (umbrella, etc.); to share an apartment [VC]
hézuò	合作	to cooperate [SC/V]; cooperation
mào hé shén lí	貌合神離	in appearance together, in spirit apart/friends or allies in appearance only
tiān zuò zhī hé	天作之合	a Heaven-made match (marriage)

huā
to spend, to be flowery, blurred

花

huābuqi	花不起	cannot afford to spend (so much): 花不起這麼多錢。 *huābuqi zhème duō qián* [VC]
huāfèi	花費	to spend money, to cost [CC/V]; the cost
huā héshàng	花和尚	profligate monk
huāhuāgōngzǐ	花花公子	a playboy
huāhuālǜlǜ	花花綠綠	colorful
huāhuāshìjiè	花花世界	world of sensual pleasures
huā qián	花錢	to spend money [V O]
huāshao	花稍	to be pretty, to be romantic, to be fond of opposite sex [CC/SV]
huā tiān jiǔ dì	花天酒地	world of women and wine/to indulge oneself in worldly pleasures
huāxiàng	花項	items of expense: 沒甚麼花項。 *Méi shénme huāxiàng.* There is no occasion to spend. [SC/N]
huāxiāo	化消	expenses: 東西都漲價了。花消太大。 *Dōngxi dōu zhǎngjiàle. Huāxiāo tài dà.* Things are more expensive now. (Our) expenses have increased a lot. [CC/N]
huāyǎn	花眼	blurred eyes [SC/N]
huā yán qiǎo yǔ	花言巧語	to speak with flowery, deceiving words
huāzhīzhāozhǎn	花枝招展	the branches of flowers sway; be gorgeously dressed
tóu hūn yǎn huā	頭昏眼花	dizzy
yǎnhuā	眼花	eyes become blurred/cannot see clearly: 看得我眼花。 *Kànde wǒ yǎnhuā.* I've read so much that my eyes have become blurred. [SP/V]
yǎn huā liáo luàn	眼花撩亂	dazzled (by the sight of things)

huàchú	化除	to abolish, to remove (prejudices): 化除成見 *huàchú chéngjiàn* [CC/V]
huà dí wéi yǒu	化敵為友	to convert enemy into friend
huà gāngé wéi yùbó	化干戈為玉帛	"beat swords into plowshares"/to put an end to war and have peace
huàhé	化合	to combine in chemical process: 化合物 *huàhéwù*, (chemical) compound [CC/V]
huàmíng	化名	to disguise one's name, to adopt a pseudonym [V-O]
huàshēn	化身	transformation of Buddha in different manifestations, a personification (of love, piety, etc.) [SC/N]
huàshí	化石	fossil [SC/N]
huàxué	化學	chemistry [SC/N]
huàyàn	化驗	to do chemical analysis [CC/V]; chemical analysis
huàyù	化育	to grow and change naturally [CC/V]; such growth and change
huà zhěng wéi líng	化整為零	to break up whole into parts/to take care of things one by one
huàzhuāng	化妝	to apply makeup: 化妝品 *huàzhuāngpǐn*, cosmetics [V-O]
huàzhuāng	化裝	to dress in disguise [V-O]
biǎomiànhuà	表面化	to bring to the surface
chūn fēng huà yǔ	春風化雨	the kindly influence of a good teacher
èhuà	惡化	to worsen, to deteriorate
fēnghuà	風化	customs, public morals: 風化區 *fēnghuà qū*, red-light district [CC/N]
jiàohuàzi	叫化子	a beggar, also *jiàohuāzi* or *huāzi*
ōuhuà	歐化	to Europeanize: 歐化句子 *Ōuhuà jùzi*, Europeanized sentences
wénhuà	文化	civilization, culture [CC/N] 有文化 *yǒu wén huà* educated [VO]
xiàndàihuà	現代化	to modernize
zàohuà	造化	creation, operation of nature, good luck: 這都是你的造化。 *Zhè dōu shì nǐde zàohuà.* These are all your good luck. [CC/N]

huàbào	畫報	illustrated magazine or newspaper [N]
huà bǐng chōng jī	畫餅充饑	to draw a cake to satisfy hunger/a Barmecide feast
huàfēn	畫分	to divide in parts [CC/V]
huàfú	畫符	to write or draw spells or incantations [V-O]
huàgòng	畫供	to sign affidavit [V-O]
huà guǐ yi, huà gǒu nán	畫鬼易，畫狗難	It is easier to paint a ghost than a dog.
huà hǔ lèi quǎn	畫虎類犬	to paint the tiger but looks like a dog/fail to achieve what one set out to do, to describe something unsucessfully
huà huàr	畫畫兒	to draw a picture [V O]
huà huóle	畫活了	to paint something very vividly
huàjiā	畫家	a painter [SC/N]
huàjiàng	畫匠	(derogatory) commercial artist [SC/N]
huàjiè	畫界	to draw the boundary [V-O]
huà lóng diǎn jīng	畫龍點睛	to add the pupil while painting the eye of a dragon/to make the critical touch
huàméi	畫眉	to draw eyebrows [V-O]; the grey thrush
huà shé tiān zú	畫蛇添足	to paint a snake with feet/superfluous
huàshī	畫師	(courtesy) painter [SC/N]
huàtú	畫圖	to paint, to draw [V-O]; a painting, a drawing
huàxiàng	畫像	to portray; portrait [VO/N]
huàyā	畫押	to make a sign (especially of an illiterate) in lieu of signature [V-O]
huàyàngzi	畫樣子	rough draft [SC/N]; to draw a model [V-O]
huàzhǎn huì huàzhǎnlǎn	畫展 = 繪畫展覽	picture show; art exhibition; exhibition of paintings [N]

huānhū	歡呼	to shout cheerfully: 歡呼萬歲 *huānhū wànsuì*, to shout *banzai* [CC/V]
huānhǔr	歡虎兒	happy tiger cub/a lively child: 這個小孩兒歡虎兒似的。 *Zhèige xiǎoháir huānhǔr sìde.* This child is as happy and gay as a tiger cub.
huānjù	歡聚	to have a happy reunion, to meet happily together: 大家歡聚一堂。 *Dàjia huānjù yì táng.* Everybody is happy together. [SC/V]
huānlè	歡樂	to be happy, delighted [CC/SV]
huānlóng	歡龍	happy dragon (= 歡虎兒 *huānhǔr*)
huānqìng	歡慶	to joyfully celebrate [V]
huānsòng	歡送	to give farewell party: 歡送會 *huānsònghuì*, farewell party [SC/V]
huān tiān xǐ dì	歡天喜地	to be overjoyed
huānxǐ	歡喜	to be happy, delighted [CC]
huānxiào	歡笑	to laugh heartily [CC/V]
huānxīn	歡心	joy, love [SC/N]
huānxīn	歡欣	to be exultant: 歡欣鼓舞 *huānxīn gǔwǔ*, to dance for joy [CC/SV]
huānxǐ yù kuáng	歡喜欲狂	crazy with happiness/overjoyed
huānxù	歡叙	to meet for happy reunion [CC/V]
huānyán	歡顏	happy countenance [SC/N]
huānyàn	歡宴	to entertain guests with banquet: 歡宴賓客。 *huānyàn bīnkè* [CC/V]
huānyíng	歡迎	to welcome: 受歡迎。 *shòu huānyíng*, to be well-liked, well received: 他那本書很受歡迎。 *Tā nèiběn shū hěn shòu huānyíng.* That book of his is well received. [SC/V]
huānyù	歡娛	to enjoy oneself [CC/V]
huānyuè	歡悅	to be pleased [CC/SV]
huānyuè	歡躍	to jump for joy [CC/V]
xǐhuan	喜歡	to like [CC/V]

huánbào	還報	to pay back [CC/V]; retribution
huánběn	還本	to recover capital invested: 夠還本 *gòu huánběn*, to come out even [V-O]
huánhún	還魂	the soul returns, dead person revives [V-O]
huánjī	還擊	to fight back; to return fire = 回擊 *huíjī* [V]
huánjià	還價	to haggle [V-O]
huánjìng	還敬	to return courtesy [VO]
huánkǒu	還口	to talk back [V-O]
huánlǐ	還禮	to return courtesy, to salute back, to give gift in return [V-O]
huánqián	還錢	to pay back money (owed to somebody)
huánqīng	還清	to repay in full [VC]
huán rénqíng	還人情	to make gift in return
huánshǒu	還手	to strike back [V-O]
huánsú	還俗	to return to secular life [V-O]
huánxiāng	還鄉	to return to one's native place [V-O]
huányuàn	還願	to redeem a vow pledged before Buddha [V-O]
huányuán	還原	to be restored to the original shape or position [V-O]
huán zhài	還債	to pay debt [V O]
huán zhàng	還賬	to repay loan [V O]
huánzuǐ	還嘴	to answer back in abuse or self-defense [V-O]
guīhuán	歸還	to return [V]
yǐ yáhuányá	以牙還牙	tooth for tooth; to take revenge

huí

回   to return

huíbài	回拜	to return a visit [VO]
huíbào	回報	to bring back a report [V-O]
huídá	回答	to answer [CC/V]; a reply
huígù	回顧	to look back [SC/V]
huíguó	回國	to return to one's native country [V-O]
huíhuà	回話	to report (on errand), to answer charges [V-O]
huí jiā	回家	to return home [V O]
huíjiàn	回見	see you again (= 回頭兒見 *huítóur jiàn*)
huíjìng	回敬	to send present in return, to propose a toast in return: 回敬一杯 *huíjìng yìbēi*, to offer a drink in return [VO]
huíkòu	回扣	a kickback [SC/N]
huílǐ	回禮	to return a salute, to give a return gift [V-O]
huímìng	回命	to return with message [V-O]
huíshēng	回聲	echo [SC/N]
huíshǒu	回手	to return a blow [V-O]
huí tóu shì àn	回頭是岸	to turn the head and there is the shore/to repent and salvation is at hand
huítóu(r)	回頭(兒)	to turn the head; to repent, to reform [V-O]; later: 回頭兒見 *Huítóur jiàn.* See you later. [Adv]
huíwèi	回味	to savor enjoyment
huíxiǎng	回想	to recall, to reflect, to consider
huíxìn	回信	to answer a letter [V-O]; letter in reply
huíyì	回憶	to reminisce [SC/V]
huíyīn	回音	an answer, an echo [SC/N]
huízuǐ	回嘴	to talk back, to retort [V-O]
làng zǐ huí tóu	浪子回頭	the prodigal son's return

huìchē	會車	to drive passing each other [VO]
huìhé	會合	to assemble, to join forces [CC/V]
huìhuà	會話	conversation
huìjiàn	會見	to meet, to see (visitor) [CC/V]
huìkǎo	會考	nationally unified examination [SC/V, N]
huì kè	會客	to see guests or visitors [V O]
huì lā huì chàng	會拉會唱	to know how to play a Chinese violin and to sing Chinese opera
huìmiàn	會面	to meet face to face [V-O]
huìshī	會師	to join forces for battle, rendezvous [V-O]
huìshuǐ	會水	to be good at swimming [V-O]
huìtán	會談	to talk; conversation; [V/N]
huìtóng	會同	jointly (manage): 會同管理 *huìtóng guǎnlǐ*
huìwù	會悟	to realize (the truth) [CC/V]
huìwù	會晤	to meet or see personally [CC/V]
huì xiàyǔ	會下雨	It is going to rain.
huìxīn	會心	silent appreciation: 會心的微笑 *huìxīnde wēixiào,* a smile of understanding
huìyǎn	會演	to perform jointly; joint performance [V/N]
huìyì	會意	to appreciate silently; one of the six principles of Chinese character formation [VO]
huìzhàn	會戰	to meet for great battle
huì zhàng	會賬	to pay the bill (as in a restaurant) [V O]
huì zuò	會做	can do, knows how to do (something) [V O]
xuéhuìle	學會了	to have learned it [VC]
yì xué jiù huì	一學就會	to learn quickly (of a fast learner)

huó dào lǎo, xué dào lǎo, xué bùliǎo	活到老, 學到老, 學不了。	Live to old age, learn to old age, can't learn everything
huódòng	活動	to move around, to exercise; to run for (an office): 活動一官半職 *huódòng yì guān bàn zhí*, to run about to get an official post [CC/V] to be active [SV]; activities
huógāi	活該	it served you right, one deserves (to be punished, etc.): 他活該挨打。誰叫他那麼壞呢。 *Tā huógāi áidǎ. Shéi jiào tā nàme huài ne.* He deserves to be spanked. Who asked him to be so bad.
huó jiàn guǐ	活見鬼	Utter nonsense! Impossible!
huójù	活劇	a drama in real life [SC/N]
huó kòuzi	活扣子	a knot that can be easily untied
huólù	活路	a way out, a chance to live [SC/N]
huómái	活埋	to bury alive [SC/N]
huópo	活潑	to be lively, energetic [CC/SV]
huór	活兒	work: 幹活兒 *gàn huór*, to do work
huó shòuzuì	活受罪	to suffer terribly
huóshuǐ	活水	fresh current [SC/N]
huó sǐrén	活死人	a walking corpse, a useless person
huótour	活頭兒	something worth living for: 連戲都不能看，還有甚麼活頭兒? *Lián xì dōu bùnéng kàn, hái yǒu shénme huótour?* What does one want to live for if he can't even go to the opera?
huóyè	活頁	loose leaf (album): 活頁文選 *huóyè wénxuǎn*, selected readings in loose leaf [SC/N]
huóyòng	活用	to make flexible use of [SC/V]
huóyuè	活躍	to be very active, lively: 他在政治方面很活躍。 *Tā zài zhèngzhi fāngmiàn hěn huóyuè.* He is very active in politics. [CC/SV]
huózhuō	活捉	to capture alive [SC/V]
shēng lóng huó hǔ	生龍活虎	live dragon and tiger/very much alive and vivid
yǎnghuó	養活	to raise (children), to support (parents): 養活 *yǎnghuó*, to bring life back to (orphan, animal, etc.) [VC]

jíchéng	集成	a grand compendium
jígǔ	集股	to form a stock company [V-O]
jíhé	集合	to assemble, to muster [CC/V]
jíhuì	集會	to hold a meeting [CC/V]
jíjǐn	集錦	collection of choice items of art or quotations [VO/N]
jíjù	集聚	to assemble in one place [CC/V]
jíquán	集權	to centralize [VO]; centralization: 中央集權 *Zhōngyāng jíquán*
jí shǎo chéng duō	集少成多	"many a little makes a mickle"
jí sī guǎng yì	集思廣益	to benefit by group discussion
jítǐ	集體	collective: 集體創作 *jítǐ chuàngzuò*, work done by many participants; 集體領導 *jítǐ lǐngdǎo*, collective leadership; 集體農場 *jítǐ nóngchǎng*, collective farm; 集體安全 *jítǐ ānquán*, collective security; 集體結婚 *jítǐ jiéhūn*, mass wedding
jítuán	集團	a group of persons or nations: 共產集團 *gòngchǎn jítuán*, the Communist block of nations
jí yè chéng qiū	集腋成裘	to make a garment by piecing together little pieces of fur/Many small contributions will make a great sum.
jíyì	集議	to hold a meeting to discuss [CC/V]
jíyóu	集郵	to collect postal stamps [V-O]: 集郵家 *jíyóujiā*, a philatelist
jízhōng	集中	to concentrate: 集中注意力 *jízhōng zhùyìlì*, to concentrate one's mind [VO]; 集中營 *jízhōngyíng*, concentration camp
jízī	集資	to collect capital for a business enterprise [V-O]

jìchóu	記仇	to bear a grudge [V-O]
jìde	記得	to remember, can recall: 我記得他是誰。 *Wǒ jìde tā shì shéi.* I remember who he is.
jìgōng	記功	to give credit for meritorious work [V-O]
jìguà	記掛	to think of, to be concerned about [CC/V]
jìguò	記過	to give a demerit [V-O]
jìhaor	記號兒	a mark, a sign: 做個記號兒就不會忘了。 *Zuòge jìhaor jiù búhuì wàngle.* Make a sign so that we will not forget. [SC/N]
jìlù	記錄	to record [CC/V]; minutes of meetings
jìmíng	記名	to register the name: 記名投票 *jìmíng tóupiào*, to sign one's name on ballot in voting [V-O]
jìqǔ	記取	to recall, to remember: 記取教訓 *jìqǔ jiàoxùn*, learn a lesson [CC/V]
jìshì	記事	to record events [V-O]; written records, chronicles
jìshìr	記事兒	to remember things (the first time a child shows its memory): 那時我才記事兒。 *Nàshí wǒ cái jìshìr.* At that time I began to remember things. [V-O]
jìxialai	記下來	to put down in writing [VC]
jìxingr	記性兒	the memory power: 我的記性兒太壞。 *Wǒde jìxingr tài huài.* My memory is too bad. [SC/N]
jìyì	記憶	to remember [CC/V]; memories: 記憶力 *jìyìlì*, memory power (= 記性兒 *jìxingr*)
jìzǎi	記載	to put down in writing [CC/V]; written records
jìzhàng	記賬	to make an entry in an account, to charge to an account [V-O]
jìzhě	記者	a newspaper reporter [SC/N]
jìzhu	記住	to bear in mind: 記住別忘了。 *Jìzhu bié wàng le.* Keep this in mind and don't forget. [VC]
bǐjì	筆記	to take notes [SC/V]; notes
sǐjì	死記	to resort to rote memory [SC/V]
sùjì	速記	to take shorthand [SC/V]

jiābān	加班	to work overtime; to work an extra shift [V-O]
jiābèi	加倍	to double [V-O]
jiāēn	加恩	to show favor [VO]
jiāfǎ	加法	addition (math.) [SC/N]
jiāgōng	加工	to do extra work [VO]; processing [N]: 食品加工 *shípǐn jiāgōng*, food processing
jiāhài	加害	to inflict injury on (someone) [VO]
jiāhào	加號	sign of addition (+)
jiājiǎng	加獎	to award praise [VO]
jiājǐn	加緊	to intensify, to become tense
jiāméng	加盟	to join the league, alliance [V-O]
jiāmiǎn	加冕	to be coronated [V-O]; coronation
jiāqiáng	加強	to strengthen, to intensify [VO]
jiārù	加入	to join, to enter [VC]
jiāsù	加速	to accelerate, to increase speed [VO]
jiātiān	加添	to augment, to increase [CC/V]
jiā yán jiā cù	加鹽加醋	to add salt and vinegar/to add freely to the original version in retelling
jiāyìn	加印	to apply the name chop or seal (on document) [V-O]; to make more printed copies [SC/V]
jiā yóu	加油	to add oil, to fill gasoline [V O]
jiā yóu(r)	加油(兒)	to encourage, to root (football team) [V-O]
jiāzhòng	加重	to add weight, to increase (penalty) [VO]
biàn běn jiā lì	變本加厲	to be more severe, cruel, violent
gèngjiā	更加	all the more [Adv]
yì jiā yī shì èr	一加一是二	One plus one is two.

jiàn bude rén	見不得人	to be unpresentable
jiàndì	見地	perception, viewpoint: 這個人很有見地。 *Zhèige rén hěn yǒu jiàndì.* This person is very clear-sighted.
jiàn fēng zhuǎn duò	見風轉舵	to turn the rudder with the wind/to be an opportunist
jiàn fèngr jiù zuān	見縫兒就鑽	to see a crack, enters/to behave like a social climber (a go-getter, a self-seeking person)
jiàngāodī	見高低	to see who beats whom, to see who is better
jiànguài	見怪	to take offense: 請別見怪。 *Qǐng bié jiànguài.* Please don't blame me. [VO]
jiàn guài bú guài	見怪不怪	to become inured to the unusual, weird, or uncanny
jiànguǐ	見鬼	to see the ghost/nonsense [VO]; also, 活見鬼 *huó jiànguǐ*
jiànjiě	見解	見識 *jiànshi*, viewpoint, and 了解 *liǎojiě*, understanding, judgment [CC/N]
jiàn jǐng shēng qíng	見景生情	to recall old memories at familiar sights
jiàn qián yǎn kāi	見錢眼開	(of blind person) to open his eyes to money if offered/to be influenced by money
jiànqīng	見輕	(illness) to get better: 他的病見輕了。 *Tāde bìng jiànqīng le.* He is getting better.
jiàn rén jiàn zhì	見仁見智	each according to his lights
jiàn rén jiù shuō	見人就說	to talk about it to whoever he sees
jiànshi	見識	insight, judgement [CC/N]
jiàn shìmian	見世面	to get to know the world
jiàn tiānrì	見天日	to see the sky and sun/injustice redressed
jiànwài	見外	to be considered as an outsider: 請你不要見外。 *Qǐng nǐ búyào jiànwài.* Please don't treat me as an outsider. (used to urge one to accept gift or invitation)
jiànwén	見聞	what one sees and hears, general knowledge: 他見聞很廣。 *Tā jiànwén hěn guǎng.* His knowledge is very broad. [CC/N]
jiànxí	見習	to get practical experience by actual work [CC/V]
kànjiàn	看見	to see [VC]
mèngjiàn	夢見	to see in dream [VC]
pèngjiàn	碰見	to run into (somebody, something) [VC]
tīngjiàn	聽見	to hear [VC]
wénjiàn	聞見	to smell [VC]
yùjiàn	遇見	= 碰見 *pèngjiàn*
zàijiàn	再見	Good-by [SC/V, N]

63

jiǎngdào	講道	to preach, to moralize [V-O]
jiǎnghé	講和	to hold peace talks, to negotiate peace, to settle differences amicably [V-O]
jiǎnghuà	講話	to talk informally [V-O]
jiǎngjià(r)	講價(兒)	to bargain over prices [V-O]
jiǎng jiāoqing	講交情	to care about friendship, to gain special favor through friendship: 你講交情不講? *Nǐ jiǎng jiāoqing bùjiǎng?* Do you care about our friendship?
jiǎngjiě	講解	to explain (as teacher to student) [CC/V]
jiǎngjiu	講究	to be particular about (clothing): 講究穿 *jiǎngjiu chuān*; matter to be taken into account [CC/SV]; 他這樣做，一定有甚麼講究。 *Tā zhèiyang zuò, yídìng yǒu shénme jiǎngjiu.* There must be something in his doing so.
jiǎnglǐ	講理	to be reasonable; to settle disputes by appealing to reason [V-O]
jiǎng miànzi	講面子	to be particular about appearances, to save someone's face [V O]
jiǎngmíng	講明	to explain clearly [VC]
jiǎngqiú	講求	to study carefully, to delve into, to be fond of: 講求外表 *jiǎngqiú wàibiǎo*, to pay special attention to appearances [CC/V]
jiǎng (rén) qíng	講(人)情	to ask for special favor, to intercede for another [V-O]
jiǎngshòu	講授	to teach, to lecture, to offer (academic courses) [CC/V]
jiǎngtái	講台	a lecture platform, a lecturn [SC/N]
jiǎngtáng	講堂	a lecture hall, a classroom [SC/N]
jiǎngxí	講習	to hold discussion meetings, to conduct training classes [CC/V]
jiǎngxué	講學	to lecture on academic subjects [V-O]
jiǎngyǎn	講演	to lecture (to students), to give a public lecture [V-O]; a lecture
jiǎngyì	講義	lecture notes, usually given to students [VO/N]

jiāo báijuànr	交白卷兒	to hand in examination paper without answers
jiāochāi	交差	to render a report upon completion of an assignment [V-O]
jiāodài	交代	to transfer duties: 交代差事 *jiāodài chāishì;* to bid, to order: 交代他不要多嘴。 *Jiāodài tā búyào duōzuǐ.* Tell him not to talk too much.
jiāodao	交道	personal relations: 很難跟他打交道。 *Hěn nán gēn tā dǎ jiāodao.* It's very hard to get along with him.
jiāohé	交合	to have sexual intercourse [CC/V]; sexual intercourse
jiāohuàn	交換	to change, to interchange, to exchange: 交換教授 *jiāohuàn jiàoshòu,* exchange professor [CC/V]
jiāojì	交際	social intercourse: 交際花兒 *jiāojìhuār,* a social butterfly
jiāoliú	交流	to flow in opposite directions [SC/V]; alternating current; interchange: 文化交流 *wénhuà jiāoliú,* cultural interchange
jiāo (péng) yǒu	交(朋)友	to make friends [V-O]
jiāoqing	交情	交往 *jiǎowǎng,* social dealings, and 情誼 *qíngyì,* friendship/friendship [CC/N]
jiāoshe	交涉	to negotiate, to discuss [CC/V]; negotiation, discussion
jiāotán	交談	to talk with
jiāotì	交替	to come one after another: 新舊交替 *xīn jiù jiāotì,* the new come after the old have gone (in personnel shake-up)
jiāo tóu jiē ěr	交頭接耳	to whisper into each other's ears, to talk confidentially
jiāowǎng	交往	to associate with [CC/V]; social or business dealings
jiāo xuéfèi	交學費	to pay tuition
jiāoyì	交易	to do business, to engage in trade: 證券交易所 *zhèngquàn jiāoyìsuǒ,* stock market
jiāoyóu	交遊	to make friends [CC/V]; circle of friends
jiāoyùn	交運	to have a spell of good fortune [V-O]
jiāozhàn	交戰	to go to war: 交戰國 *jiāozhànguó,* belligerent [V-O]
chéngjiāo	成交	to close a business transaction [V-O]

jiàocài	叫菜	to call for takeout orders from restaurant [V-O]
jiàogēge	叫哥哥	a singing grasshopper [N]; to call one's older brother [V-O]
jiàohǎn	叫喊	to shout; to yell [V]
jiàohǎor	叫好兒	to shout "bravo" [V-O]
jiàohào	叫號	to yell out, to shout out [CC/V]
jiàohuan	叫喚	to shout [CC/V]
jiàohuāzi	叫化子	a beggar
jiàojiēde	叫街的	a beggar (roving the streets and crying for pity)
jiào kǔ lián tiān	叫苦連天	to constantly complain of hardship
jiàomài	叫賣	to cry goods for sale [CC/V]
jiàomén	叫門	to call for a door to be opened, to knock on the door [V-O]
jiàoqū	叫屈	to complain of unfair treatment [V-O]
jiào tā chūqu	叫他出去	to let him go out
jiào xiǎojie	叫小姐	to call a prostitute to entertain
jiàoxiāo	叫囂	to shout, to scream [CC/V]
jiào Zhāngsān	叫張三	to be called Chang San, to call Chang San
jiàozhenr	叫真兒	to be too serious about [SV]
jiàozuo	叫做	to be called: 這就叫做 "自討苦吃"。 *Zhè jiù jiàozuo "zì tǎo kǔ chī."* This is called "self-inflicted hardship." 我們把孔子叫做至聖先師。 *Wǒmen bǎ Kǒngzǐ jiàozuo zhì shèng xiān shī.* We call Confucius the greatest sage and teacher.
jiàozuòr	叫座兒	to be popular, to have good box office [VO/SV]

jiébài	結拜	to become sworn brothers or sisters
jiébàn(r)	結伴(兒)	to form companionships [V-O]
jiéchóu	結仇	to become enemies: 跟誰結仇 *gēn shéi jiéchóu?*
jiécún	結存	to leave a balance of: 結存一千塊錢。 *jiécún yìqiān kuài qián*, leaves a balance of 1,000 dollars; such balance
jié fà fū qī	結髮夫妻	partners by the first marriage
jiégòu	結構	construction, structure: 動賓結構 *dòngbīn jiégòu*, verb-object construction [CC/N]
jiéguǒ	結果	to bear fruit [V-O]; to finish off, to kill (person) [VO] outcome, result [VO/N]; as a result [VO/Adv]
jiéhūn	結婚	to get married [V-O]
jiéjú	結局	the final outcome, the last act (of a play) [SC/N]
jiélùn	結論	summary, conclusion [SC/N]
jiéqīn	結親	to unite in marriage [V-O]
jiéshè	結社	to form a club [V-O]
jiéshéng	結繩	to tie knots on cords as means of reckoning or recordkeeping before the invention of writing [V-O]
jiéshì	結識	to make the acquaintance of, to become friends with [CC/V]
jiésù	結束	to wind up, to end (war, quarrel, etc.) [CC/V]
jiésuàn	結算	= 結賬 *jiézhàng* [CC/V]
jiéyè	結業	to graduate [V-O]; graduation
jiéyuàn	結怨	to become deadly enemies [V-O]
jiéyuán	結緣	to lay the basis for future relationship or intimacy [V-O]
jiézhàng	結賬	to clear or close account [V-O]
bājie	巴結	to fawn on, to toady
gōujié	勾結	to conspire, to work in collusion with

jiěcháo	解嘲	to justify one's action, to answer criticism [V-O]
jiěchú	解除	to relieve, to eliminate, to annul: 解除婚約 jiěchú hūnyuē, to annul an engagement (to marry) [CC/V]
jiědá	解答	to answer (questions), to solve (problems) [CC/V]
jiěfàn	解犯	to deliver a prisoner under guard [V-O]
jiěfàng	解放	to liberate, to set free: 解放黑奴 jiěfàng hēinú, to set the Negro slaves free [CC/V]
jiěhèn	解恨	to quench hatred, to get even with the enemy [V-O]
jiějiù	解救	to save [CC/V]
jiějué	解決	to settle, to solve (problems), to put an end to the difficulties, to kill a person off: 先把他解決了。 xiān bǎ tā jiějué le. Take care of him first. [CC/V]
jiěkāi	解開	to untie, to solve (a riddle) [VC]
jiěmènr	解悶兒	to dispel sadness, to kill time [V-O]
jiěnáng	解囊	to loosen the purse string/to donate money for worthy cause [V-O]
jiěquàn	解勸	to exhort, to calm down [CC/V]
jiěsàn	解散	to scatter, to breakup, to dissolve (Parliament): 解散議會 jiěsàn yìhuì [CC/V]
jiěshì	解釋	to explain, to clarify, to expound [CC/V]; an explanation
jiěshuō	解說	to explain [CC/V]; an explanation
jiěshǒur	解手兒	to relieve oneself, to urinate [V-O]
jiětǐ	解體	to disintegrate, to fall to pieces [V-O]
jiětuō	解脫	to set free, to liberate from worldly cares [CC/V]; such liberation, freedom [CC/V]
jiěwéi	解圍	to raise seige, to save someone from embarrassment [V-O]
jiěyōu	解憂	to allay grief or sorrow [V-O]
jiěyuē	解約	to annul a contract [V-O]

jìnbī	進逼	to press hard [CC/V]
jìnbīng	進兵	to dispatch troops, to order an attack on the enemy [V-O]
jìnbù	進步	to make progress, to be progressive, to improve [VO/SV]; an improvement
jìnchū	進出	entrance and exit, receipt and expenditure [CC/N]; to go in and out [V]
jìngōng	進攻	to mount an attack on (the enemy) [CC/V]
jìnhuà	進化	to evolve, to develop [CC/V]; evolution
jìnhuò	進貨	to stock (a shop) with goods [V O]
jìnjiǔ	進酒	to urge someone to drink (at a banquet) [V O]
jìnkǒu	進口	an entrance, imports: 進口貨 *jìnkǒuhuò*, imported goods [SC/N]
jìnkuǎn	進款	income, revenue, receipts [SC/N]
jìnqián	進錢	to receive money [V-O]; money received [SC/N]
jìnqǔ	進取	to make progress, to advance further and further, to be aggressive: 進取心 *jìnqǔxīn*, enterprising mind [CC/V]
jìnqu	進去	to go in [VC], also used as complement to other verbs
jìntuì	進退	to go forward or retreat/decision to do or not to do: 進退兩難 *jìn tuì liǎng nán*, equally difficult to go on or retreat [CC/N]
jìnxiāng	進香	to offer incense [V-O]
jìnxiàng	進項	= 進款 *jìnkuǎn* [SC/N]
jìnxíng	進行	to proceed, to advance, to make moves for an office: 進行工作 *jìnxíng gōngzuò* [CC/V]
jìnxiū	進修	to pursue further studies, to take an advanced course [CC/V]
jìnyán	進言	to offer suggestions, to make recommendations [V-O]
jìnyè	進謁	to see (superior) [CC/V]
jìnzhǎn	進展	to advance, to make progress [CC/V]; advance, progress
jìnzhàn	進站	to arrive: 火車就要進站了。 *Huǒchē jiùyào jìn zhànle.* The train is approaching the station soon.
jìnzhàng	進賬	to enter into account [V-O]; money income, receipts [SC/N]
tīngbujìnqu	聽不進去	can't stand listening to (something boring) [VC]

jǔbàn	舉辦	to initiate, to undertake, to sponsor [CC/V]
jǔbīng	舉兵	to take up arms [V-O]
jǔcuò	舉措	an act, action, any measure taken [CC/N]
jǔdòng	舉動	an act, a move, activity: 一舉一動 *yì jǔ yí dòng*, every move [CC/N]
jǔfā	舉發	to expose (the wrongdoing of someone), to accuse publicly [CC/V]
jǔjiā	舉家	the whole family [N] 舉家南遷。 *Jǔjiā nán qiān* The whole family moved south.
jǔlì	舉例	to give examples [V-O]; an example, illustration
jǔ mù wú qīn	舉目無親	to be stranded in a foreign land, far away from one's kin
jǔ qí bú dìng	舉棋不定	to hesitate about a chess move/shilly-shally
jǔqilai	舉起來	to raise up (hands, flags, etc.) [VC]
jǔshì	舉世	all the world: 舉世聞名 *jǔshì wén míng*, known all over the world, internationally famous [SC/N]
jǔshì	舉事	to raise the standard of revolt (= *jǔyì*) [V-O]
jǔshǒu	舉手	to raise hands: 舉手贊成 *jǔshǒu zànchéng*, to show approval by raising hands (for voting) [V-O]
jǔxíng	舉行	to put into operation, to hold (meeting, ceremony) [CC/V]
jǔ yī fǎn sān	舉一反三	to learn by analogy
jǔzhǐ	舉止	behavior, conduct: 舉止大方 *jǔzhǐ dàfang*, to carry oneself in a graceful manner [CC/N]
jǔzhòng	舉重	to lift weight [V-O]; weightlifting
jǔ zú qīng zhòng	舉足輕重	to play decisive role
duō cǐ yì jǔ	多此一舉	action unnecessarily taken
gāo jǔ hóng qí	高舉紅旗	to raise the red flag high (PRC)
xuǎnjǔ	選舉	to elect, an election [CC]
yì jǔ liǎng dé	一舉兩得	one action two gains/to kill two birds with one stone

kāibukāi	開不開	can't open [VC]
kāicǎi	開彩	to draw the lottery [V-O]
kāi chéng bù gōng	開誠布公	to act with honesty and justice
kāichú	開除	to expel (a student from school, a person from party membership) [CC/V]
kāi dānzi	開單子	to make out a list [V O]
kāidāo	開刀	to operate (surgical); to be operated on; to punish [V O]
kāi fángjiān	開房間	to rent a hotel room (often for illicit love)
kāiguān	開關	open-close/a switch [CC/N]
kāihuà	開化	to be civilized: 未開化國家 *wèikāihuà guójiā*, uncivilized country [CC/V]
kāi huǒ	開火	to start a boarding arrangement [V-O]
kāi huǒr	開火兒	to open fire (in a battle) [V-O]
kāi kǒu	開口	to open mouth/to speak up: 開口大笑 *kāi kǒu dà xiào*, to laugh broadly; to break (dam) or (dam) breaks [V-O]
kāikǒuxiào	開口笑	open-mouth-smile/a kind of pastry
kāiluó	開鑼	to begin beating the gong/to begin an opera [V-O]
kāi mèn jiàn shān	開門見山	to open the door to see the mountain/to speak without beating around the bush
kāimíng	開明	liberal, enlightened, progressive [CC/SV]
kāishǐ	開始	to begin, a beginning [CC]
kāi shuǐ	開水	boiled water [SC/N]; to turn on the water [V O]
kāitōng	開通	to break through obstructions [VC]; liberal, modern-minded: 他父母很開通 *Tā fùmǔ hěn kāitōng.* His parents are modern-minded. [CC/SV]
kāitōur	開頭兒	to begin [VO]; the beginning
kāi wánxiào	開玩笑	to poke fun at
kāi wèi	開胃	to be appetizing [VO/SV]; to tease: 別拿我開胃。 *Bié ná wǒ kāiwèi.* Don't tease me. [V-O]
kāixiāo	開消	expenses: 開消很大 *Kāixiāo hěn dà.* The operating expenses are heavy. [CC/N]
kāixīn	開心	to make fun of somebody: 別拿我開心。 *Bié ná wǒ kāixīn.* Don't make fun of me. [V-O]; to be happy [SV]
dǎkāi	打開	to open [VC]
nákāi	拿開	to take something away [VC]

kàn
to look at, to examine, to read

看

kàn bìng	看病	to see a doctor; to examine a patient [V O]
kànbuchulai	看不出來	cannot see clearly, cannot figure out: 看不出來他是誰。 *kànbuchulai tā shì shéi*, cannot figure out who he is [VC]
kànbúshùnyǎn	看不順眼	to look disgusting, revolting
kànchūan	看穿	= 看透 *kàntòu* [VC]
kàndāile	看呆了	watch intensely [VC]
kàndeguòyǎnr	看得過眼兒	to look agreeable, passable
kàn fēngtou	看風頭	to watch the direction (head) of wind/to change one's position on the basis of the situation at the moment (an opportunist)
kànhǎo	看好	to anticipate improvement [VC]
kàn hóngle yǎn	看紅了眼	to behold so intensely that the eyes become reddish/to be jealous, to covet
kànjiǔ	看酒	to serve wine: 茶房！看酒！ *Cháfáng! Kànjiǔ!* Waiter! Serve the wine! [V-O]
kànkāi	看開	= 看透 *kàntòu* [VC]
kàn miànzi	看面子	to watch the countenance of someone/to do something for favor of someone: 要不是看你的面子，我才不會替他辦那件事呢。 *Yàobúshì kàn nǐde miànzi, wǒ cái búhuì tì tā bàn nèijiàn shì ne.* If not for your sake, I would never do that for him.
kànqīng	看輕	to look down upon, to slight [VC]
kànshang	看上	to have one's eye on, to have a liking for (a girl, an object): 你怎麼會看上他？ *Nǐ zěnme huì kànshang tā?* How can you have a liking for her? [VC]
kàntòu	看透	to see through (a trick, problem), to be no longer serious about it: 他甚麼都看透了，一點兒也不在乎。 *Tā shénme dōu kàntòule, yìdiǎnr yě búzàihu.* He has seen through everything. He doesn't care a bit. [VC]
kànzhǎng	看漲	to anticipate a rise in price [VC]
kànzhe bàn	看著辦	to act as one sees fit: 這件事你看著辦吧。 *Zhèijiàn shì, nǐ kànzhe bàn ba.* On this matter, you do as you see fit.
kànzhòng	看中	= 看上 *kànshang* [VC]
kànzhòng	看重	to think greatly (of somebody, or his idea) [VC]

kàngdí	抗敵	to resist the enemy [VO]
kàng jié bú fù	抗節不附	to maintain moral integrity and not to depend on others
kàngjù	抗拒	to resist: 我們得抗拒敵人的侵略。 *Wǒmen děi kàngjù dírénde qīnluè.* We must resist the enemy's aggression. [CC/V]
kàngmìng	抗命	to defy order: 司令要你去，你可不能抗命不去。 *Sīlìng yào nǐ qù, nǐ kě bùnéng kàngmìng búqù.* The commander wants you to go. You shouldn't defy his order. [V-O]
kàng mìng jù dí	抗命拒敵	to defy the order and to oppose the enemy
kàngshēngsù	抗生素	anti-biotics
kàngshuì	抗稅	to refuse to pay tax [V-O]
kàngwèi	抗衛	to fight to defend [CC/V]
kàngyì	抗議	to protest [V-O]; a protest; 你應當提出抗議才對。 *Nǐ yīngdāng tíchū kàngyì cái duì.* It won't be right if you don't lodge a formal protest.
kàngzāi	抗灾	to fight natural calamities [VO]
kàngzhàn	抗戰	war of resistance (from 抗日戰爭 *kàng rì zhànzhēng*, war of resisting Japan) [SC/N]; 我們抗了八年的戰才把日本打敗了。 *Wǒmen kàngle bānián de zhàn cái bǎ Rìběn dǎbài le.* Not until we fought eight years of war did we defeat Japan [V-O]
kàng zhèn	抗震	anti-seismic [VO]
kàng zhì bù qū	抗志不屈	to maintain moral integrity and never submit to the crooked/to be a man of lofty ambition and high virtue.
fēn tíng kàng lǐ	分庭抗禮	to meet as equals: 你是誰？怎麼敢跟他分庭抗禮呢？ *Nǐ shì shéi? Zěnme gǎn gēn tā fēn tíng kàng lǐ ne?* Who are you? How dare you meet with him as equals?

kǎochá	考察	to inspect [CC/V]; an inspection
kǎodìng	考訂	to study and settle problems of age, authorship, edition, and textual differences [CC/V]
kǎohé	考核	to examine; to check [V]
kǎogǔ	考古	to work as an archaeologist: 我明年要到中國去考古。*Wǒ míngnian yào dào Zhōngguo qù kǎogǔ.* I am going to China to do some archaeological work next year. [VO]; archaeology (also 考古學 *kǎogǔxué*)
kǎojiù	考究	to be exquisite: 她的衣裳真考究。 *Tāde yīshang zhēn kǎojiù.* Her dresses are really exquisite; to be fastidious about: 她真考究穿。 *Tā zhēn kǎojiù chuān.* She is really fastidious about clothing. [CC/SV]; to examine carefully: 把原因考究出來就知道怎麼回事了。 *Bǎ yuányīn kǎojiùchūlai jiù zhīdao shì zěnme huí shì le.* When we find out the reasons (we) will know what it is all about. [CC/V]
kǎojù	考據	to do research (particularly on textual criticism), to seek proofs for data [CC/V]
kǎojuàn (r)	考卷(兒)	examination paper [SC/N]
kǎolǜ	考慮	to consider, to think over: 這件事，你得好好地考慮考慮。 *Zhèijiàn shì, nǐ děi hǎohāorde kǎolǜkaolǜ.* Regarding this matter, you must think it over carefully. [CC/V]
kǎoqǔ	考取	to pass an examination (= 考上 *kǎoshàng*) [VC]
kǎoshàng	考上	to pass an examination: 你考上了北大沒有? *Nǐ kǎoshàngle Běidà méiyou?* Did you pass the entrance examination for Pekin University? [VC]
kǎoshēng	考生	examinee [N]
kǎoshì	考試	to examine, to take an examination [VO]; examination
kǎowèn	考問	to interrogate [CC/V]
kǎo xué	考學	to take a school entrance examination
kǎoyàn	考驗	to test: 時代考驗青年。 *Shídài kǎoyàn qīngnian.* This age is putting (our) youth to the test. [CC/V]; a test: 他缺點太多，是經不起考驗的。 *Tā quēdiǎn tài duō, shì jīngbùqǐ kǎoyàn de.* He has too many shortcomings. He just cannot stand the test.
kǎozhèng	考證	= 考據 *kǎojù* [CC/V]
kǎozhòng	考中	to pass an examination (= 考上 *kǎoshàng*) [VC]
dàkǎo	大考	big examination/final examination
yuèkǎo	月考	monthly examination

kèdízhìshèng	克敵制勝	to defeat the enemy and win the battle
kèdīngkèmǎo	克丁克卯	to be very careful 他工作克丁克卯。 *Tā gōngzuò kèdīngkèmǎo.* He works very carefully and seriously.
kèfú	克服	to overcome: 克服困難 *kèfú kùnnán*, to overcome difficulties [VC]
kèfù	克復	to recover: 克復失地 *kèfù shīdì*, to recover the lost territory [VC]
kèkòu	克扣	to embezzle part of what should be issued [V]
kè jǐ	克己	to overcome selfishness, to be unselfish [VO/SV]
kèjiǎn	克減	to cut down 克減工錢 *kèjiǎn gōngqián.* to cut down the salary. [V]
kè jìn jué zhí	克盡厥職	to perform fully the functions of an office
kè jìn xiào yǎng	克盡孝養	to discharge all the filial duties to one's parents
kè qín kè jiǎn	克勤克儉	to have capacity for industry and thrift: 老王克勤克儉，日子過得一天比一天好。 *Lǎo Wáng kè qin kè jiǎn, rìzi guòde yìtiān bǐ yìtiañ hǎo.* Old Wang is both industrious and thrifty. His life is better everyday.
kèsī	克私	to overcome selfishness: 克私為公 *kèsī wèi gōng*, to repress the private for the public [VO]
kèxiǎng	克享	can enjoy: 克享天年 *kèxiǎng tiānnián*, can enjoy long life
kèyù	克慾	to overcome desires [VO]
kè yù xiū xíng	克慾修行	to subdue the passions and cultivate moral conduct
kèzhì	克制	to control: 克制情感 *kèzhì qínggǎn*, to control one's emotions; to rule over (territory) [CC/V]
rǒu néng kè gāng	柔能克剛	softness can overcome strength: 你柔能克剛，說幾句好話不就完了嗎？ *Nǐ rǒu néng kè gāng, shuō jǐjù hǎohuà bú jiù wánle ma?* Since softness can overcome strength, you say a few nice words (to apologize) and the matter will end there.

kuānchàng	寬暢	to be free from worry; to be happy/cheerful: 心裏很寬暢 *xīnli hěn kuānchàng*; spacious; wide: 小孩子應該在寬暢的地方玩。 *Xiǎoháizi yīnggāi zài kuānchàng de dìfāngwán.* Children should play in spacious places. [S V/ Adj.]
kuānchǎng	寬敞	to be spacious; roomy; commodious: 宿舍很寬敞。 *Sùshè hěn kuānchang.* The dorm is very spacious.; = 寬暢 *kuānchàng* [S V/Adj]
kuān dà bāo róng	寬大包容	to be broadminded and tolerant
kuān dà rén ài	寬大仁愛	to be generous and merciful
kuān dà shū chàng	寬大舒暢	with broad and enlightened mind/to be cheerful and liberal
kuān dà yǒu yú	寬大有餘	abundance and wealth/well-to-do
kuān guǎng bó dà	寬廣博大	vast and extensive in scope and field of knowledge, etc.
kuān hóng dà liàng	寬洪大量	to be liberal minded, tolerant, magnanimous: 他一向寬洪大量才不會跟那些小人一般見識呢。 *Tā yíxiàng kuān hóng dà liàng cái búhuì gēn nèixie xiǎorèn yì bān jiàn shì ne.* As a magnanimous person, he will never behave like those hypocrites.
kuānróng	寬容	to pardon (offenses, person), to tolerate: *kuānróng zhèngcè,* tolerant policy [SC/V]
kuānshù	寬恕	to pardon (person, wrongdoing): 看在他父親的面子上，把他寬恕了吧。 *Kàn zai tā fùqinde miànshang, bǎ tā kuānshùle ba.* For his father's sake, let's forgive him. [SC/V]
kuānsōng	寬鬆	to be less crowded: 過了北京，擁擠的火車站略為寬鬆了一些 *Guòle Běijīng, yōngjǐ de huǒchē lüèwèi kuānsōng le yìxiē.* After leaving Beijing, the crowded train became less crowded.; to feel relaxed: 她聽了大家伙兒勸慰的話，心裏寬鬆多了。 *Tā tīngle dàjiāhuǒr quànwèi de huà, xīnli kuānsōng duō le.* After being comforted by others, she felt better.; to be well-off: 日子過好了，手頭寬鬆了。 *Rìzi guòhǎo le, shǒutóu kuānsōng le.* We now live a better life and have more money.; to be loose: 我喜歡穿寬鬆的褲子。 *Wǒ xǐ huan chuān kuānsōng de kùzi.* I like wearing loose pants. [SV/Adj]
kuānwèi	寬慰	to comfort (person): 要寬慰父母，就得好好兒念書。 *Yào kuānwèi fùmǔ, jiù děi hǎohāor niànshū.* In order to comfort one's parents, one has to study hard. [CC/V]; to be happy: 你好好兒地念書才能讓父母感到寬慰。 *Nǐ hǎohāorde niànshū cái néng ràng fùmǔ gǎndào kuānwèi.* Only by studying hard can you make your parents feel happy. [SV]
kuānxiàn	寬限	to extend date (of delivery, etc.): 寬限一個月 *kuānxiàn yíge yuè,* to extend the time-limit with a month's grace [VO]
kuānxīn	寬心	to relax [V-O]; not worried: 他總是很寬心。 *Tā zǒngshi hěn kuānxīn.* He is always very relaxed. [SV]
kuān yī jiě dài	寬衣解帶	to remove the upper clothing and loosen the belt
kuān yǐ dài rén, yàn yǐ zé jǐ	寬以待人嚴以責己	to be lenient in treating others, to be strict in treating oneself.
kuānzhǎi	寬窄	broad and narrow/width [CC/N]

lā cháng liǎn	拉長臉	to pull a long face
lā cháng xiàn(r)	拉長線(兒)	to draw a long line/to leave something for future decision
lāche	拉扯	to involve others by loose talk: 請別把我拉扯進去。 *Qǐng bié bǎ wǒ lāche jìnqu.* Please don't involve me. [CC/V]
lādǎo	拉倒	to pull down: 他把樹拉倒了。 *Tā bǎ shù lādǎole.* He pulled down the tree. to forget it: 這件事我看還是拉倒吧。 *Zhèijiàn shì wǒ kàn háishi lādǎo ba.* I think we should forget about this matter. [RC/V]
lā dùzi	拉肚子	to have loose bowels [V O]
lā guānxi	拉關係	to draw relations with someone/to try to draw close to influential people: 跟他拉不上關係。 *Gēn tā lābushang guānxi.* Can't draw close to him.
lā húqinr	拉胡琴兒	to play a Chinese fiddle
lājià	拉架	to mediate between two parties quarreling or fighting [V-O]
lā jiāoqing	拉交情	= *la guanxi*
lā kè	拉客	to solicit customers (esp. streetwalkers) [V O]
lālong	拉攏	to draw to one's side: 你拉攏他做甚麼? *Nǐ lālong tā zuò shénme?* Why do you draw him to your side? to draw people with different views together: 你替他們兩個拉攏拉攏。 *Nǐ tì tāmen liǎngge lālonglalong.* You do something to get those two together. [CC/V]
lā mǎimai	拉買賣	= 拉生意 *lā shēngyi*
lā pítiaor	拉皮條(兒)	= 拉馬 *lā mǎ*, to act as a pimp
lā shēngyi	拉生意	to solicit business
lā shǐ	拉屎	to move bowels [V O]
lāta	拉遢	to be untidy, dirty [SV]
lāxiàshuǐ	拉下水	to corrupt someone.; to drag someone into the mire; to get in; to make an accomplice of someone: 他會把你拉下水的。 *Tā huì bǎ nǐ lāxiàshuǐ de.* He will get you involved in it. [V]
lā yìnggōng	拉硬弓	to draw a stiff bow/to force someone to do something against his will
lā yìpìgu zhài	拉一屁股債	to owe a mountain of debts

77

láibīn	來賓	guest [SC/N]
láide	來得	the manner in which one does something: 你這句話來得厲害。 *Nǐ zhèi jù huà láide lìhai.* Your words are most telling.
láidejí	來得及	(There is) enough time to do something [VC]
láihuí(r)	來回(兒)	a round trip: 來回票 *láihuí piào,* a roundtrip ticket [CC/N]
láilì	來歷	origin, background, source: 來歷不明 *Láilì bùmíng.* The origin is not known. [SC/N]
lái lóng qù mò	來龍去脈	a sequence of events, cause and effect
láilù bùmíng	來路不明	unidentified; of unknown origin: 來路不明的飛機 *láilù bùmíng de fēijī* unidentified airplane [Adj/V]
láinián	來年	next year [SC/TW]
láirén	來人	a messenger; a call for someone to come (usually servants): 來人啊! *lái rén a;* a call to get attention to someone coming: 來人啦! *Lái rén la!* Some is coming! [SC/N]
láishēng	來生	next life [SC/TW]
lái shì xiōngxiōng	來勢洶洶	to break in in full fury, to come to look for trouble
láitou(r)	來頭(兒)	position or social status: 他的來頭不小。 *Tāde láitou bùxiǎo.* He is very influential socially, something worth doing: 這種遊戲還有甚麼來頭呢。 *Zhèizhǒng yóuxì hài yǒu shénme láitou ne.* This kind of game is not worth playing.
láiwǎng	來往	to come and go/to exchange visits: 我們早就不來往了。 *Wǒmen zǎo jiu bùláiwǎng le.* We don't see each other anymore. [CC/V]; friendly intercourse: 你跟他有來往嗎? *Nǐ gēn tā yǒu láiwǎng ma?* Do you have any dealings with him? [CC/V]
láixìn	來信	your letter: 來信收到了。 *Láixìn shōudàole.* Your letter has been received. [SC/N]; to write a letter (to someone): 你很久沒給我來信了。 *Nǐ hěn jiǔ méi gěi wǒ láixìn le.* You haven't written me a letter for a very long time. [V-O]
láiyì	來意	Intention of one's coming: 他的來意不善。 *Tāde láiyì búshàn.* His intention is not good. [SC/N]
láizhe	來着	marker to indicate action that occurred a short while ago: 他說他姓甚麼來着? *Tā shuō tā xìng shénme láizhe?* What did he say his surname was?
méi lái yǎn qù	眉來眼去	to exchange glances, to communicate with eyes

líbié	離別	to take leave of: 我們離別以後沒通過信。 *Wǒmen líbié yǐhòu méi tōngguo xìn.* We have not written to each other since we said goodbye. [CC/V]
líbùliǎo	離不了	cannot be separated from: 他那種人離不了女人。 *Tā nèizhong rén líbùliǎo nǚrén.* His kind of people can't live without women. [VC]
lí chóu bié hèn	離愁別恨	grief of parting
lígér	離格兒	to deviate from standard: 說話別離格兒。 *Shuōhuà bié lígér.* Talk must be within limit. [V-O]
líhūn	離婚	to divorce: 他們老早離婚了。 *Tāmen lǎo zǎo líhūnle.* Those two were divorced a long time ago. [V-O]
líjiān	離間	to sow dissention between or among: 你得小心小人離間我們。 *Nǐ děi xiǎoxin xiǎorén líjiān wǒmen.* You must watch the wicked person's sowing dissention between us. [CC/V]
líkāi	離開	to depart from (place, person): 小孩兒離不開父母。 *Xiǎoháir líbùkāi fùmǔ.* Children can't leave their parents. [VC]
lípǔ(r)	離譜(兒)	to be off or below standard, to be irregular: 這件事做得有點兒離譜了。 *Zhèijiàn shì zuòde yǒu diǎnr lípǔ le.* This matter was handled a little irregularly. [V-O]
líqí	離奇	to be unbelievably strange, to be mysterious [CC/SV]
lí qún suò jū	離群索居	to live the life of a recluse
lísàn	離散	to be scattered about, to be separated from one another: 一家人因為戰爭都離散了。 *Yìjiā rén yīnwei zhànzhēng dōu lísànle.* The whole family was separated from one another because of the war. [CC/V]
lí xiāng bèi jǐng	離鄉背井	to be away from one's native place
líxiū	離休	retirement of a veteran cadre; to retire with honors; to leave one's post and rest: 他父親早就離休了。 *Tā fùqin zǎo jiù líxiū le.* His father retired with honors long ago. [V]
líxīnlì	離心力	centrifugal force
lí zhèr hěn jìn	離這兒很近	very close to here
bēi huān lí hé	悲歡離合	sorrows and joys, separations and reunions/facts of life
fēnlí	分離	to be separated: 他們不願意分離。 *Tāmen búyuànyi fēnlí.* They don't want to be separated. [CC/V]
pànlí	叛離	to rebel [CC/V]

lǐcái	理財	to administer financial affairs [VO]
lǐcǎi	理睬	to heed the presence of (someone), to take notice of: 他不理睬我。 *Tā bùlǐcǎi wǒ.* He doesn't take notice of me. [CC/V]
lǐfà	理髮	to cut hair, to have a haircut [V-O]
lǐ fán zhì jù	理繁治劇	to manage difficulties and regulate the trouble
lǐhuì	理會	to realize, understand (a situation, an explanation), to pay attention to: 他常常不理會人。 *Tā chángchang bùlǐhuì rén.* He doesn't often pay attention to people. [CC/V]
lǐjiā	理家	to manage domestic affairs: 張太太真會理家。 *Zhāng Tàitai zhēn huì lǐjiā.* Mrs. Zhang is really a good housekeeper. [V-O]
lǐjiě	理解	to comprehend [CC/V]; comprehension
lǐjiělì	理解力	ability to comprehend: 他的理解力很高。 *Tāde lǐjiě lì hěn gāo.* His ability to comprehend is very high.
lǐ luàn jiě fēn	理亂解紛	to control the chaos and mediate disputes
lǐlùn	理論	theory [SC/N]; to discuss, to argue [V]
lǐsāng	理喪	to manage the funeral ceremony [V-O]
lǐshì	理事	to attend to a matter [VO]; director (of a firm, organization, etc.)
lǐshū	理書	to revise a book [V-O]
lǐxiǎng	理想	to be ideal [SC/SV]; an idea
dàilǐ	代理	to act in place of [CC/V]: 主任病了。 誰代理他的職務？ *Zhǔrèn bìng le. Shéi dàilǐ tāde zhíwù?* The chairman is sick. Who acts in his place?
xiūlǐ	修理	to repair; to punish (Taiwan slang): 那個不良少年昨天被警察好好兒修理了一次。 *Nèige bùliáng shàonian zuótian bèi jǐngchá hǎohāor xiūlǐ le yícì.* That juvenile delinquent was punished well by the police yesterday. [CC/V]

lián běn dài lì	連本帶利	both principal and interest
liánbì	連璧	to join the jade/to combine two good things [V-O]
liánhuànr	連串兒	a series of (disasters, mishaps, etc.): 一連串兒的不幸事件。 *yì liànchuànrde búxìng shìjiàn*, a series of unfortunate incidents [VO/N]
lián dǎ dài mà	連打帶罵	with both beating and cursing
liándàiguānxi	連帶關係	the relationship or connection (between two things)
liánhào	連號	consecutive numbers, firms of the same owner, the hyphen [SC/N]
liánhé	連合	to join (efforts, pieces together) [CC/V]
liánhuán	連環	a chain of rings linked together: 連環圖 *liánhuántú*, comic strips [SC/N]
liánjiē	連接	= 接連 *jiēlián* continuously: 我接連看了三個病人。 *Wǒ jiēlián kànle sānge bìngren.* I saw three patients in succession. [CC/Adv]
liánlèi	連累	to cause or bring trouble to another: 我連累你了。 *Wǒ liánlèi nǐ le.* I have caused you trouble. [CC/V]
liánlián	連連	continuously: 連連點頭 *liánlián diǎntóu*, to nod repeatedly [Adv]
liánluò	連絡	to get in touch with: 你跟他連絡一下。 *Nǐ gēn tā liánluò yíxià.* You get in touch with him. [CC/V]; 連絡處 *Liánluò chù*, Liaison office.
liánmáng	連忙	quickly, without hesitation: 他看見老板來了，就連忙過去打招呼。 *Tā kànjian lǎobǎn láile, jiù liánmáng guòqu dǎ zhāohu.* As soon as he saw his boss coming, he quickly went over to greet him. [Adv]
liánnián	連年	year after year: 連年旱災 *liánnián hànzāi*, famine year after year [VO/TW]
liánpiān	連篇	page after page: 連篇錯字 *liánpiān cuò zi*, wrong characters all over the essay [VO/Adv]
liánrèn	連任	to serve another term of office [V-O]
liánshū	連書	to write syllables together to form words [SC/V]
liánxù	連續	continuously: 連續下了三天雨。 *liánxù xiàle sāntiān yǔ*, rained continuously for three days [CC/Adv]
liányòng	連用	to use together; to use in succession; to go consecutively = 連起來使用 *liánqǐlai shǐ yòng* 這兩個字不能連用。 *Zhèi liǎng ge zì bùnéng liányòng.* These two characters don't go together. [V]

liánbāng	聯邦	federation, confederate [VO/N]
liánbāng zhèngfǔ	聯邦政府	federal government
liándà	聯大	abbreviation for 聯合國大會 *Liánhéguó Dàhuì*, United Nations General Assembly
liándān	聯單	duplicate or joint forms for receipt, etc. [SC/N]
liánhé	聯合	to unite: 我們聯合起來，誰也不怕。 *Wǒmen liánhéqilai shéi yě búpà.* When we unite, we will not be afraid of anyone. [CC/V]
liánhéguó	聯合國	United Nations
liánhé zhèngfǔ	聯合政府	coalition government
liánhuānhuì	聯歡會	a get together party
liánjūn	聯軍	allied troops [SC/N]
liánluò	聯絡	= 聯絡 *liánluò* (p. 81) [CC/V]
lián mèi ér lái	聯袂而來	to come together
liánmíng	聯名	to sign together: 我們聯名申請。 *Wǒmen liánmíng shēnqǐng.* We apply with joint signatures. [VO/Adv]
liánpiào	聯票	connection tickets for journey [SC/N]
liánqilai	聯起來	to unite, to connect [VC]
liánshū	聯書	to sign jointly [SC/V]
liánxi	聯系	to make connection (with someone): 為了這件事的成功，你應當跟他聯系聯系。 *Wéile zhèijiàn shì de chénggōng, nǐ yīngdāng gēn tā liánxilianxi.* You ought to contact him for the success of this venture. [CC/V]
liánxiǎng	聯想	to remind one of something or someone [SC/V]
liányìhuì	聯誼會	social, fellowship party
liányīn	聯姻	to be related by marriage [V-O]
liányíng	聯營	to manage jointly: 公私聯營 *gōng sī liányíng*, to manage jointly between government and private citizens [SC/V]

列   to arrange in order, to enumerate, to classify

liè biǎo	列表	to prepare a chart, table, schedule, etc. [V O]
lièchē	列車	a train of wagons/railroad train [SC/N]
lièdān	列單	to draw up a list [V-O]
lièdǎo	列島	archipelago [SC/N]
lièguó	列國	the different countries: 春秋列國 *chūnqiū lièguó*, the city-states at the time of Confucius [SC/N]
lièjǔ	列舉	to give a list of (names, crimes): 列舉人名，罪狀。 *lièjǔ rénmíng, zuìzhuàng* [CC/V]
lièmíng	列名	to enter or appear on a list of names of persons [V-O]
lièqiáng	列強	a group of strong nations/the Great Powers [SC/N]
lièrù	列入	to enter as an item (of agenda, list, etc.): 請把這件事列入議程 *Qǐng bǎ zhèijiàn shì lièrù yìchéng.* Please include this matter in the agenda. [RC/V]
Lièwèi	列位	= 各位 *Gèwèi* Gentlemen! or Ladies and Gentlemen! [SC/N]
lièxí	列席	to be present at meeting, to be observers at conference [V-O]
lièzhuàn	列傳	biographies, especially section on biographies in different dynastic histories [SC/N]
bìngliè	並列	to be listed side by side [SC/V]
bìnglièshì	並列式	parallel style
hángliè	行列	row or column [CC/N]
kāiliè	開列	to draw up a list: 你把要買的東西開列一個單子吧。 *Nǐ bǎ yào mǎi de dōngxi kāiliè yíge dānzi ba.* You ought to draw up a list of the things you want to buy. [CC/V]
xiàliè	下列	the following: 請解釋下列各名詞。 *Qǐng jiěshì xiàliè gè míngcí.* Please explain the following nouns. [SC/V]

lǐngbān	領班	foreman [VO/N]
lǐng bīng	領兵	to command troops [V O]
lǐngdài	領帶	to lead troops [CC/V]; necktie [SC/N]
lǐngdān	領單	receipt on delivery [SC/N]
lǐngdì	領地	territory under jurisdiction [SC/N]
lǐngháng	領航	to pilot (navigation, aviation, etc.) [V-O]
lǐnghuí	領回	to get back [VC]
lǐnghuì	領會	to understand, to comprehend: 這個問題太複雜，小孩子恐怕不能領會。 *Zhèige wèntí tài fùzá, xiǎoháizi kǒngpà bùnéng lǐnghuì.* This problem is too complicated, I'm afraid that children cannot understand. [CC/V]
lǐngjiào	領教	to receive instructions/to get someone's opinion, to pay a visit; 明天我再來領教。 *Míngtian wǒ zài lái lǐngjiào.* I will come to see you again tomorrow. [V-O]
lǐnglù	領路	to lead the way; to show the way = 帶路 *dàilù* [V]
lǐnglüè	領略	to grasp, to understand [CC/V]
lǐngqíng	領情	to accept with thanks, to accept the sentiment but not the gift: 你的好意，我領情就是了。 *Nǐde hǎoyì wǒ lǐngqíng jiùshi le.* I accept your thoughtfulness with thanks (but I can't accept the gift). [V-O]
lǐngqǔ	領取	to receive [CC/V]
lǐngshòu	領受	to receive formally (awards, baptism, etc.) [CC/V]
lǐngtóu(r)	領頭(兒)	to lead the way, to be first [V-O]
lǐngwù	領悟	to comprehend (truth, doctrine, significance) [CC/V]
lǐngxiān	領先	to head the list (of sponsors, actors, etc.) [VO]
lǐngxiè	領謝	to show appreciation [V-O]
lǐngyǎng	領養	to adopt: 領養一個小孩兒。 *lǐngyǎng yíge xiǎoháir*, to adopt a child [CC/V]
lǐngzuì	領罪	to offer apology [V-O]
rènlǐng	認領	to claim (lost property, dog, etc.) [CC/V]
màolǐng	冒領	to make false claim on (lost property, etc.) [SC/V]

liúbì	流弊	defects that have been passed down/malpractice, shortcoming [SC/N]
liúbiàn	流變	flowing and change/the development [CC/N]
liúchǎn	流產	to have a miscarriage; to fail to materialize: 他的計劃不幸流產了。 *Tāde jìhuà búxìng liúchǎn le.* Unfortunately, his plan did not materialize. [V-O]
liúchuán	流傳	to circulate; to spread; 謠言流傳得很快。 *Yáoyán liúchuán de hěnkuài.* Rumors spread quickly. [V]
liúdòng	流動	to drift, to move about [CC/V]; mobile, liquid (assets): 流動財產 *liúdòng cáichǎn* [SV]
liúfāng	流芳	to leave a good name: 萬世流芳 *Wànshì liúfāng*, to leave a good name to posterity [VO]
liúfàng	流放	to exile, to send to: 他被流放到新疆去了。 *Tā bèi liúfàng dào xīnjiāng qù le.* He was exiled to *Xīnjiāng*. [CC/V]
liú hàn	流汗	to perspire [V O]
liúlǎn	流覽	to glance over (books) [SC/V]
liúlàng	流浪	to travel freely, to drift from one place to another [CC/V]
liú lèi	流淚	to shed tears [V O]
liúlì	流利	to be fluent: 他的中國話說得很流利。 *Tāde Zhōngguóhuà shuōde hěn liúlì.* His Chinese is really fluent. [CC/SV]
liúlí shī suǒ	流離失所	to wander about lost or homeless
liúlián	流連	to loiter, to linger; 流連忘返 *Liúlián wàng fǎn*, to indulge in pleasures and forget to return [CC/V]
liúluò tā xiāng	流落他鄉	to drift about in strange places (other than native place)
liúlù	流露	to reveal, to show unintentially: 真情流露 *zhēnqíng liúlù*, true sentiments were revealed [CC/V]
liú shuǐ	流水	flowing water [SC/N]; to flow [V O]
liútōng	流通	to circulate (air, currency, etc.) [CC/V]; to flow through [VC]
liúwáng	流亡	to live as a refugee (abroad): 流亡海外 *liúwáng hǎiwài* [CC/V]
liúxiànxíng	流線型	streamlined style: 流線型火車 *liúxiànxíng huǒchē*, streamlined train
liúxíng	流行	to be fashionable, to be generally accepted [CC/SV]
liú xuě	流血	to shed blood
liúyán	流言	rumors, hearsay (especially malicious) [SC/N]

lùndiǎn	論點	point of discussion [SC/N]
lùndiào	論調	tone of discussion [SC/N]
lùnduàn	論斷	judgement, opinion [CC/N]
lùn gōng xíng shǎng	論功行賞	to reward on merit
lùnjià	論價	to discuss price [V-O]
lùn jiāoqing	論交情	to consider friendship: 論交情，你不應該反對他。 *Lùn jiāoqing, nǐ bùyīnggāi fǎnduì ta.* Considering your friendship with him, you should not have opposed him.
lùnjù	論據	grounds for discussion [SC/N]
lùnlǐ	論理	according to reason [VO/Adv]; logic
lùnshuō	論說	a treatise, essay [SC/N]
lùntí	論題	proposition, theme [N]
lùnwén	論文	thesis, dissertation: 博士論文 *bóshì lùnwén*, doctoral dissertation [SC/N]
lùnzhàn	論戰	war of discussion/controversy in journals, papers, etc. [SC/N]
lùnzhèng	論證	evidence, proof [SC/N]
lùnzhù	論著	published works [CC/N]
lùnzuì	論罪	to consider one's guilt, to sentence (according to offense) [V-O]
biànlùn	辯論	to debate [CC/V]; a debate
búlùn	不論	regardless of: 不論你怎麼樣 *búlùn nǐ zěnme yàng*, regardless of what you do [SC/Adv]
tǎo lùn	討論	to discuss [VO]
wúlùn	無論	= *búlùn* [VO/Adv]
yánlùn	言論	published statements: 總統言論 *Zǒngtǒng yánlùn*, President's speeches [CC/N]
yǐ shì lùn shì	以事論事	to consider the matter itself (not to involve personalities)
yúlùn	輿論	public opinion [SC/N]

luòbǎng	落榜	to fail to pass the examination (one's name not appearing on the roster) [V-O]
luòcǎo	落草	to join the bandits [V-O]
luòchéng	落成	to be completed (of buildings): 落成典禮 *luòchéng diǎnlǐ*, dedication ceremony [VC]
luòdì	落地	to touch the ground: 落地窗 *luòdì chuāng*, French window; 落地式電視 *luòdìshì diànshì*, console television set [VO]
luòfà	落髮	to cut off the hair/to become a Buddhist monk or nun [V-O]
luò huā liú shuǐ	落花流水	thoroughly, whole-heartedly: 把敵人打得落花流水。*Bǎ dírén dǎde luò huā liú shuǐ.* Route the enemy completely.
luòhòu	落後	to be backward: 落後國家 *luòhòu guójiā*, underdeveloped countries [VO/SV]
luòkōng	落空	to end up with nothing [V-O]
luòlèi	落淚	to shed tears, to weep [V-O]
luòluò dàfāng	落落大方	to be very poised and dignified
luòpò	落魄	to be down and out, to be a failure [V-O]
luòshí	落實	to realize, to put into effect: 那是落實毛主席指示的重要措施 *Nà shi luòshí Máo Zhǔxí zhǐshì de zhòngyào cuòshī.* That is an important measure to realize Chairman Mao's instructions. (PRC); 落實政策 *luòshí zhèngcè* to put policy into effect [VC]
luòshuǐ	落水	to fall into the water, to become a prostitute [V-O]
luòshuǐgǒu	落水狗	a dog that falls into the water/a defeated person: 打落水狗 *Dǎ luòshuǐgǒu*, to hit a person who has been defeated
luòtāngjī	落湯雞	chicken drenched and about to be feathered/a person drenched through
luòwǔ	落伍	to drop behind others, to become outdated: 思想落伍 *sīxiǎng luòwǔ*, thinking is backward [V-O]
luòxialai	落下來	to drop down, to fall (as leaves from the tree) [VC]
luòxuǎn	落選	to fail in election or competition [V-O]
luòyǔ	落雨	to rain [V-O]
línglíng luòluò	零零落落	in piecemeal fashion

mǎibàn	買辦	compradore [CC/N]
mǎibuqǐ	買不起	can afford to buy [VC]
mǎifāng	買方	the buying party in a contract [SC/N]
mǎiguān	買官	to buy official post/to pay bribe to obtain official post [V-O]
mǎihǎo	買好	to try to secure goodwill, friendship, etc. (of person), to try to please: 買他的好 *mǎi tāde hǎo*, to please him [V-O]; to be through buying: 買好了就走。 *Mǎihǎole jiù zǒu.* Will leave after buying is done. [VC]
mǎijìn	買進	to buy in (goods) [VC]
mǎikè	買客	customer at shops [SC/N]
mǎi kōng mài kōng	買空賣空	buy empty sell empty/to speculate on stocks, to cheat by empty talk
mǎilùqián	買路錢	blackmail money paid for immunity for robbers, money demanded by robbers
mǎimài	買賣	to buy and sell, to trade [CC/V]; 買賣 *mǎimai*, business: 買賣好嗎? *Mǎimai hǎo ma?* Is business good? [CC/N]
mǎimíng	買名	to buy fame/to cater to publicity by sordid methods (V-O)
mǎi rénxīn	買人心	to buy people's hearts/to win people's hearts through favors [V O]
mǎitōng	買通	to pay bribe to: 你把他買通了就沒問題了。 *Nǐ bǎ tā mǎitōngle jiù méi wèntí le.* There will be no problem if you have bribed him. [VC]
mǎixiào	買笑	to buy smiles/to visit prostitutes [V-O]
mǎizhǔ	買主	customer, buying party [SC/N]
mǎizuì	買醉	to buy drink/to have a drinking spree [V-O]
bùmǎizhàng	不買賬	won't do others a favor, won't yield to pressure

mài běnshi	賣本事	to sell ability/to show off skill [V O]
màibǔ	賣卜	to be a fortune teller [V-O]
màichàng	賣唱	to sell singing/to be a professional singer [V-O]
màichū	賣出	to sell out [VC]
màidǐ	賣底	to sell the bottom/to betray the secret [V-O]
màiguāi	賣乖	to sell good behavior/to show off cleverness, good behavior, etc. [V-O]
màiguānzi	賣關子	to keep people guessing; to stop a story at climax to keep the listeners in suspense 他就喜歡賣關子。 *Tā jiù xǐhuan màiguānzi.* He enjoys keeping people guessing.
màiguó	賣國	to sell the country/to be a traitor: 賣國賊 *màiguózéi*, a traitor [V-O]
màijì	賣技	to sell skill/to be a professional artist [V-O]
màijià	賣價	the selling price [SC/N]
màilì	賣力	to sell strength/to put in extra energy in work [V-O]; to be hard-working [SV]
màiliǎn	賣臉	to sell face/to disregard the loss of face, to sell looks: 唱歌兒的賣臉不賣身。 *Chànggērde mài liǎn búmài shēn.* The singsong girls sell their looks, but not their bodies. [V-O]
màinòng	賣弄	to show off: 賣弄文墨 *màinòng wénmò*, to show off one's writings [CC/V]
màiqiào	賣俏	to sell cuteness/to flirt [V-O]
mài rénqíng	賣人情	to sell fellowship/to do favor
mài wén wéi shēng	賣文為生	to sell writing for a living
màixiào	賣笑	to sell smiles/to be a prostitute [V-O]
màiyì	賣藝	to sell art/to be an acrobat [V-O]
màiyín	賣淫	to sell lewdness/to be a prostitute [V-O]
mài yǒu qiú róng	賣友求榮	to betray friends to obtain promotion
màizuǐ	賣嘴	to sell mouth/to show off forensic skill, to indulge in clever talk [V-O]

măn buzàihu	滿不在乎	to be totally unconcerned: 他對那件事滿不在乎。 *Tā duì nèijiàn shì măn búzàihu.* He is totally unconcerned with that matter.
măn chéng fēng yǔ	滿城風雨	the city is full of wind and rain/the city is full of rumors: 他們兩個 的事鬧得滿城風雨。 *Tāmen liǎngge de shì nàode măn chéng fēng yǔ.* Rumors about the two of them have spread all over town.
măn fù láo sāo	滿腹牢騷	to have a grudge against everything
măn kǒu dāying	滿口答應	to make profuse promises
măn kǒu hú yán	滿口胡言	to be full of stupid talk
măn miàn chūn fēng	滿面春風	spring wind fills the face/to radiate happiness: 他近來滿面春風得 意得很。 *Tā jìnlai măn miàn chūn fēng déyìde hěn.* Recently he radiates happiness and is having a ball.
mănmù	滿目	to be eyeful: 商店琳琅滿目 *Shāngdiàn línláng mănmù.* The store is fully stocked.
mănyì	滿意	to satisfy, to be satisfied [V-O/SV]
măn yǐwéi	滿以為	to be fully convinced (but . . .): 我滿以為他會當選，沒想到會輸得 這麼慘。 *Wǒ măn yǐwéi tā huì dāngxuǎn, méixiǎngdào huì shūde zhème cǎn.* I was fully convinced that he would win the election. Unexpectedly, he suffered a big loss.
mănyuè	滿月	full moon [SC/N]; to be one month old [V-O]; celebration of baby's first full month.
măn zài ér guī	滿載而歸	to come back loaded (with honors, profit, etc.)
mănzú	滿足	to be satisfied [CC/SV]; to satisfy [V]
măn zuǐ rén yì dàodé, măn dùzi nán dào nǚ chāng	滿嘴仁義道德， 滿肚子男盜女娼	mouth full of humanity, righteousness, and moral principles; stomach full of being thieves for a male and a prostitute for a female/to be a hypocrite
măn zuǐ yīngwén	滿嘴英文	mouth filled with English/to keep on speaking English
mănzuò	滿座	to have a full house: 今天戲園子一定滿座。 *Jīntian xìyuánzi yídìng mănzuò.* Today the theatre will certainly have a full house. [SC/V]
bǎomǎn	飽滿	to be vigorous: 他的精神總是很飽滿。 *Tā de jīngshen zǒng shì hěn bǎomǎn.* He is always full of vigor. [CC/SV]
yuánmǎn	圓滿	to be satisfactory: 結果圓滿 *Jiéguǒ yuánmǎn.* The result is satisfactory. [CC/SV]

mídèng	迷瞪	to become infatuated with something; 迷迷瞪瞪的樣子 *mímidèngdengde yàngzi*, to look infatuated [CC/V]
míguǎi	迷拐	to drug and kidnap [CC/V]
míhu	迷糊	to be unclear, blurred; 迷迷糊糊 *mímihuhu*, in a daze, difficult to make out [CC/SV]
míhún	迷魂	to infatuate the soul/to be infatuated, to be bewildered: 迷魂湯 *míhúntāng*, soup of infatuation/enticing words [V-O]
míhuò	迷惑	to tempt, to confuse, to mislead [CC/V]
míle xīn	迷了心	to be thoroughly infatuated
míliàn	迷戀	to love blindly: 他竟然會迷戀一個妓女。 *Tā jìngrán huì míliàn yíge jìnǚ.* He went so far as to blindly love a prostitute. [SC/V]
mílù	迷路	to lose one's way: 我因為迷了路怎麼也找不著他的家。 *Wǒ yīnwèi míle lù, zěnme yě zhǎobuzháo tā de jiā.* Because I lost the way, I simply couldn't find his home. [V-O]
míluàn	迷亂	to be bewildered [CC/SV]
mínǐ	迷你	transliteration of mini-: 迷你裙 *mínǐqún*, miniskirt [VO]
mírén	迷人	to charm, to be charming: 迷人精 *mírénjīng, charmer, enchanter* [VO/SV]
míshī fāngxiàng	迷失方向	to lose one's bearings
míwǎng	迷惘	to be lost, confused [CC/SV]
míxìn	迷信	to believe blindly [SC/V]; superstition: 破除迷信 *pòchú míxìn*, to eradicate superstition [SC/N]
mízuì	迷醉	to be fascinated by (new ideas, etc.): 迷醉新思想 *mízuì xīn sīxiǎng* [CC/V]
cáimí	財迷	one who is crazy for wealth [SC/N]
hūnmí zhuàngtài	昏迷狀態	in a comatose state
sèmí	色迷	one who is infatuated with women [SC/N]
xìmí	戲迷	one who is an avid opera fan [SC/N]
zhí mí búwù	執迷不悟	to be obstinately foolish, to be hopelessly confused

nábàn	拿辦	to arrest and punish [CC/V]
nábùchūshǒu	拿不出手	not to be presentable: 恐怕我的禮物拿不出手。*Kǒng pà wǒde lǐwù nábùchūshǒu.* I am afraid my gifts are not good.
nábuqilai	拿不起來	cannot lift, (figuratively) cannot handle: 他真無能。甚麽事都拿不起來。*Tā zhēn wúnéng. Shénme shì dōu nábuqilai.* He is really incompetent. He can't handle anything. [VC]
nábúzhù	拿不住	can't control: 他拿不住小王。*Tā nábúzhù Xiǎo Wáng.* He can't manipulate Xiao Wang.
nábuzhǔn	拿不準	to be in doubt; to be not sure of; to feel uncertain: 目前還有三個州的投票情況拿不準。*Mùqián háiyǒu sān ge zhōu de tóu piào qíng kuàng nábuzhǔn.* For now, the results of voting in three states are not clear.
nábuzhù rén	拿不住人	can't keep people under control: 拿不住人，別想當主管。*Nábuzhù rén, bié xiǎng dāng zhǔguǎn.* If one can't keep people under his control, he shouldn't think of becoming boss.
nádà	拿大	to pretend to be superior; give oneself airs 我不喜歡動不動就拿大的人。*Wǒ bùxǐ huan dòngbudòng jiù nádà de rén.* I don't like people who often put on airs. [V]
nádàdǐng	拿大頂	to stand on one's head [V-O]
nádìng zhǔyì	拿定主意	to make up one's mind
náhuò	拿獲	to capture 一個小時就把敵人全部拿獲了。*Yí ge xiǎoshí jiù bǎ dírén quán bù náhuòle.* The enemy was captured in one hour.
nájiàzi	拿架子	to put on airs: 他拿甚麽臭架子，誰不知道他是誰。*Tā ná shénme chòu jiàzi. Shéi bùzhīdao tā shi shéi.* What smelly airs is he putting on? Who doesn't know who he is? [V-O]
nánie	拿捏	to purposely put obstacles in the way of someone, to pretend to conform to the rules of propriety [CC/V]
ná qián búdàng qián huā	拿錢不當錢花	to spend money recklessly
ná qiāng zuò shì	拿腔作勢	to pretend to be important
náquán	拿權	to get control of; to be in the saddle; to wield power 他現在拿權。*Tā xiànzài náquán.* He is in power now. [V-O]
nárén	拿人	to make things difficult for others; to raise difficulties 他動不動就拿人一手。*Tā dòngbudòng jiù nárén yìshǒu.* He always makes things difficult for others. [V]
náshì	拿勢	to have the power [V-O]
náshǒu	拿手	to be good at, to excel in: 他對足球很拿手。*Tā duì zúqiú hěn náshǒu.* He is very good at football. [VO/SV]
ná zéi dàng hǎorén	拿賊當好人	to treat a thief as a good person
názhǔyì	拿主意	to make a decision; to make up one's mind 他這人不善拿主意。*Tā zhè rén búshàn názhǔyì.* He is not good at making decisions. [V O]

niànbáile zì	念白了字	to read a character incorrectly
niàndao	念叨	to remember someone by talking: 他常常念叨着你。*Tā chángcháng niàndaozheni.* She often remembers you in her talks; *niànniandaodao.* to grumble: 他老是在那兒念念叨叨。*Tā lǎo shi zài nàr niànniandaodao.* He is always grumbling.
niànfó	念佛	to chant Buddhist scriptures, to say prayers to Buddha [V-O]
niàn jiāoqing	念交情	to care about friendship
niànjīng	念經	to chant religious scriptures
niànjiù	念舊	to remember old friends, old times, etc. [VO/SV]
niàn něiyixì	念哪一系	to study in which department
niànniànbúwàng	念念不忘	never to forget
niànniàn yǒu cí	念念有詞	to mumble: 他總是念念有詞，不知道說些甚麽。*Tā zǒng shi niànniàn yǒu cí, bùzhīdao shuō xie shénme.* He is always mumbling. Nobody knows what he is talking about.
niàn shū	念書	to read books, to study [V O]
niànsòng	念誦	to read aloud 念誦詩文*niànsòng shīwén* to read poems aloud [V]
niàntou	念頭	idea, thought, intention: 為了一個女人，他不知道轉了多少念頭。*Wèile yíge nǚren, tā bùzhīdao zhuǎnle duōshao niàntou.* For a woman he has tried many things (in order to win her).
niàn xiǎoxué	念小學	to study in an elementary school
niànzhū	念珠	rosary [SC/N]
búniànjiùè	不念舊惡	to forget and forgive old grudges
jìniàn	紀念	to commemorate: 這棵樹是為了紀念我母親種的。*Zhèikē shù shi wèile jìniàn wǒ mǔqīn zhòng de.* This tree was planted to commemorate my mother. [CC/V] commemoration: 結婚紀念 *jiéhūn jìniàn*, wedding momentos, wedding anniversary
liúniàn	留念	to keep as a memento (used in sending a picture, etc.): 大哥留念 *Dàgē liúniàn*, To my brother (oldest) [CC/V]
xiǎngniàn	想念	to think of, to miss: 他很想念他母親。*Tā hěn xiǎngniàn tā mǔqin.* He misses his mother a lot. [CC/SV]

pà
to fear, to be afraid of   怕

pàde shi	怕的是	What I am afraid of is: 怕的是明天下雪不能開車。*Pàde shi míngtian xiàxuě bùnéng kāichē.* What I am afraid of is that it will snow tomorrow and we won't be able to drive.
pà dézuì rén	怕得罪人	to be afraid of offending people
pà guǐ	怕鬼	to be afraid of ghosts [V O]
pà guǐ jiào mén	怕鬼叫門	to be afraid that a ghost may knock on the door: 不做虧心事，不怕鬼叫門。*Búzuò kuīxīn shì, búpà guǐ jiào mén.* If one has not done anything discreditable, he is not afraid that a ghost may knock on his door.
pà jiàn rén	怕見人	to be afraid of seeing people, bashful
pà lǎopó	怕老婆	to be henpecked
pà qián pà hòu	怕前怕後	to be afraid of front and back/to be afraid of everything, to worry too much
pàrén	怕人	to be shy: 這個小孩兒怕人。*Zhèige xiǎoháir pàrén.* This child is shy. to be terrifying, shockingly bad: 這張畫兒真怕人。*Zhèizhāng huàr zhēn pà rén.* This picture is really terrifying. [VO/SV]
pàsào	怕臊	to be bashful [VO/SV]
pà shénme	怕甚麼	What are you afraid of? Don't be afraid.
pàshēng	怕生	to be shy with strangers = 認生 *rènshēng* 這小孩兒怕生。*Zhè xiǎoháir pàshēng.* This kid is shy with strangers. [V]
pàshì	怕事	to be afraid of getting involved, don't want to be bothered: 這個人怕事的不得了。你最好別找他。*Zhèige rén pàshìde budeliǎo. Nǐ zuìhǎo bié zhǎo ta.* This man hates to be bothered. You'd better not disturb him. [VO]
pàsǐ	怕死	to be afraid of death [V O]
pàxiū	怕羞	to be bashful: 女孩兒多半兒怕羞。*Nǚhair duōbànr pàxiū.* Most girls are bashful. [VO/SV]
hàipa	害怕	to fear, to be afraid of, to be scared [VO]
kǒngpà	恐怕	perhaps: 他恐怕不會來了。*Tā kǒngpà búhuì láile.* Perhaps he will not come. [CC/Adv]

pǎobù	跑步	to run [VO]
pǎochāi	跑差	to run errands [V-O]
pǎochē	跑車	a race car, sports car [SC/N]
pǎodānbāng	跑單幫	to travel back and forth with profit making goods
pǎodào	跑道	runway, athletic track [SC/N]
pǎodiào	跑調	to be out of tune [VO]
pǎodiàole	跑掉了	to have escaped, to have run away [VC]
pǎogǒu	跑狗	to have a dog race [V-O]; dog race
pǎojiē	跑街	to run errands [V-O]; errand boy
pǎo lái pǎo qù	跑來跑去	to run around
pǎo lóngtào	跑龍套	to act insignificant roles in Chinese opera, to serve in a supporting role: 我只能替人家跑跑龍套而已。*Wǒ zhǐ néng tì rénjia pǎopao lóngtào éryì.* What I can do is only serve in a supporting role for others.
pǎomǎ	跑馬	to have a horse race; to have a wet dream [V-O]; horse race
pǎo mǎtóu	跑碼頭	to travel from one port to another/to make a living in wandering around (magicians, singers, etc.)
pǎotángde	跑堂的	waiter in a restaurant
pǎotí	跑題	to be off the subject: 你的文章跑題了。*Nǐde wénzhāng pǎotí le.* Your essay is off the topic. [VO]
pǎotuǐ	跑腿	to run on errand [V-O]; footman, messenger
pǎo xīnwén	跑新聞	to run around to gather news (reporter)
dǎpǎole	打跑了	to chase somebody (or a dog) away by beating [VC]
gēn rén pǎole	跟人跑了	to run away with someone
sàipǎo	賽跑	to run a race [V-O]

píng'ān	平安	to be peaceful, safe: 一路平安 *yílù píng'ān*, all the way peaceful/bon voyage [CC/SV]
píngděng	平等	to be equal [CC/SV]; equality: 男女平等 *nán nǚ píngděng*, equality between male and female
píngdìng	平定	to subjugate (rebels) and restore peace [VC]; to be peaceful: 這個地方很平定。*Zhèige dìfang hěn píngdìng.* This place is peaceful. [SV]
píngfán	平凡	to be commonplace: 一件很平凡的事 *yíjian hěn píngfánde shì*, a commonplace thing; 那個人可不平凡。*Nèi ge rén kě bùpíngfán.* That person is really unusual. [CC/SV]
píngfēn	平分	To divide equally: 我們平分這些東西。*Wǒmen píngfēn zhèxie dōngxi.* We will divide these things equally. [SC/V]
pínghé	平和	to be moderate [CC/SV]
pínghéng	平衡	to be evenly balanced [CC/SV]
pínghua	平滑	to be smooth and even [CC/SV]
píngjìng	平靜	to be peaceful and quiet: 這個地方很平靜。*Zhèige dìfang hěn píngjìng.* This place is very quiet and peaceful. [CC/SV]
píngjūn	平均	to be evenly distributed, on the average: 平均一個人賺多少錢? *Píngjūn yíge rén zhuàn duōshao qián?* On the average how much does a person earn? [CC/SV]
píngmín	平民	common people [SC/N]
píngpíng	平平	to be so-so, nothing special: 近來一切平平。沒有甚麼可說的。*jìnlai yíqiè píngpíng. Méiyou shénme kěshuōde.* Recently everything is so-so. There is nothing worth saying. [CC/SV]
píngshí	平時	usually: 平時我不睡午覺。*Píngshí wǒ búshuì wǔjiào.* Usually I don't take a noon-nap. [SC/TW]
píngtǎn	平坦	to be level: 道路平坦。*Dàolù píngtǎn.* The road is level. [CC/SV]
píngwěn	平穩	to be steady, safe [CC/SV]
píngxìn	平信	ordinary mail [SC/N]
píng xīn jìng qì	平心靜氣	to be calm, cool
píngxíng	平行	to be parallel [SV]
píng yì jìn rén	平易近人	to be personable and accessible

pòchǎn	破產	to declare bankruptcy [V-O]; bankruptcy
pòchú	破除	to overcome, to eradicate (prejudices, obstacles, superstition): 破除迷信 *pòchú míxìn*, to eradicate superstition [CC/V]
pòfèi	破費	to spend money (used by guests to host after dinner or receipt of gifts): 破費，破費！今天讓您破費了。*Pòfèi, pòfèi! Jīntian ràng nín pòfèi le.* Today you spent too much money. [V-O]
pògé	破格	to take exception [V-O]
pòguā zhī nián	破瓜之年	age sixteen (girl), age 64 (women)
pò guànzi	破罐子	a broken jar/unchaste woman, a physical wreck [SC/N]
pòhuài	破壞	to damage: 破壞名譽 *pòhuài míngyù*, to damage the reputation; to destroy: 破壞家庭 *pòhuài jiātíng*, to destroy a family [CC/V]
pòlàn	破爛	torn and rotten/torn-down, ragged [CC/SV]
pòlànr	破爛兒	junk: 撿破爛兒過活 *jiǎn pòlànr guòhuó*, to make a living by picking up junk
pòliè	破裂	to break, to be broken: 感情破裂 *gǎnqíng pòliè*, friendship is broken, to stop loving each other [CC/V]
pòluò	破落	to decline [CC/V]
pòsǎngzi	破嗓子	broken voice, lost voice [SC/N]
pòshāngfēng	破傷風	tetanus infection
pòsuì	破碎	to be piecemeal, to be broken up [CC/SV]
pòtiānhuāng	破天荒	to be unprecedented: 他破天荒第一次來。*Tā pòtiānhuāng dìyícì lái.* He breaks all precedents to come for the first time.
pòtír	破題兒	the opening sentence of essay in civil examinations defining the theme; (figuratively) the first thing [VO/N]
pòtǔ	破土	to break ground (for construction)
pòxiǎo	破曉	daybreak [VO/N]
pòzhàn	破綻	a flaw (secret, argument) [SC/N]
shì rú pò zhú	勢如破竹	It's like splitting bamboo/with irresistible force
yì yǔ dào pò	一語道破	to hit the point with one remark

qǐ
to rise; to begin

起

qǐbīng	起兵	to raise troops/to go to war [VO]
qǐcǎo	起草	to prepare a draft [V-O]
qǐchéng	起程	to start the journey [VO]
qǐchū	起初	at the beginning [Adv]
qǐchuáng	起床	to get out of bed [V-O]
qǐfēi	起飛	to take off (airplane, economy): 經濟起飛 *Jīngjì qǐfēi*. The economy took off. [CC/V]
qǐhòng	起鬨	to make an uproar [V-O]
qǐjiā	起家	to raise the fortunes of the family, to be prosperous in one's career: 他是做生意起家的。*Tā shi zuò shēngyi qǐjiā de.* He raised the fortunes of his family by doing business. [V-O]
qǐjiàn	起見	motive, purpose: 為了省錢起見 *Wèile shěng qián qǐjiàn*, for the purpose of saving money
qǐjìn(r)	起勁(兒)	to be energetic: 他做事真起勁兒。*Tā zuòshì zhēn qǐjìnr.* He is really energetic when he does things. [VO/SV]
qǐjū	起居	rising and resting/one's everyday life style: 他近來起居很正常。*Tā jìnlai qǐjū hěn zhèngcháng.* His recent behavior is very normal. [CC/N]
qǐlai	起來	to rise, to get up; as a verbal complement in neutral tone, it indicates the beginning of an action: 說起話來沒有完。*Shuōqi huà lai méiyou wán.* When one starts talking, there will be no end. 說起來，話長。*Shuōqilai, huà cháng.* It's a long story when one starts to talk about it. [VC]
qǐlì	起立	to stand up 全體起立 *Quántǐ qǐlì* All rise. [V]
qǐmíng	起名	to give a name [V-O]
qǐsè	起色	improvement: 他的病有點兒起色。*Tāde bìng yǒu diǎnr qǐsè.* His illness is improving/He is a little better. [SC/N]
qǐshēn	起身	to start a journey [V-O]
qǐshǒu	起手	to start [VO]
qǐshì	起誓	to take an oath, to swear [V-O]
qǐtóu(r)	起頭(兒)	to begin: 誰起的頭兒? *Shéi qǐde tóur?* Who started it? [V-O]
qǐyì	起義	to raise a righteous revolt [V-O]
kànbuqǐ	看不起	to look down upon (somebody or something) [VC]
mǎideqǐ	買得起	can afford to buy [VC]

qiángbào	強暴	to violate: 強暴少女 *qiángbào shàonǚ*, to rape a young girl [CC/V]
qiángbiàn	強辯	to argue forcefully; to call white black, refuse to admit one's mistake: 他錯了還要強辯。*Tā cuòle hái yào qiángbiàn*. Even when he has made a mistake, he still won't admit it. [SC/V]
qiáng cí duó lǐ	強辭奪理	to exaggerate by rhetoric
qiángdào	強盜	a robber [SC/N]
qiángdiào	強調	to emphasize, to reiterate: 他一直強調他反對的理由。*Tā yìzhí qiángdiào tā fǎnduì de lǐyóu*. He constantly reiterates the reasons for his opposition. [SC/V]
qiánggàn	強幹	to do something by force [SC/V]
qiánghàn	強悍	to be powerful, brutal [CC/SV]
qiánghéng	強橫	to be arrogant, brutal [CC/SV]
qiánghuà	強化	to strengthen 強化記憶 *qiánghuà jìyì* to strengthen the memory [V]
qiángjiān	強姦	to rape [SC/V]
qiángjiàn	強健	to be physically strong [CC/SV]
qiǎngpò	強迫	to force, coerce (somebody to do something) [SC/V]
qiǎngpò jiàoyù	強迫教育	compulsory education
qiángshèng	強盛	to be strong and prosperous (nation): 中國現在可強盛起來了。*Zhōngguó xiànzài kě qiángshèngqilai le*. China is now really strong and prosperous. [CC/SV]
qiángyìng	強硬	to be unyielding: 敵人的態度很強硬。*Díren de tàidu hěn qiángyìng*. The enemy's attitude is very unyielding. [CC/SV]
qiángyǒulì	強有力	to be powerful: 一個強有力的國家。*Yíge qiángyǒulìde guójiā*, a powerful country
qiǎngzhì zhíxíng	強制執行	to carry it out by force
qiángzhuàng	強壯	to be powerful, strong [SC/SV]
miǎnqiǎng	勉強	to do something against one's will: 你要是不願意，請別勉強。*Nǐ yàoshi búyuànyi, qǐng bié miǎnqiǎng*. If you are not willing, please don't force yourself; to strive to do one's best: 我實在做不了，你一定要我做，我只好勉強試試。*Wǒ shízài zuòbuliǎo, nǐ yídìng yào wǒ zuò, wǒ zhǐhǎo miǎnqiǎng shìshi*. I really can't do it. Since you insist, I will try my best.

qièchí	切齒	to grind one's teeth in hatred: 切齒之恨 *qièchí zhī hèn* [VO]
qièdàng	切當	to be very appropriate, to the point [SC/SV]
qiēduàn	切斷	to cut in two, to amputate [VC]
qièfū zhī tòng	切膚之痛	sorrow close to the skin/heartfelt sorrow
qiègǔ zhī hèn	切骨之恨	hatred to the bones
qièhé	切合	to be fitting; to fit: 切合事實 *qièhé shìshí*, to correspond to the facts [SC/SV]
qièjì	切記	be sure to remember
qièjì	切忌	to avoid by all means 切忌受涼 *qièjì shòu liáng* to avoid catching cold by all means [V]
qièjìn	切近	to be close to (reality), to be close at (home) [CC/SV]
qièqiè	切切	be sure to: 切切記住 *qièqiè jìzhu*, be sure to remember [Adv]
qièshēn	切身	to be close, personal, intimate: 切身問題 *qièshēn wèntí*, personal problem to be taken care of immediately; 切身之痛 *qièshēn zhī tòng*, sorrow that hits close to home [VO/SV]
qièshí	切實	to be practical: 切切實實 *qièqieshíshí*; in earnest: 切切實實地做事 *qièqieshishìde zuòshì*, to work in earnest [SV]
qièzhòng shíbì	切中時弊	to hit closely the shortcomings of the day
búqiè shíjì	不切實際	to be unrealistic, not practical: 他的話一點兒都不切實際。*Tāde huà yìdiǎnr dōu búqiè shíjì.* His words are not practical at all.
guānqiè	關切	to be concerned about: 他對我的事情一向很關切。*Tā duì wǒde shìqing yíxiàng hěn guānqiè.* He has always been very concerned about my affairs. 他對我很關切。*Tā duìwǒ hěn guānqiè.* He is very concerned about me. [CC/SV]
mìqiè	密切	to be close, intimate: 他們倆的關係很密切。*Tāmen liǎ de guānxi hěn mìqiè.* The relationship between the two of them is very close. to pay close attention to: 請你密切注意他的行動。*Qǐng nǐ mìqiè zhùyì tāde xíngdòng.* Please pay close attention to his activities. [CC/SV]
qīnqiè	親切	to be warm and sincere: 他的態度很親切。*Tāde tàidu hěn qīnqiè.* His attitude is very warm and sincere. [CC/SV]
pòqiè	迫切	to be urgent: 這件事很迫切。*Zhèijiàn shì hěn pòqiè.* This matter is very urgent. [CC/SV]

qīn'ài	親愛	to be affectionate, dear: 親愛的母親 *qīnàide mǔqin*, my dear mother [CC/SV]
qìngjia	親家	relatives by marriage (note special pronunciation for *qīn*) [SC/N]
qīnjìn	親近	to associate closely with: 親近小人 *qīnjìn xiǎorén*, to associate closely with dishonorable men [CC/V]; to be close, intimate [SV]; close friends or relatives
qīnkǒu	親口	personally: 親口答應 *qīnkǒu dāyìng*, to promise personally [SC/Adv]
qīnmì	親密	to be very intimate [CC/SV]
qīnniáng	親娘	one's own mother [SC/N]
qīnqǐ	親啟	letter writing form used after addressee's name: 王大年先生親啟 *Wáng Dànián Xiānsheng qīnqǐ*, "personal" for Mr. Wang Danian [SC/V]
qīnrè	親熱	to be warm and affectionate (with people) [CC/SV]
qīnrén	親人	a relative [SC/N]
qīnshàn	親善	to be friendly: 中美親善 *Zhōng Měi qīnshàn*. China and the U.S. are friendly. [CC/SV]
qīnshēn	親身	personal: 親身經驗 *qīnshēn jīngyàn*, personal experience [SC/Adj]
qīnshēng	親生	one's own (children, parents): 親生子女，親生父母 *qīnshēng zǐnǚ, qīnshēng fùmǔ* [SC/Adj]
qīnshì	親事	wedding [SC/N]
qīnsuí	親隨	personal attendant [SC/N]
qīnxìn	親信	confidant, right-hand man [CC/N]
qīnzì	親自	personally: 親自出馬 *qīnzì chūmǎ*, to deal with something personally [CC/Adv]
qīnzuǐ	親嘴	to kiss: 親他/她的嘴 *qīn tāde zuǐ*, kiss her or him, or 跟他親了個嘴 *gēn tā qīnle ge zuǐ* [V-O]
chéngqīn	成親	to marry [V-O]
jiéqīn	結親	to unite by marriage [V-O]
xiāng qīn xiāng ài	相親相愛	to be deeply attached to each other: 他們是親兄弟，當然應該相親相愛。 *Tāmen shì qīn xiōngdì, dāngran yīnggāi xiāng qīn xiāng ài.* They are blood brothers. Of course they should love each other dearly.

qǐng'ān	請安	to inquire after someone's health, to wish the best of health [V-O]
qǐngbiàn	請便	please make yourself at home, do as you please
qǐng cáishen	請財神	to call upon the god of wealth
qǐngdiào	請調	to ask for transferring: 請調報告 *qǐngdiào bàogào* transferring appeal [V]
qǐngjià	請假	to ask for leave: 請病假 *qǐng bìngjià*, to ask for sick leave; 請事假 *qǐng shìjià*, to ask for business leave [V-O]
qǐngjiǎn	請柬	invitation card or letter [SC/N]
qǐngjiào	請教	to ask for advice [V-O]
qǐng jìn	請進	Please come in.
qǐngkè	請客	to give a party, to be host: 今天我請客。 *Jīntian wǒ qǐngkè.* Today I am the host. 我請你的客。 *Wǒ qǐng nǐde kè.* I invite you (You are my guest). [V-O]
qǐngqiú	請求	to beg, request, to demand [CC/V]
qǐngshì	請示	to beg for instructions: 你要是不向上司請示，做錯了事誰負責？ *Nǐ yàoshi búxiàng shàngsī qǐngshì, zuòcuòle shì shéi fùzé?* If you don't get instructions from your superior, who is going to be responsible if something is done wrong? [V-O]
qǐngtiē	請帖	invitation card [SC/N]
qǐngwèn	請問	May I ask: 請問你貴姓？ *Qǐngwèn nǐ guìxìng?* May I ask what your surname is? 請問吧。 *Qǐng wèn ba.* Please ask.
qǐng yīsheng	請醫生	to call a doctor
qǐngyuàn	請願	to demand (usually at popular demonstration) [V-O]
qǐngzuì	請罪	to confess guilt and ask for punishment [V-O]
kěnqǐng	懇請	to beg earnestly [SC/V]
pìnqǐng	聘請	to appoint: 聘請(家庭教師) *pìnqǐng jiājiào (jiāting jiàoshī)*, to hire a home tutor [CC/V]
shēnqǐng	申請	to make application: 申請工作 *shēnqǐng gōngzuò*, to apply for a job [CC/V]

qiúcái	求才	to look for talent [V-O]
qiúdài	求貸	to ask for a loan [V-O]
qiúhé	求和	to beg for peace by offering surrender [V-O]
qiúhūn	求婚	to ask for a girl's hand [V-O]
qiújiàn	求見	to seek an interview [CC/V]
qiújiào	求教	to ask for advice [V-O]
qiújiù	求救	to ask for help [V-O]
qiúmíng	求名	to set one's mind to obtain fame [V-O]
qiúqīn	求親	to ask for marriage between two families; to ask for help from relatives [V-O]
qiúqíng	求情	to ask for special consideration, to make an appeal on friendship [V-O]
qiúráo	求饒	to ask for pardon [V-O]
qiú rén	求人	to ask others for help: 我是沒事絕不求人的。 *Wǒ shì méishì jué bù qiú rén de.* If I don't have anything important, I will never ask others for help. [V O]
qiú shì	求事	to seek a job [V O]
qiúxué	求學	to seek knowledge, to go to school or college for studies [V-O]
qiú zhī bù dé	求之不得	just what one wished for: 那真是一件求之不得的事。 *Nà zhēn shi yíjian qiú zhī bù dé de shì.* That is just what one wished for.
bù qiú yǒu gōng, zhǐ qiúwú guò	不求有功 只求無過	to seek no rewards for accomplishment, but only to be free from mistakes.
kě yù ér bù kě qiú	可遇而不可求	something unique that may come only by chance
lì qiú shàng jìn	力求上進	to try to get ahead (in studies, career, etc.)
yǒu qiú bì yìng	有求必應	(of god, gentlemen) never refuses a request

qǔbǎo	取保	to ask somebody to act as guarantor [V-O]
qǔcái	取材	to get material for a writing assignment [V-O]
qǔdài	取代	to substitute; to replace: 沒人可以取代他。 *Méirén kěyǐ qǔdài tā.* Nobody can replace him. [V]
qǔdào	取道	to go by way of: 我們取道香港到中國去。 *Wǒmen qǔdào Xiānggǎng dào Zhōngguó qù.* We go to China by way of Hong Kong. [V-O]
qǔdé	取得	to obtain (consent, degree, wealth, etc.) 取得學位 *qǔdé xuéwèi*, to receive a degree [CC/V]
qǔdì	取締	to ban (publications, etc.); to deprive (person) of certain rights [CC/V]
qǔ dōngxi	取東西	to fetch things
qǔjué	取決	to make decision: 我們家的事由太太取決。 *Wǒmen jiā de shì yóu tàitai qǔjué.* In our family, the wife makes the decision. [VO]
qǔlè(r)	取樂（兒）	(to do something) to have fun: 他專門罵人取樂（兒）。 *Tā zhuānmen màren qǔlè(r).* He especially enjoys scolding people. [V-O]
qǔmíng(r)	取名（兒）	to give or to be given a name: 他取名（兒）大強。 *Tā qǔmíng(r) dàqiáng.* He was given the name (Da Qiang). 大強是他爸爸給他取的名兒。 *Dàqiáng shi tā bàba gěi tā qǔ de míngr.* (Da Qiang) is the name his father gave him [V-O]
qǔnuǎn	取暖	to stay warm: 他在壁爐前取暖。 *Tā zài bìlú qián qǔnuǎn.* He tries to stay warm in front of the fireplace. [V]
qǔ qí biàn	取其便	choose it for its convenience: 我們這樣決定不過是取其便而已。 *Wǒmen zhèyang juédìng búguò shì qǔ qí biàn éryǐ.* We made such a decision only because of its convenience.
qǔ qián	取錢	to get money [V O]
qǔqiǎo	取巧	to take short cut, to choose the easy way: 喜歡投機取巧的人常常會失望。 *Xǐhuan tóujī qǔqiǎo de rén chángcháng huì shīwàng.* Those who enjoy speculation and shortcuts are often disappointed. [V-O]
qǔ rén zhī shàn	取人之善	to take a person's good points
qǔshě	取捨	the power of judgment in taking or rejecting [CC/N]
qǔshèng	取勝	to win victory [V-O]
qǔxiāo	取消	to cancel (appointment, treaty, contract, etc.) [CC/V]
qǔxiào(r)	取笑（兒）	to make fun, to make fun of (somebody): 別取笑他。 *Bié qǔxiào tā.* Don't make fun of him. [VO/TV]
yì wú kě qǔ	一無可取	nothing worth mentioning: 這個人真是一無可取。 *Zhèige rén zhēn shi yì wú kě qǔ.* This person really has nothing to offer.

qùbìng	去病	to drive away illness [V-O]
qùchu	去處	a place to go: 沒有個去處 *méiyǒu ge qùchu*, there is no place to go (for visits, recreation, etc.); whereabouts: 不知去處 *bùzhī qùchu*, whereabouts unknown [SC/N]
qùde	去得	to be worth a visit; *qùbude*, to be unfit to go
qùdiào	去掉	to put off; to get rid of: 去掉怪異思想 *qùdiào guàiyì sīxiǎng* to get rid of strange ideas. [V]
qùdú	去毒	(Chinese medicine) to reduce poison in the body system [V-O]
qùhú(r)	去核(兒)	to remove the stone of fruits, pitted: 去核(兒)紅枣(兒) *qùhú(r) hóng zǎo(r)*, pitted red dates [V-O]
qùhuǒ	去火	(Chinese medicine) to reduce combustion in body system [V-O]
qùliú	去留	the question of leaving or staying, resigning or continuing (position), dismissing or retaining [CC/N]
qùpí	去皮	to remove the skin, to exclude the packing (net weight) [V-O]
qùrèn	去任	= 去職 *qùzhí* to leave an official position
qùshēng	去聲	falling tone [SC/N]
qùshì	去世	to depart from the world/to pass away [V-O]
qùshǔ	去暑	to drive away summer heat: 西瓜真可謂是去暑佳品。 *Xīguā zhēn kěwèi shì qùshǔ jiāpǐn.* Watermelon is really a good thing to help stay cool. [VO]
qùwū	去污	to remove dirt; to clean: 去污粉 *qùwūfěn* cleanser [V]
qùxiàng	去向	direction: 不知去向 *bùzhī qùxiàng*, don't know the direction or destination [SC/N]
qùxié	去邪	to ward off evil spirits [V-O]
qùzhí	去職	to leave an official position [V-O]
guòdequ	過得去	to be able to cross; to be presentable [VC]
shuō lái shuō qù	說來說去	to talk about something over and over again
xìn kǒu shuō qu	信口說去	reckless talking

ràngbù	讓步	to make concessions [V-O]
ràngdào	讓道	to let pass; to yield = 讓路[V-O]
ràng fēnliang	讓分量	to give the customer a little more of what he is buying
rànggei	讓給	to yield (One's rights) to
ràngguò(r)	讓過(兒)	to yield, to give in: 那兩個人一吵起來，誰也不讓過兒。 *Nèi liǎngge rén yì chǎoqilai, shéi yě búràngguòr.* When these two men start to quarrel, neither will give in to the other. [V-O]
ràngjià(r)	讓價(兒)	to reduce the price: 要是你不讓點兒價，我就不買。 *Yàoshi nǐ búràng diǎnr jià, wǒ jiù bùmǎi.* If you don't reduce the price a little, I won't buy it. [V-O]
ràng jiǔ	讓酒	to offer wine: 客人都坐好了，怎麼還不讓酒。 *Kèren dōu zuòhǎole, zěnme hái búràngjiǔ?* The guests have all been seated. Why don't you offer them a drink? [V O]
ràngkāi	讓開	to make way for someone: 汽車來了，請讓開。 *Qìchē lái le; qǐng ràngkāi.* A car is coming; please make way. [VC]
ràng lí	讓梨	to show fraternal affection (allusion to the story of K'ung Yung, who let his elder brother have the bigger pear) [V O]
ràng lù	讓路	to step aside to let other people pass [V O]
ràngrang	讓讓	to make a polite gesture: 讓讓他就是了，來不來在他。 *Ràngrang jiu shi le. Lái bulai zài tā.* We made a polite gesture to invite him. It's up to him whether he comes or not.
ràngrén	讓人	to yield to others [V-O]
Ràng tā qu shìshi	讓他去試試	Let him try it.
ràngwèi	讓位	to abdicate the throne in favor of someone else; to give up one's seat or position to another [V-O]
ràngyú	讓與	to cede (one's rights to someone else): 把房產全讓與李四。 *Bǎ fángchǎn quán ràngyú Lǐ Sì.* To cede one's right to a property to Li Si.
ràngzhe	讓著	to give (someone) the better of an argument: 他年紀小，你就讓著他點兒。 *Tā niánji xiǎo, nǐ jiu ràngzhe tā diǎnr.* Since he is younger, you just give him the better of the argument.
ràngzuò(r)	讓座(兒)	to give one's seat to a lady or an older person, to invite someone to take a seat [V-O]

rèài	熱愛	to love ardently: 羅密歐熱愛朱麗葉。 *Luómĕiōu rèài Zhūlìyè.* Romeo loves Juliet ardently. [SC/V]
rèchéng	熱誠	to be earnest, enthusiastic [CC/SV]
rèhōnghōngde	熱烘烘的	red-hot
rèhūhūde	熱呼呼的	very hot (of food)
rèhuo	熱和	to be warm (person or temperature), friendly, affectionate [CC/SV]
rèliè	熱烈	(of feelings) to be warm, passionate, fervent, ardent: 他的情緒很熱烈。 *Tāde qíngxu hĕn rèliè.* His emotion is very fervent. [CC/SV]
rèmén(r)	熱門(兒)	hot door/any commodity in great demand [SC/N]; popular: 熱門兒人物 *rèménr rénwù*, persons who make frontpage news [Adj]
rè'nào	熱鬧	to be jolly, noisy, boisterous: 熱熱鬧鬧 *rère'naonāo*, very jolly; [CC/SV]
rè'nào(r)	熱鬧(兒)	noisy fun in which many people take part, stage shows and stunts, merry-making: 人家辦生日晚會，咱們去湊個熱鬧兒吧。 *rénjia bàn shēngrì wănhuì, zámen qù còu ge rè'nàor ba.* They are celebrating a birthday. Let's go have some fun together.
rèqíng	熱情	to be passionate [SC/SV]: passionate feelings or love
rèsĭ	熱死	to be unbearably hot: 這種天氣能把人熱死。 *Zhèizhong tiānqi néng bă rén rèsĭ.* This kind of weather can really kill people with the heat. [VC]
rè tāng	熱湯	hot soup [SC/N]; to heat the soup [V-O]
rèxiàn	熱線	hot line (telephone line between the White House and Kremlin) [SC/N]
rèxīn	熱心	to be enthusiastic, ardent, zealous, earnest: 這個人辦事很熱心。 *Zhèige rén bànshì hĕn rèxīn.* This man does things very enthusiastically. 他熱心公益。 *Tā rèxīn gōngyì.* He is enthusiastic about public wellbeing. [SC/SV]
rè xīnchang	熱心腸	to be enthusiastic, sincere, zealous: 這個人熱心腸，誰的忙他不幫? *Zhèige rén rè xīnchang. Shéide máng tā bùbāng?* This person is enthusiastic. He will help anybody.
rèzhao	熱著	to fall victim to heat stroke [VC]
rèzhòng	熱中	to be restless, impatient; to hanker for (official preferment). 他對賭博很熱中。 *Tā duì dŭbo hĕn rèzhòng.* He likes to gamble. 他熱中名利。 *Tā rèzhòng mínglì.* He hankers for fame and fortune. [CC/SV]

rènchū	認出	to recognize: 我沒認出她是誰。 *Wǒ méi rènchū tā shì shéi.* I didn't recognize her. [V]
rèncuò	認錯	to admit one's fault, to mistake someone (or thing) for another: 他認錯人了。 *Tā rèncuòle rén le.* He mistook one person for another. [V-O]
rènde	認得	to be able to recognize (character, person); 我認得這個字(人)。 *Wǒ rènde zhèige zì (or rén).* I know this character (or person).
rèndìng	認定	to affirm, to put one's finger on [VC]
rèn gāndiē	認乾爹	to recognize one as godfather
rènkě	認可	to approve, to endorse, to give legal force to [VO]
rènle	認了	to accept without protest: 我輸多少錢也認了。 *Wǒ shū duōshao qián yě rènle.* No matter how much I have lost, I accept the loss (not going to try to win it back)
rènlǐng	認領	to adopt (a child), to claim a lost article [CC/V]
rènmìng	認命	to accept one's fate [VO]
rènqīn	認親	to recognize relatives, especially first meeting on wedding day between both sides [V-O]
rènshēng	認生	to recognize strangers/to be shy (said of children) [VO]
rènshi	認識	to recognize, to know (= 認得 *rènde)* [CC/V]
rènshū	認輸	to admit defeat (gambling, fighting, etc.) [V-O]
rènwéi	認為	to consider to be, to consider that . . . , to think: 王同志不這樣認為。 *Wáng Tóngzhì bú zhèyang rènwéi.* Comrade Wang doesn't think this way. (PRC) [CC/V]
rènxǔ	認許	to approve, to acknowledge [CC/V]
rènzhēn	認真	to make earnest effort to do something, to take seriously [VO]
rènzì	認字	to recognize characters, to be literate (= 識字 *shí zì)* [V-O]
rènzéi zuò fù	認賊作父	to take a thief as one's father/unfilial, disloyal
liù qīn bú rèn	六親不認	to be unfeeling toward everybody, to be utterly devoid of human feelings

róngbuxià	容不下	can't take it (because of limited capacity) [VC]
róngjī	容積	volume as measured in cubic units [SC/N]
róngliàng	容量	capacity [SC/N]
róngliàng	容諒	to forgive and forget [CC/V]
róngmào	容貌	appearance; looks: 她容貌俊秀。 *Tā róngmào jùnxiù.* She is good looking. [N]
róngnà	容納	to accept (ideas, views, suggestions): 政府官員都要有能容納大眾意見的雅量。 *Zhèngfǔ guānyuán dōu yào yǒu néng róngnà dàzhòng yìjiàn de yǎliàng.* Government officials should all have the capacity to accept opinions from the masses. [CC/V]
róngqì	容器	container [N]
róngqíng	容情	to be lenient, to make special allowance for [V-O]
róngràng	容讓	to be tolerant [V]
róngrěn	容忍	to tolerate [CC/V]
róng rén zhī guò	容人之過	to tolerate other's mistakes
róngshēn	容身	to have somewhere to stay: 無地容身 *wú dì róng shēn*, nowhere to live, ashamed to show one's face [V-0]
róngshù	容恕	to forgive, to pardon [CC/V]
róng wǒ jǐ tiān	容我幾天	Please give me a few days' grace
róngxī	容膝	to accept the knee/a tiny spot [V-O/N]
róngxiàn	容限	limitation, limit of capacity [SC/N]
róngxǔ	容許	to permit [CC/V]; perhaps, maybe [Adv]
róngyi	容易	to be easy [CC/V]
kuānróng	寬容	to be tolerant [SV/V]

rùchǎng	入場	to enter [V-O]
rùěr	入耳	to be pleasant to hear [VO/SV]
rùgǎng	入港	to enter port [V-O]
rùhuǒ	入伙	to join a gang; [V-O]
rùjí	入籍	to be naturalized: 他已經入了美國籍了。 *Tā yǐjing rùle Měiguo jí le.* He has already been naturalized as an American. [V-O]
rùjìng	入境	to enter country [V-O]
rùkǒu	入口	entrance, imports [SC/N]
rùmén(r)	入門(兒)	to be initiated into a subject [V-O]; a primer or introduction (of a subject): 漢語入門 *hànyǔ Rùmén*, Mandarin Primer
rùmí	入迷	to be enchanted, enraptured: 他下棋下得入迷了，甚麼事都不管 了。 *Tā xiàqí xiàde rùmíle, shénme shì dōu bùguǎn le.* He is so much interested in playing chess that he doesn't tend to any other business. [V-O]
rùmó	入魔	to be completely bewitched; to go the way of the devil [V-O]
rùshuì	入睡	to fall asleep = 入夢 *rù mèng* [V-O]
rùshǒu	入手	to commence, to start [V-O]; a start
rùtǔ	入土	to be buried [V-O]
rùwéi	入闈	to live incommunicado during period of examination (of official in charge of government examinations) [V-O]
rùwèir	入味兒	to be interesting, to be tasteful [V-O]
rùwǔ	入伍	to enter military service [V-O]
rùxuǎn	入選	to be selected (for a job, contest, etc.) [V-O]
rùyǎn	入眼	to be pleasing to the eye [V-O]
rùyuàn	入院	to enter the hospital/to be hospitalized [V-O]

sàichǎng	賽場	racing area [N]
sàichē	賽車	to race cars [V-O]
sàichuán	賽船	to run a boat race [V-O]
sàidēng	賽燈	to show off lanterns (as at the lantern festival) [V-O]
sàigǒu	賽狗	to have a dog race [V-O]
sàiguo	賽過	to excell: 張家的三個女孩子長得一個賽過一個。 *Zhāngjiā de sānge nǚháizi, zhǎngde yí ge sàiguo yí ge.* As for the Changs' daughters, each is prettier than the last. [VC]
sàihuì	賽會	a religious festival (with parades of idols, stilts, floats, etc.); an exposition [SC/N]
sàimǎ	賽馬	to hold a horse race [V-O]; horse race
sàipǎo	賽跑	to hold a race [V-O]
sàiqiú	賽球	to play a ball game [V-O]
sàiquán	賽拳	to match fingers (drinking game) [V-O]
sàishì	賽事	race; competition [N]
sài tiānxiān	賽天仙	to rival the beauty of a fairy
sàitǐng	賽艇	racing boat [N]
sàixīshī	賽西施	to rival the beauty of Hsi Shih (an historical beauty)
sài yīngtao	賽櫻桃	to rival a cherry (as to size and color of a girl's mouth)
bǐsài	比賽	to have a contest: 今天我們比賽寫字。 *Jīntiān wǒmen bǐsài xiězì.* Today we will have a contest for writing characters. [CC/V]; a contest; 寫字比賽 *xiězì bǐsài*, writing contest
jìngsài	競賽	to compete; [V]

shāngbiāo	商標	trademark [N]
shāngdiào	商調	to consult so as to transfer goods/people [V]
shāngdìng	商定	to decide after discussion [VC]
shāngjì	商計	to discuss = 商量 *shāngliang*, 商議 *shāngyì* [V]
shāngliang	商量	to discuss: 商量商量 *shāngliangshāngliang*, to discuss a bit [CC/V]
shāngqià	商洽	to meet someone, to discuss [V]
shāngquè	商榷	to discuss together (problems, business, etc.) [CC/V]
shāngtán	商談	to discuss, to confer [CC/V]
shāngtǎo	商討	to discuss (from 商量 *shāngliang* and 討論 *tǎolùn*) [CC/V]
shāngyì	商擬	to propose to, to suggest [CC/V]
shāngnì	商議	to discuss [CC/V]
shāngyuō	商約	to decide (together to do something) [CC/V]
shāngzhàn	商戰	trade war [N]
shāngzhuó	商酌	to discuss (situation, etc.), (from 商量 *shāngliang* and 斟酌 *zhēnzhuó*)
cóngshāng	從商	to go into business as a career [V-O]
cuòshāng	措商	to deliberate, to discuss [CC/V]
jīngshāng	經商	to engage in business [V-O]
miànshāng	面商	to discuss personally [SC/V]
xiéshāng	協商	to discuss together (terms, procedures, etc.) [SC/V]

shàngbān	上班	to go to work [V-O]
shàngcāo	上操	to go to drill [V-O]
shàngchǎng	上場	to appear on scene, market, or stage [V-O]
shàngdàng	上當	to fall into a trap, to be cheated: 今天我上了個大當。 *Jīntiān wǒ shàngle ge dà dàng.* I was badly cheated today. [V-O]
shàngdiào	上吊	to hang oneself [V-O]
shàngdòng	上凍	to freeze (of river, lake, etc.) [V-O]
shànggōng	上工	to report for work (usually labor work) [V-O]
shànghuǒ(r)	上火(兒)	to be inflamed with anger, to get angry [V-O]
shàngjǐn	上緊	to affix tightly: 把螺絲上緊 *Bǎ luòsi shàngjǐn*, to affix the screw tightly [VC]
shàngjìn	上勁	to do something energetically; to encourage: 他今天光給我上勁。 *Tā jīntiān guāng gěi wǒ shàngjìn.* She has encouraged me all day today. [V-O]
shàngjìn	上進	to make progress (esp. in studies) [SC/V]
shàngkǒu	上口	easy to read [V-O]
shànglai	上來	to come up [VC]; also used as complement to other verbs
shàngliè	上列	above-mentioned [SC/Adj]
shàngshēng	上升	to go up (skyward) [SC/V]
shàngsi	上司	boss; supervisor [N]
shàngshǒu	上手	to get in one's hand [V-O]
shàngsuàn	上算	it pays to (do something): 坐飛機比較上算。 *Zuò fēijī bǐjiǎo shàngsuàn.* Comparatively, it pays to go by plane. [VO/SV]
shàngtiān	上天	to go up to the heavens, to die [V-O]; the sky above [SV/N]
shàngxiāng	上香	to offer incense at temple [V-O]
shàngxiàng	上相	to be photogenic [VO/SV]
shàngyǎn	上眼	to appeal to the eye: 看不上眼 *kàn búshàngyǎn*, to disdain, to hold in contempt [V-O]
shàngyìng	上映	to show, to be shown, now showing

shèbeì	設備	to provide (facilities) [CC/V]; facilities, equipment: 這個學校設備不錯。 *Zhèige xuéxiaò shèbèi búcuò.* The facilities of this school are not bad.
shèdìng	設定	to set up (laws, regulations, etc.) [CC/V]
shèfǎ	設法	to think of ways to, to try to: 我們得設法省錢。 *Wǒmen děi shèfǎ shěng qián.* We have to try to save money. [V-O]
shèfáng	設防	to set up defense [V-O]
shèfú	設伏	to waylay; to lay an ambush [V]
shèguǎn	設館	to give private tutoring [V-O]
shèjì	設計	to design, to draw up a blueprint, to contrive [CC/V]
shèjú	設局	to set up a situation: 設騙局 *shè piànjú*, to lay a plan for swindle [V-O]
shèlì	設立	to establish: 設立學校 *shèlì xuéxiào*, to establish a school [CC/V]
shèquāntào	設圈套	to trap; to shill
shèshēnchǔdì	設身處地	to put oneself in somebody else's position; to be considerate
shèshī	設施	arrangement, provisions, facilities [CC/N]
shèxí	設席	to set up banquet at [V-O]
shèxiàn	設限	to limit [V]
shèxiǎng	設想	to imagine
shèyàn	設宴	to give a dinner; to give a banquet [V-O]
shèyíng	設營	to quarter; to encamp; to billet [V-O]
shèzhì	設置	to arrange [CC/V]; arrangement
shèzuò	設座	to set up seats/to give dinner at: 設座華國飯店 *shèzuò Huáguó Fàndiàn*, to give a dinner at the (Huaguo) Restaurant [V-O]
chénshè	陳設	display, arrangement (of furniture, etc.) [CC/N]

shēngbìng	生病	to fall ill [V-O]
shēngcài	生菜	raw vegetable, salad [SC/N]
shēngchǎn	生產	to produce, to give birth to children: 你太太甚麼時候生產? *Nǐ tàitai shénme shìhòu shēngchǎn?* When is your wife going to have the baby? = 生孩子 [CC/V]
shēng huā miào bǐ	生花妙筆	gifted pen
shēnghuo	生活	to live; 吃生活 *chī shēnghuo*, (Shanghai dialect) to get a beating [CC/V]
shēnghuǒ	生火	to build a fire [V-O]
shēngjì	生計	to plot [V-O]; means of livelihood [SC/N]
shēnglì	生利	to bear interest, to make profit [V-O]
shēng lóng huó hǔ	生龍活虎	live dragon and live tiger/extremely vivid or forceful
shēnglù	生路	way out, ways to make a living [SC/N]
shēngmìng	生命	life [CC/N]
shēngqì	生氣	to get angry [V-O]; vitality [SC/N]
shēngshì	生事	to cause trouble [V-O]
shēngsǐ	生死	life and death: 生死關頭 *shēngsǐ guāntou*, a grave crisis between life and death; 生死之交 *shēngsǐ zhī jiāo*, lifetime friendship [CC/N]
shēngxī	生息	to bear interest [V-O]
shēngxìng	生性	one's born nature [SC/N]
shēngyǎng	生養	to give birth to and bring up (children) [CC/V]
shēngyi	生意	business: 做生意 *zuò shēngyi*, to do business; [SC/N]
shēngzhǎng	生長	to grow, to grow up: 生長得很好 *shēngzhǎngde hěnhǎo*, to grow up well [CC/V]
shēngzhí	生殖	to grow, multiply, to reproduce: 生殖器 *shēngzhíqì*, sexual organs [CC/V]
shēngzǐ	生子	to give birth to a son [V-O]
shēngzì	生字	new characters, new words [SC/N]
wú shì shēng fēi	無事生非	to make uncalled for trouble

shībài	失敗	to fail, to be defeated [CC/V]
shīcháng	失常	to be abnormal [VO]
shīdiào	失掉	to lose: 失掉民心 *shīdiào mínxīn* to lose people's support [V]
shīhé	失和	to quarrel, to have differences of opinion, do not get along [VO]
shīhuǒ	失火	to have fire: 房子失火了。*Fángzi shīhuǒ le.* The house is on fire. [V-O]
shījiǎo	失腳	to slip on the ground [VO]
shījìng	失敬	to fail in courtesy or etiquette [VO], also 失禮 *shīlǐ*
shīkǒu	失口	to say something carelessly [V-O], also 失言 *shīyán*
shīliàn	失戀	to be disappointed in love [V-O]
shīmián	失眠	to suffer from insomnia [V-O]
shīmíng	失明	to become blind [VO]
shīsàn	失散	to scatter, to disperse [CC/V]
shīshēn	失身	to lose virginity [V-O]
shīshì	失事	to run into trouble, to have an accident: 飛機失事了。 *Fēijī shīshì le.* The plane crashed. [V-O]
shīwàng	失望	to lose hope, to be disappointed [V-O]
shīxiào	失效	to become invalid [V-O]
shīxìn	失信	to fail to keep promise [V-O]
shīxué	失學	to be forced to drop out of school [V-O]
shīyè	失業	to be unemployed [V-O]
shīyì	失意	to be disappointed: 情場失意 *qíngchǎng shīyì*, disappointed in love [VO/SV]
shīyuē	失約	to fail to meet appointment, to break promise [V-O]
shīzōng	失踪	to lose traces/to be missing [V-O]
wàn wú yì shī	萬無一失	complete success assured

shíbié	識別	to know the difference, to distinguish [CC/V]
shíbiélì	識別力	power of discrimination
shícái	識才	to know the talent [V-O]
shícáizūnxián	識才尊賢	to know and respect the talent
shíduōcáiguǎng	識多才廣	to be knowledgeable and versatile
shíhuò	識貨	to know the goods/to have good judgement for goods [VO]
shíjīnghènwǎn	識荊恨晚	to regret to have made your acquaintance so late
shípò	識破	to penetrate; to see through; [V]
shíqù(r)	識趣(兒)	to know the subtleties/to be tactful, know the right thing to do [VO/SV]
shírén	識人	to know people/to be able to distinguish between good and bad people [VO]
shíshíwùzhě wéijùnjié	識時務者為俊杰	Whosoever understands the times is a great man.
shítúlǎomǎ	識途老馬	an old horse which knows the way [N]
shíxiàng	識相	to be able to read the countenance/to know what is right to do, to be tactful: 他要是稍微識相點兒，也不會讓人家笑話他。 *Tā yàoshi shāowei shíxiàng diǎnr, yě búhuì ràng rénjia xiàohua tā.* If he is a little tactful, he will not be laughed at by people. [VO/SV]
shízì	識字	to know characters/to be able to read [V-O]
cáishí	才識	ability and insight (from 才能 *cáinéng* and 見識 *jiànshì*) [CC/N]
jiànshi	見識	insight, intellectual discrimination [CC/V]
mù bú shí dīng	目不識丁	eyes cannot read the character *ding*/to be completely illiterate
shǎngshí	賞識	to appreciate (a person's ability): 老王的上司很賞識他的工作。 *Lǎo Wáng de shàngsī hěn shǎngshí tāde gōngzuò.* Lao Wang's superior appreciates his work very much. [CC/V]
xiāngshí	相識	to know each other [SC/V]
xuéshí	學識	knowledge and insight (from 學問 *xuéwèn* and 見識 *jiànshì*) [CC/N]

shǐbànr	使絆兒	to plot against; to stumble [V]
shǐbude	使不得	cannot be used: 這把刀子使不得。 *zhèibǎ dāozi shǐbude.* This knife cannot be used. [VC]
shǐbuliǎo	使不了	cannot use (so much): 買書使不了這麼多錢。 *Mǎi shū shǐbuliǎo zhème duō qián.* One doesn't need so much money for buying books. [VC]
shǐde	使得	will do: 昨兒買的那件大衣使得嗎? *Zuór mǎide nèijiàn dàyī shǐde ma?* Is that coat (that you) bought yesterday all right? [VC]
shǐ guāi nòng qiǎo	使乖弄巧	to play tricks
shǐ guǐjì	使詭計	to play tricks
shǐ huài	使壞	to willfully make someone suffer, to hurt, to destroy [VC]
shǐhuan	使喚	to order servants, (children) about: 他會使喚人。 *Tā huì shǐhuan rén.* He knows how to order people around. [CC/V]
shǐhuanrén	使喚人	servant, attendant
shǐjìn(r)	使勁(兒)	to exert effort, to put out strength: 使勁兒念書 *shǐjìnr niànshū,* to study hard [V-O]
shǐmìng	使命	official mission: 上次他沒有完成使命。 *Shàngcì tā méiyou wánchéng shǐmìng.* Last time he didn't complete his mission. [SC/N]
shǐnǚ	使女	a maidservant [SC/N]
shǐqì	使氣	to act on impulse or in fit of anger [V-O]
shǐ rén nánshòu	使人難受	to make people feel bad
shǐ shǒuduàn	使手段	to use strategy to maneuver
shǐtú	使徒	(Christian) disciples [SC/N]
shǐ xìngzi	使性子	to be temperamental: 他喜歡使性子是因為父母把他慣壞了。 *Tā xǐhuan shǐ xìngzi shì yīnwèi fùmǔ bǎ tā guànhuài le.* She is temperamental because her parents spoiled her. [V-O]
shǐ xīnyǎnr	使心眼兒	to use holes of intelligence supposed to be in the heart to act intelligently
shǐ yǎnsè	使眼色	to ogle, to make signs with the eyes
shǐyòng	使用	to use, to employ: 外國人不會使用筷子。 *Wàiguó rén búhuì shǐyòng kuàizi.* Foreigners do not know how to use chopsticks. [CC/V]

shìchē	試車	trial run 明兒試車。 *Míngr shìchē.* The trial run will be tomorrow. [V-O/N]
shìgōng(r)	試工(兒)	to try out a workman or employee [V-O]
shìhūn	試婚	to try out a marriage [V-O]; a trial marriage [SC/N]
shìjīnshí	試金石	a touch stone
shìjuàn	試卷	examination paper [SC/N]
shìshi	試試	to have a try
shìtàn	試探	to explore [CC/V]
shìtí	試題	examination questions or topics [SC/N]
shìwèn	試問	May I ask, formula in asking questions, especially in classroom exercises [CC/V]
shìxiǎng	試想	just think 試想你這樣做，別人會怎樣看? *Shìxiǎng nǐ zhè yàng zuò, bié rén huì zěnyàng kàn?* Just think what others will think if you do it this way. [V]
shìyǎn	試演	to rehearse [V-O]; a rehearsal [SC/N]
shìyàn	試驗	to experiment [CC/V]; an experiment: 試驗管 *shìyànguǎn*, test tube
shìyìng	試映	to preview (a movie) [V]
shìyòng	試用	to try out (person, utensil); to be on probation: 試用期間我不敢請假。 *shìyòng qījiān wǒ bùgǎn qǐngjià.* During probation, I dare not ask for leave. [CC/V]
shìzhǐ	試紙	Litmus paper [SC/N], also 試驗紙 *shìyànzhǐ*
bǐshì	筆試	written examination [SC/N]
chángshì	嘗試	to try out [CC/V]; an attempt, a trial
jiāngshì	監試	to monitor an examination [V-O]
kǎoshì	考試	to take an examination, to examine [CC/V]; an examination
kǒushì	口試	oral examination [SC/N]
yìngshì	應試	to go to take an examination [V-O]

shōubīng	收兵	to withdraw troops [V-O]
shōucáng	收藏	to collect (curios, rare books, etc.) [CC/V]
shōuchǎng	收場	to wind up [V-O]; end, ending (of a play): 收場太令人難受了。 *Shōuchǎng tài lìng rén nánshòu le.* The ending makes people very sad.
shōuchéng	收成	harvest: 今年的收成特別好。 *Jīnniánde shōuchéng tèbié hǎo.* This year's harvest is especially good. [SC/N]
shōufù	收復	to recover (lost territory): 收復失地 *shōufù shīdì* [CC/V]
shōugōng	收工	to wind up work [V-O]
shōugòu	收購	to buy for business or collection [CC/V]
shōuhuí	收回	to take back, to rescind (order) [VC]
shōuhuò	收獲	harvest, results (of study, exploration, etc.) [CC/N]
shōují	收集	to collect; to gather: 收集信息 *shōují xìnxī* to gather information [V]
shōujù	收據	a receipt, also 收條兒 *shōutiáor* [SC/N]
shōulǎn	收攬	to win over (people's support): 收攬民心 *shōulǎn mínxīn* [CC/V]
shōulǐ	收禮	to receive present = 收受禮物 *shōushòu lǐwù* [V-O]
shōuliú	收留	to accept (orphan, relative) for care [CC/V]
shōumǎi	收買	= 收購 *shōugòu*; to win (popular support): 收買人心 *shōumǎi rén xīn* [CC/V]
shōuróng	收容	to provide housing for (refugees): 收容難民 *shōuróng nànmín* [CC/V]
shōurù	收入	to receive [CC/V]; income
shōushi	收拾	to tidy up, to manage: 不可收拾 *bùkě shōushi*, unmanageable; to punish: 好好收拾收拾那個壞蛋。 *Hǎohāo shōshishoushi nèige huàidàn.* Take good care of that rascal. [CC/V]
shōusuō	收縮	to shrink up, to curtail (business, deals) [CC/V]
shōuwěi	收尾	ending (of story, affair) [VO/N]
shōuyǎng	收養	to keep and raise (orphan) [CC/V]
shōuyīn	收音	to receive radio message: 收音機 *shōuyīnjī*, a radio [V-O]
shōuzhī	收支	receipt and expenditure [CC/N]

shòubuliǎo	受不了	can't stand it [VC]
shòuchǒng	受寵	to receive favor from superior: 受寵若惊 *shòuchǒng ruò jīng*, to be overwhelmed by superior's favor [V-O]
shòuhài	受害	to suffer, to be murdered [V-O]
shòuhuì	受賄	to accept bribe [V-O]
shòujīng	受精	to conceive, to be fertilized [V-O]
shòukàn	受看	to be good to look at [VO/SV]
shòukǔ	受苦	to suffer [V-O]
shòulèi	受累	to be involved on account of others: 受勞累 *shòuláolèi*, to suffer hardship [V-O]
shòulǐ	受理	(of court) to accept a complaint [CC/V]
shòunàn	受難	to suffer hardship, to die a martyr [V-O]
shòupiàn	受骗	to be cheated [V-O]
shòuqì	受氣	to suffer petty annoyances: 受氣包兒 *shòuqì bāor*, person subjected to daily persecutions [V-O]
shòuqū	受屈	to suffer an injustice [V-O]
shòurǔ	受辱	to be humiliated [V-O]
shòushāng	受傷	to be injured [V-O]
shòutīng	受聽	to be good to hear [VO/SV]
shòutuō	受託	to be entrusted to do something by a friend [V-O]
shòuxǐ	受洗	to be baptized [V-O]
shòuyòng	受用	to be physically comfortable, enjoyable: 天熱喝杯冰茶很受用。*Tiān rè hē bēi bīngchá hěn shòuyòng.* On a hot day, it is very enjoyable to drink a cup of ice tea. [VO/SV]
shòuyùn	受孕	to become pregnant
shòuzuì	受罪	to suffer: 受洋罪 *shòu yáng zuì*, to suffer something difficult to explain [V-O]
nánshòu	難受	to feel unhappy, to be uncomfortable [SC/SV]

shǔbuguòlai	數不過來	cannot reckon how many: 人太多，我數不過來。 *Rén tài duō, wǒ shǔbuguòlai.* There are so many people that I can't count them. [VC]
shǔbuqīng	數不清	cannot reckon how many [VC]
shǔbushàng	數不上	cannot be counted as one: 好學生裏頭怎麼也數不上他。 *Hǎo xuésheng litou zěnme yě shǔbushàng tā.* No matter how you do it, he can't be counted as one of the good students. [VC]
shǔbúshèngshǔ	數不勝數	numerous
shǔdiǎn	數點	to count up [CC/V]
shǔjiǔhántiān	數九寒天	the coldest days of the year
shǔláibǎo	數來寶	the rhythmic story-telling to clapper accompaniment
shǔluò	數落	to scold: 成天家數落他，你有沒有個完呢？ *Chéngtiānjia shǔluò tā, nǐ yǒu méiyou ge wán ne?* Scolding him day in and day out, don't you have an end?
shǔmà	數罵	to enumerate faults and scold/to scold [CC/V]
shǔ mǐ ér cuī	數米而炊	to count grains before cooking/to be extremely poor
shǔshuō	數說	to enumerate faults [CC/V]
shǔshùr	數數兒	to count the number [V-O]
shǔsuàn	數算	to count and reckon [CC/V]
shǔ tā cōngming	數他聰明	to count him as the intelligent one
shùwǎngzhīlái	數往知來	to know the future by thinking of the past
shǔ yī shǔ èr	數一數二	to count at the top (number one or number two): 他是美國數一數二的科學家。 *Tā shì Měiguó shǔ yī shǔ èr de kēxuéjiā.* He is a top American scientist.
shǔzhe	數着	to count as (the best, the ablest, etc.): 朋友裏頭數着他最有錢了。 *Péngyoulitou, shǔzhe tā zuì yǒuqián le.* Among friends, count him as the richest.

shuōbudìng	說不定	maybe: 他說不定已經走了。 *Tā shuōbudìng yǐjīng zǒule.* Maybe he has already left. [Adv]
shuōbuguòqu	說不過去	to be unreasonable: 他這種作風真說不過去。 *Tā zhèizhǒng zuòfēng zhēn shuōbuguòqu.* His way of doing things is really unreasonable. [VC]
shuōbulái	說不來	hard to say; cannot get along: 彼此說不來。 *bǐcǐ shuōbulái,* cannot get along with each other [VC]
shuōbushàng	說不上	cannot be considered: 這張畫說不上傑作。 *Zhèi zhang huà shuōbushàng jiézuò.* This painting cannot be considered a masterpiece. [VC]
shuōchuān	說穿	to expose (a secret): 說穿了一錢不值。 *Shuōchuānle yì qián bùzhí.* When the secret is exposed, it is worth nothing. [VC]
shuō dōng dào xī	說東道西	to speak of East and West/to engage in random talk, also 說長道短 *shuō cháng dào duǎn,* 說天道地 *shuō tiān dào dì,* 說三道四 *shuō sān dào sì*
shuōfú	說服	to convince (another) [VC]
shuōhuà	說話	to speak; to talk; to chat; to say [V-O]
shuōhuǎng	說謊	to tell a lie [V-O]
shuōkāi	說開	to explain, to allay fears; to have become current [VC]
shuōliūle zuǐ	說溜了嘴	to make a slip of the tongue: 我本來不想告訴他，可是我說溜了嘴了。 *Wǒ běnlái bùxiǎng gàosù ta. Kěshi wǒ shuōliūle zuǐ le.* I didn't want to tell him, but I made a slip of the tongue.
shuōmíng	說明	to explain; to illustrate [V]
shuōpò	說破	to expose (secret) [VC]
shuōpòzuǐ	說破嘴	to talk oneself hoarse (in futile long persuasion)
shuōqilai	說起來	to mention, in regard to: 說起來話長 *shuōqilai huà cháng,* if one starts talking, it will be a long story. 說起話來沒有完。 *Shuōqihuàlai méiyou wán.* There will be no end when one starts talking. [VC]
shuōqīngchǔ	說清楚	to state clearly: 不知道我說清楚了沒有? *Bù zhīdào wǒ shuōqīngchu le méiyǒu?* I wonder if I have stated clearly. [V]
shuō rénqing	說人情	to plead for leniency because of friendship
shuōshū	說書	to tell stories (of professional story-tellers): 說書的 *shuōshūde,* story-teller [V-O]
shuōzhe wánr	說着玩兒	do not mean what one says: 我是說着玩兒的 *Wǒ shì shuōzhe wánr de.* I didn't mean what I said.
shuō dà huà	說大話	to boast [V-O], to talk big

sǐbǎn	死板	to be inflexible, rigid [SC/SV]
sǐbié	死別	to part and never see each other again [SC/V]
sǐ búyào liǎn	死不要臉	to be devoid of shame
sǐdǎng	死黨	partisans sworn to the death [SC/N]
sǐděng	死等	to wait forever [SC/V]
sǐdí	死敵	eternal enemy [SC/N]
sǐduìtou	死對頭	deadly foe: 他是我的死對頭。 *Tā shì wǒde sǐduìtou.* He is my deadly foe. [SC/N]
sǐguǐ	死鬼	(abuse) devil: 你這個死鬼。 *Nǐ zhèige sǐguǐ.* You devil! [SC/N]
sǐ hútongr	死胡同兒	dead alley
sǐjié	死結	a tightly-tied knot; a long-standing grudge [SC/N]
sǐkěn	死啃	to work hard on eating from a piece of bone, to read without digesting [SC/V]
sǐlù	死路	dead end, fatal route [SC/N]
sǐ pí lài liǎn	死皮賴臉	shamelessly: 他死皮賴臉求了一天。 *Tā sǐ pí lài liǎn qiúle yìtiān.* He shamelessly begged for a whole day.
sǐ qù huó lái	死去活來	to be half dead: 他被打得死去活來。 *Tā bèi dǎde sǐ qù huò lái.* He was beaten half to death.
sǐrén	死人	(abuse) a dunce, a dead person [SC/N]
sǐshuǐ	死水	stagnant water [SC/N]
sǐwáng	死亡	to die [CC/V]
sǐxiàng	死相	a teasing remark in disgust: 看你那個死相! *kàn nǐ nèige sǐxiàng!* Take a look at yourself! [SC/N]
sǐxīn	死心	to give up hope [V–O]
sǐxīnyǎnr	死心眼兒	single-minded
sǐ yào qián	死要錢	to be dead set on getting money
sǐyìng	死硬	to be irreconcilable [SC/SV]; 死硬派 *sǐyìngpài*, diehard faction
sǐzuì	死罪	death penalty [SC/N]
èsǐ	餓死	*to die* to die of hunger, to be extremely hungry [VC]
kěxiàosǐle	可笑死了	to be extremely funny, laughable [VC]

sòngbié	送別	to send off [V–O]
sòngbìn	送殯	to attend funeral [V–O]
sònggěi	送給	to give: 這本書就送給你了。 *Zhèi běn shū jiù sònggěi nǐ le.* The book was given to you.; to give as a gift: 他去年送給他父母一套房。 *Tā qùnián sònggěi tā fùmǔ yítào fáng.* Last year, he gave his parents a set of apartments as a gift.
sòng hányī	送寒衣	to send winter clothing/to burn paper clothing for the dead at the end of the 10th lunar month
sònghuà	送話	to send words; to give opponent grounds for attack by using ill advised statement [V–O]
sònghuò	送貨	to deliver goods = 運送貨物 *yùnsòng huòwù*
sònglǎo	送老	to give burial ceremony to deceased parents (= 送終 *sòngzhōng*) [V–O]
sòlǐ	送禮	to give gift [V–O]
sòngmìng	送命	to risk one's life [V–O]
sòngqián	送錢	to send money, to waste money [V–O]
sòngrénqíng	送人情	to do a favor for friendship; to give a present
sòngsāng	送喪	to attend funeral [V–O]
sòngshén	送神	to send spirits away after offering sacrifice [V–O]
sòngsǐ	送死	to walk into a trap [VO]
sòng wǎng yíng lái	送往迎來	to send off the going and welcome the coming/to meet and send off visitors
sòng xìn	送信	to deliver a letter [V O]
sòng xìnr	送信兒	to send message through third party [V O]
sòngxíng	送行	to send off [V–O]
sòngzàng	送葬	to attend funeral [V–O]
sòngzào	送竈	to send off kitchen god for New Year holiday, on the 23rd day of the 12th lunar month [V–O]
sòngzhōng	送終	= 送老 *sònglǎo* [V–O]
sòngzǒu	送走	to show someone the way out: 我剛把客人送走。 *Wǒ gāng bǎ kèrén sòngzǒu.* I just walked the guests out.

suànbude	算不得	cannot be considered as (unusual, rare, etc.) [VC]
suànbuliǎo	算不了	cannot be reckoned as: 算不了一回事。 *Suànbuliǎo yìhuí shì.* This is nothing. [VC]
suànfǎ	算法	arithmetic [SC/N]
suànguà	算卦	to practice divination, to tell fortune [V–O]
suànjì	算計	to calculate, to plot ruin or injury (of someone): 小心被人家算計。 *Xiǎoxīn bèi rénjia suànjì.* Be careful about another's plot against you. [CC/V]
suànle	算了	let it be, do not bother anymore: 不去算了。 *Búqù suànle.* If you don't go, forget it.
suànmìng	算命	to tell fortune; 算命的 *suànmìngde*, fortune-teller [V–O]
suànqilai	算起來	all counted or considered: 算起來還是這個好。 *suànqilai háishi zhèige hǎo.* All considered, this one is still better. [VC]
ouànchang	算上	to include, to count in: 你組織旅行別忘了把我算上。 *Nǐ zuzhi lǚxíng bié wàngle bǎ wǒ suànshang.* If you are organizing a tour, don't forget to include me. [VC]
suànshù	算術	arithmetic [SC/N]
suànshùr	算數兒	to count, to be taken seriously: 你說的話算數兒不算數兒? *Nǐ shuōde huà suànshùr bu suànshùr?* Are you serious about what you say? [V–O]
suàntí	算題	to solve a math problem; arithmetical question [V/N]
suànzhàng	算賬	to reckon accounts, to ask for bill to pay; to get even (for revenge): 回頭我跟你算賬。 *Huítóu wǒ gēn nǐ suànzhàng.* I'll get even with you later. [V–O]
bǐsuàn	筆算	to calculate with a pen [SC/V]
dǎsuàn	打算	to plan, to intend to [CC/V]
dǎ suànpan	打算盤	to calculate on abacus; to calculate costs and benefits: 他就會打如意算盤。 *Tā jiù huì dǎ rúyì suànpan.* He always indulges himself in wishful thinking.
jìsuàn	計算	to reckon, to compute: 計算機, *jìsuànjī*, calculator [CC/V]
pánsuàn	盤算	to ruminate in mind [SC/V]
xīnsuàn	心算	to calculate mentally [SC/V]

tánbǐng	談柄	butt of jokes [SC/N]
tándelái	談得來	can make conversation with: 他們兩個很談得來。 *Tāmen liǎngge hěn tándelái.* The two of them can talk to each other. [VC]
tán hé róngyì	談何容易	It's so easy to talk and criticize. (It implies that it isn't so easy to do.)
tán hǔ sè biàn	談虎色變	to turn pale at the mere mention of a tiger/to get scared easily
tánhuà	談話	to talk [V–O]; conversation, talk: 他昨天的談話真有意思。 *Tā zuótiān de tánhuà zhēn yǒuyìsi.* His talk yesterday was really interesting.
tánliàn'ài	談戀愛	to be in love with: 他們兩個正在談戀愛。 *Tā men liǎng ge zhèngzài tán liàn'ài.* They are in love.
tánlùn	談論	to discuss [CC/V]; a discussion
tán qíng shuō ài	談情說愛	to talk love
tánpàn	談判	to negotiate [CC/V]; a negotiation
tántiān(r)	談天(兒)	to chat, to gossip idly [V–O]
tán tiān shuō dì	談天說地	to talk of anything under the sun
tántǔ(r)	談吐(兒)	way of talking: 談吐很風雅。 *Tántǔ heǐ fēngyǎ.* His way of talking is very cultured. [CC/V]
tán xiào fēng shēng	談笑風生	to talk in a fascinating and lively manner
tán xiào zì ruò	談笑自若	to be completely at ease while talking
tánxīn	談心	to have a heart-to-heart talk [V–O]
tán yán wēi zhòng	談言微中	talk sparingly but to the point
tán zhèngzhì	談政治	to talk politics
tánzhù	談助	material for gossip [SC/N]
jiē tán xiàng yì	街談巷議	street gossip
lǎoshēng cháng tán	老生常談	moral platitudes
xiántán	閒談	to have a leisurely talk [SC/V]
yántán	言談	a person's style or ability of conversation [CC/N]

táobēn	逃奔	to flee [CC/V]
táobì	逃避	to shirk (duty): 逃避責任 *táobì zérèn*; to refuse to face (reality): 逃避現實 *táobì xiànshí* [CC/V]
táobīng	逃兵	a deserter [SC/N]
táo bīngyì	逃兵役	to avoid military service
táochuàn	逃竄	(of bandits, rebels) to flee elsewhere [CC/V]
táodiào	逃掉	to get away with: 這次讓你逃掉了。 *Zhèi cì ràng nǐ táodiào le.* This time you got away. [VC]
táofàn	逃犯	escaped convict [SC/N]
táohuāng	逃荒	to flee from famine [V–O]
táohūn	逃婚	to run away from a wedding [V–O]
táomìng	逃命	to flee for one's life [V–O]
táonàn	逃難	to run away from disaster, to become a refugee [V O]
táonì	逃匿	to escape and to hide, to keep oneself out of sight [CC/V]
táopǎo	逃跑	to escape, to flee, to steal away [CC/V]
táoshēng	逃生	to flee for one's life (= 逃命 *táomìng*) [V–O]
táoshuì	逃稅	to evade tax [V–O]
táotuō	逃脫	to succeed in escaping [VC]
táowáng	逃亡	to flee from home: 逃亡在外 *táowáng zài wài* [CC/V]
táoxué	逃學	to play truant: 我從來沒有逃過學。 *Wǒ cónglái méi táoguo xué.* I have never played truant. [V–O]
táo zhī yāoyāo	逃之夭夭	to have escaped and is nowhere to be found
táozǒu	逃走	to run away [VC]
táozuì	逃罪	to escape from the law [V–O]

tǎoqiú	討求	to ask, beg, demand [CC/V]
tǎofá	討伐	to make war on (country, rebels) to vindicate authority [CC/V]
tǎofàn	討飯	to beg for food: 討飯的 *tǎofànde*, a beggar [V–O]
táohǎo	討好	to ingratiate oneself, to toady [V–O]
tǎohuán	討還	to get something back: 討還債務 *tǎohuán zhàiwù* to demand repayment of a debt [V]
tǎo jià huán jià	討價還價	to haggle over price
tǎojiào	討教	to seek instruction [V–O]
tǎo lǎopó	討老婆	to get a wife
tǎolùn	討論	to discuss [CC/V]; discussion
tǎo piányi	討便宜	to seek advantage: 讓他討個便宜。 *Ràng tā tǎo ge piányi.* Let him get a bargain.
tǎoqián	討錢	to ask for money [V–O]
tǎoqiǎo	討巧	to try to get something for nothing [V–O]
tǎoqiào	討俏	to beg for witty [V]
tǎoqīn	討親	to marry a wife [V–O]
tǎoqíng(r)	討情(兒)	to ask for leniency [V–O]
tǎoráo	討饒	to beg for pardon, forgiveness [V–O]
tǎoxián	討嫌	to ask for unpleasant treatment: 討人嫌 *tǎo rénxián*, to annoy people [V–O]
tǎo xífu	討媳婦	to get a wife
tǎoyàn	討厭	to incur dislike, to be annoying [V–O/SV]; to dislike [TV]
tǎozhài *tǎo huán zhàiwù*	討債 = 討還債務	to demand repayment of a debt; to dun [V–O]
tǎozhàng	討賬	to ask for payment of debt [V–O]
zì tǎo kǔ chī	自討苦吃	to walk into trouble oneself
zì tǎo méi qù	自討沒趣	to do something that will result in a rebuke or embarrassment

tíbá	提拔	to promote = 選拔提昇 *xuǎnbá tíshēng* [V]
tíbǐ	提筆	to take up pen/to write: 我很久沒有提過筆了。 *Wǒ hěn jiǔ méi yǒu tíguo bǐ le.* I have not written for a long time. [V–O]
tíchàng	提倡	to encourage; to advocate; to promote [V]
tíchéng	提成	to take a percentage [V]
tíchū	提出	to bring up (opinion): 提出意見 *tíchū yìjian* [VC]
tídào	提到	to mention, refer to: 書上提到你沒有? *Shūshang tídào nǐ méiyou?* Does the book mention you? [VC]
tífáng	提防	to guard against (enemy attack): 提防敵人進攻 *tífáng dírén jìngōng* [CC/V]
tí gāng xié lǐng	提綱挈領	to give main outline (of facts, principles, etc.)
tígāo	提高	to elevate, to heighten (vigilance): 提高警覺 *tígāo jǐngjué* [VC]
tígōng	提供	to contribute: 這個節日是福特公司提供的。 *Zhèige jiémù shì Fútè Gōngsī tígōng de.* This program is brought to you by the Ford Company. [CC/V]
tíhuò	提貨	pick up goods; to take delivery of goods = 提取貨物 *tíqǔ huòwù* [V–O]
tíjí	提及	to mention; to bring to notice = 提起 *tíqǐ*; 提到 *tídào*; 談到 *tándào* [V]
tíjià	提價	to raise price [V–O]
tíkuǎn	提款	to withdraw money [V–O]
tíliàn	提煉	to refine, extract (oil, chemicals) [CC/V]
tímíng	提名	to nominate (person for election, awards, etc.) [V–O]
tíqilai	提起來	to lift up; mentioning (someone or something): 提起來她的女兒就掉淚。 *Tíqilai tāde nǚ'er jiù diào lèi.* At the mention of her daughter, she sheds tears. [VC]
tíqīn	提親	to bring up proposal of marriage [V–O]
tíqín	提琴	a violin [SC/N]
tíshén	提神	to refresh oneself, to put on one's guard [V–O]
tíshì	提示	to point out, to give advice (to younger people) [CC/V]
títour	提頭兒	worth mentioning: 這個人沒甚麼大提頭兒。 *Zhèige rén méi shénme dà títour.* This person is not worth talking a great deal about.
tíwèn	提問	to ask a question [V]
tíxīn	提心	to worry: 你做事真讓人提心。 *Nǐ zuòshì zhēn ràngrén tíxīn.* When you do things you really make people worried.
tí xīn diào dǎn	提心吊膽	to worry a great deal
tíxǐng	提醒	to remind, to alert [CC/V]
tíyào	提要	brief summary [VO/N]
tíyì	提議	to propose [V–O]; a proposal
ěr tí miàn mìng	耳提面命	(teacher, parent) give personal advice constantly

diàobāo	調包	to substitute stealthily [V–O]
diàochá	調查	to investigate [CC/V]
diàodòng	調動	to transfer (troops, personnel) [CC/V]; 調不動 *diàobúdòng*, cannot transfer [VC]
diào hǔ lí shān	調虎離山	to lure tiger to leave mountain/to lure enemy out of position
diàohuí	調回	to recall (troops, etc.) [V]
diàorén	調人	to transfer (someone) to a new post [V–O]
diàozǒu	調走	to transfer away [VC]
tiáohé	調和	to blend (flavors), to mediate [CC/V]
tiáojì	調劑	to set right proportions, to make adjustments: 整天工作，週末到鄉下去玩玩兒，調劑調劑生活。 *Zhěngtiān gōngzuò, zhōumò dào xiāngxia qù wánwanr, tiáojìtiaoji shēnghuó.* We work all day. We should go to the country for a change. [VO]
tiáojiě	調解	to mediate, to reconcile [CC/V]
tiáonòng	調弄	= 調戲 *tiáoxì*, to flirt, and 玩弄 *wánnòng*, to make fun/to make fun of; to play (musical instrument) [CC/V]
tiáopí	調皮	to be naughty, to be tricky
tiáoqíng	調情	to flirt with, to court [V–O]
tiáotíng	調停	to settle dispute amicably [CC/V]
tiáowèi	調味	to blend flavors: 調味品 *tiáowèipǐn*, seasoning [V–O]
tiáoxì	調戲	to flirt with (a girl) [CC/V]
tiáoxiào	調笑	to ridicule, to tease [CC/V]
tiáoyǎng	調養	to recuperate [CC/V]
tiáozhěng	調整	to make adjustment, to reorganize: 調整公教人員待遇 *tiáozhěng gōngjiào rényuán dàiyù*, to make adjustments in salary and fringe benefits for civil servants and teachers [CC/V]
tiáozhì	調治	to receive medical treatment [CC/V]

tiàocáo	跳槽	to change profession (= *tiàoháng*) [V-O]
tiàochū huǒkēng	跳出火坑	to jump out of fire/to pull oneself out of a bad situation
tiàodòng	跳動	to jump about [CC/V]
tiàogāo	跳高	to do high jump [VC]
tiàoháng	跳行	to skip a line in reading; to change profession (= 跳槽 *tiàocáo*) [V-O]
tiào jǐng	跳井	to jump into well (to commit suicide) [V O]
tiàolán	跳欄	to jump hurdles [V-O]
tiào lóu	跳樓	to jump off a building [V O]
tiàopíjīn	跳皮筋	to skip and dance over a chain of rubber bands [V O]
tiàosǎn	跳傘	to parachute [V-O]; a parachute; also 降落傘 *jiàngluò sǎn*
tiàoshén(r)	跳神(兒)	to dance before the gods to exorcise evil spirits [V-O]
tiào shéng	跳繩	to skip rope [V O]
tiàoshī	跳虱	flea [SC/N]
tiàoshuǐ	跳水	to dive [V-O]
tiàowǔ	跳舞	to dance [V-O]
tiàoyuǎn	跳遠	to do broad jump [VC/V]
tiàoyuè	跳躍	to jump, hop for joy [CC/V]
bèngbeng tiàotiao	蹦蹦跳跳	to jump and skip about
gǒu jí tiào qiáng	狗急跳牆	a desparate dog jumps over a wall/take desperate measures if pushed to the wall
xiàle yítiào	嚇了一跳	to give one a start (from fright)
xīn jīng ròu tiào	心驚肉跳	to be jump with fear
xīntiào	心跳	heart palpitates: 我有點兒心跳 *Wǒ yǒu diǎnr xīntiào.* My heart palpitates a little. [SP/V]
yǎnpí tiào	眼皮跳	eyelids twitch

tīngbiàn	聽便	to let someone have his own option [V-O]
tīngchāi	聽差	to serve as a servant [V-O]; a servant
tīngcóng	聽從	to obey, to head [CC/V]
tīngguān	聽官	the sense of hearing [SC/N]
tīnghuà	聽話	to listen to someone's advice; to obey: 這個小孩兒不聽話 *zhèige xiǎoháir bùtīnghuà.* This child doesn't obey. [V-O]
tīnghòu	聽候	to await (arrival, decision, etc.) [CC/V]
tīngjian	聽見	to hear [VC]
tīngjiǎng	聽講	to hear said, to attend lectures [V-O]
tīngjué	聽覺	sense of hearing (= *tīngguān*) [SC/N]
tīngmìng	聽命	to let fate take its course [V-O]
tīnglì	聽力	the power, function of hearing [SC/N]
tīng qí zìrán	聽其自然	to let things take their natural course
tīngqǔ	聽取	to listen and hear (opinion): 聽取意見 *tīngqǔ yìjian* [CC/V]
tīngshěn	聽審	(of judge) to sit on a trial [CC/V]
tīngshū	聽書	to attend a recitation by storytellers [V-O]
tīngshuō	聽說	to hear, it is said [CC/V]
tīng tiān yóu mìng	聽天由命	to resign to fate, to be fatalistic
tīngtǒng	聽筒	earphone [SC/N]
tīngtou	聽頭	what is worth listening to
tīngwén	聽聞	to hear (story, new, etc.) [CC/V]
tīngxì	聽戲	to go to opera [V-O]
tīngxiě	聽寫	to listen and write/to dictate [CC/V]; dictation
tīngxìn	聽信	to listen and to believe [CC/V]; to wait for news, 聽信兒 *tīngxìnr* [V-O]
tīngzhòng	聽眾	the audience [SC/N]

tíngbàn	停辦	to stop operation, to close up [VO]
tíngbó	停泊	to lie at anchor [VO]
tíngchē	停車	to stop driving, to park a car: 停車場 *tíngchēchǎng*, parking lot [V-O]
tíngdang	停當	all set, all arranged [CC/SV]
tíngdiàn	停電	to stop electric supply [V-O]
tíngdùn	停頓	to bog down, to be at a standstill [CC/V]
tíngfù	停付	to stop payment [VO]
tínggōng	停工	to stop work [V-O]; a stoppage of work
tínghuǒ	停伙	to stop cooking [V-O]
tínghuǒ	停火	to cease fire (= 停戰 *tíngzhàn*) [V-O]
tíngkān	停刊	to cease publication (of periodical) [V-O]
tíngkè	停課	to suspend classes [V-O]
tíngliú	停留	to stop over during journey, to delay for a rest [CC/V]
tíng qī zài qǔ	停妻再娶	to divorce wife and remarry
tíngshuǐ	停水	to stop water supply [V O]
tíngting(r)	停停(兒)	by and by, after a while
tíngxué	停學	to give up schooling, to suspend schooling [V-O]
tíngyòng	停用	to stop using [VO]
tíngzhàn	停戰	to cease fire [V-O]; a cease fire, armistice
tíngzhí	停職	to suspend appointment, to dismiss [V-O]
tíngzhǐ	停止	to stop [CC/V]
tíngzhì	停滯	to be held up, to be blocked up [CC/V]
tíngzhu	停住	to come to a stop [VC]
bùtíngde	不停地	continuously: 不停地動 *bùtíngde dòng*, to move about continuously [Adv]

tōngbiàn	通便	to help bowel movement [V-O]
tōngcái	通才	one who has received a liberal education [SC/N]
tōngchē	通車	through train or bus, to begin operation [V-O]
tōngdá	通達	to be well versed, experienced and understanding [CC/SV]
tōngfēng	通風	to ventilate; to send secret message [V-O]
tōnggào	通告	to notify, to announce; to inform [V]
tōngguò	通過	to go through; carried as a motion [VO]
tōnghóng	通紅	to flush red all over [SV/V]= 滿臉通紅 *mǎnliǎntōnghóng*
tōngjiān	通姦	to commit adultery [V-O]
tōnglì hézuò	通力合作	to work together with everybody pitching in for a common cause
tōnglùn	通論	a general introduction (to a subject): 政治學通論 *Zhèngzhìxué Tōnglùn*, A General Introduction to Political Science [SC/N]
tōngqì(r)	通氣	to be in touch with each other; to ventilate [V-O]
tōngrong	通融	to relax or circumvent regulations to accomodate: 請通融一下, *Qǐng tōngrong yíxià.* Please make an accommodation. [CC/V]
tōngshāng	通商	to trade, to have commercial intercourse [V-O]
tōngshùn	通順	(of writing) good and clear [CC/SV]
tōngsú	通俗	to be common, popular [CC/SV]
tōngtōng	通通	all, altogether, entirely
tōngxìn	通信	to correspond: 你常跟家裏人通信嗎? *Nǐ cháng gēn jiāli rén tōngxìn ma?* Do you correspond with your family often? [V-O]
tōngzhī	通知	to notify [CC/V]
bùtōng rénqíng	不通人情	to be unreasonable in dealing with people
shuōbutōng	說不通	cannot get (person) to understand or agree; (of argument) unconvincing: 這樣實在說不通。 *Zhèyang shízài shuōbutōng.* This is really unconvincing. [VC]
Zhōngguó tōng	中國通	a China hand, an expert on China

tóngbān	同班	to go to the same class [V-O]; classmate
tóngbàn	同伴	companion [CC/N]
tóngbāo	同胞	brothers of the same mother; compatriots [VO/N]
tóngbèi	同輩	persons of the same generation [SC/N]
tóng bìng xiānglián	同病相憐	fellow sufferers (of same sickness) understand one another
tóngchuāng	同窗	to share the same window/schoolmate, classmate [V-O]
tóng chuáng yì mèng	同牀異夢	same bed different dreams/persons thrown together but having different problems or ambitions
tóngdào	同道	person of same belief or conviction [SC/N]
tóngděng	同等	to be equal, same [SC/V]
tóngwū	同屋	to share the same room [V-O]; roommate
tóng guī yú jìn	同歸於盡	to perish together
tónghángʼr)	同行(兒)	fellow craftsman, person of the same profession [SC/N]
tónghào	同好	same taste or hobby [SC/N]
tónghuà	同化	to assimilate [SC/V]
tónghuǒ	同夥	fellow worker in same shop, member of group or gang [SC/N]
tóngjū	同居	to live together, without getting married [SC/V]
tóng liú hé wù	同流合污	to associate oneself with undesirable elements or trend
tónglùrén	同路人	fellow travelers
tóngqíng	同情	to sympathize; 同情心, *tóngqíngxīn*, sympathy [SC/V]
tóngshì	同事	to work in the same firm; a colleague, coworker [V-O]
tóngxiāng	同鄉	a fellow provincial, a person from the same area [VO]
tóngxíng	同行	to travel together [SC/V]
tóngxué	同學	to go to the same school; a schoolmate [V-O]
tóngzhì	同志	comrade; gay [SC/N]
tóng zhōu gòng jì	同舟共濟	people in the same boat help each other in distress
bùtóng	不同	to be different [SC/SV]

tōudù	偷渡	to steal into another country [V]
tōu gōng jiǎn liào	偷工减料	(contractors) to save illegally on materials and labor
tōu hànzi	偷漢子	= *tōurén* 偷人 [V O]
tōu jī mō gǒu	偷雞摸狗	to steal chickens and dogs/small burglar
tōukàn	偷看	to watch without permission, to peep [SC/V]
tōukòng(r)	偷空(兒)	to manage a little time (to do something): 偷空兒看朋友 *tōukòngr kàn péngyou*, to manage a little time to see friends [V-O]
tōulǎn(r)	偷懶(兒)	to be idle or negligent at work [V-O]
tōu lóng zhuǎn fèng	偷龍轉鳳	to steal a dragon and replace with a phoenix/to steal a male child and substitute a female child
tōuqiǎo	偷巧	to do something as a shortcut [V-O]
tōuqiè	偷竊	to steal [CC/V]; a thief, thievery
tōuqíng	偷情	to have illicit relations with men or women [V-O]
tōurén	偷人	(of women) to have illicit relations with men (= 偷漢子 *tōu hànzi*) [V-O]
tōushēng	偷生	to live on without meaning or purpose [VO]
tōushuì	偷稅	to evade tax, to smuggle [V-O]
tōu tiān huàn rì	偷天換日	to steal heaven and replace the sun/audacious scheme of cheating people
tōutōur(de)	偷偷兒地	stealthily [Adv]
tōuxí	偷襲	to make a surprise attack [SC/V]
tōuxián	偷閒	to spare a few moments from work to do something else [VO]
tōuyíng	偷營	to steal camp/to attack a camp at night [V-O]
tōuzuǐ	偷嘴	to steal mouth/to steal food, to eat without permission [V-O]
xiǎo tōur	小偷兒	a petty thief [SC/N]

tuī bō zhù làng	推波助浪	to follow and hasten movement of waves/to aggravate dispute by third party
tuībúdiào	推不掉	can't shove off (duty) [VC]
tuīcè	推測	to calculate, to conjecture [CC/V]; a conjecture
tuī chén chū xīn	推陳出新	to make renovations
tuīchí	推遲	to put off; to postpone; to defer [V]
tuīcí	推辭	to decline (offer) [CC/V]
tuīdǎo	推倒	to push down, to overthrow [VC]
tuīdòng	推動	to move by pushing, to initiate [VC]
tuīduàn	推斷	to predict [CC/V]
tuī jǐ jí rén	推已及人	to place oneself in another's place/to do to others what you would do to yourself
tuījiàn	推薦	to recommend [CC/V]
tuī lái tuī qù	推來推去	to push back and forth; to make all sorts of excuses
tuīqiāo	推敲	to try to find out, to weigh words [CC/V]
tuīràng	推讓	to yield to others [CC/V]
tuīshuō	推說	to use as an excuse [V]
tuītóu	推頭	to push the head/to cut the hair [V-O]
tuī xián yú néng	推賢與能	to select the capable and put them in power
tuīxiǎng	推想	to imagine, to reckon [CC/V]
tuīxiè	推卸	to evade, to shove off (duty): 推卸責任 *tuīxiè zérèn* [CC/V]
tuī xīn zhì fù	推心置腹	to show the greatest consideration or confidence, to treat someone as oneself
tuīxuǎn	推選	to elect [CC/V]
bàn tuī bàn jiù	半推半就	(of women) half refusing and half yielding
shùn shuǐ tuī zhōu	順水推舟	to go with the current, to take advantage of favorable trend

tuōbìng	託病	to use sickness as excuse [V-O]
tuōcí	託辭	to make excuse [CC/V]; an excuse [SC/N]
tuōérsuǒ	託兒所	a day nursery
tuōfú	託福	to have blessings: 託你的福 *Tuō nǐde fú* or 託福託福 *tuōfútuōfú*. All because of your blessings. [V-O]
tuōfu	託付	to entrust: 把這件事就託付給你了。*Bǎ zhèi jiàn shì jiù tuōfu gěi nǐ le.* I will entrust this matter to you. [CC/V]
tuōgù	託顧	to entrust orphan to someone's care [V-O]
tuōgù	託故	to use some pretext: 託故不去 *tuōgù búqù*, will not go on pretext [V-O]
tuōguǎn	託管	trusteeship [CC/V]
tuōmèng	託夢	(spirit of deceased) appear in a dream to give a message [V-O]
tuōmíng	託名	to do something in someone's name, to assume false name [V-O]
tuōqíng	託情	to ask someone to put in a nice word for one [V-O]
tuō rén	託人	to entrust someone [V O]
tuōshēn	託身	to take abode in some place [V-O]
tuōshēng	託生	to be reincarnated: 他是牛託生的。*Tā shì niú tuōshēng de.* He was reincarnated from an ox. [VO]
tuō yǐ tā cí	託以他詞	to evade by making excuses
tuōyùn	託運	to have something shipped [CC/V]
bàituō	拜託	to request (of someone): 拜託你一件事。*Bàituō nǐ yíyjiàn shì.* Please do one thing for me. 拜託拜託！*Bàituō bàituō!* Thanks! [CC/V]
shòu rén zhī tuō	受人之託	I am entrusted (with something by someone)
wěituō	委託	to commission (someone), to ask someone to be reasonable for something: 委託行 *wěituō háng*, a second-hand shop [CC/V]

wán 'àn	完案	To close a case at court [V-O]
wánbèi	完備	to be complete, well provided: 這個學校的一切都很完備。*Zhège xuéxiào de yíqiè dōu hěn wánbèi.* This school is well equipped in every respect. [CC/SV]
wánbì	完畢	to come to an end, to end: 工作完畢 *Gōngzuò wánbì.* The work has been finished. [CC/V]
wánchéng	完成	to complete (project, mission, etc.): 完成任務 *wánchéng rènwù,* to complete mission [CC/V]
wándàn	完蛋	done for
wángǎo	完稿	to complete the manuscript; to finish a piece of writing [V O]
wángōng	完工	to complete work: 我們的廚房，甚麼時候完工? *Wǒmende chúfáng, shénme shíhou wángōng?* When is our kitchen going to be completed? [V-O]
wánhǎo	完好	complete and good/intact, not cracked [CC/SV]
wánhūn	完婚	to get married [V-O]
wánjié	完結	to close account; closed [CC/V]
wánjuàn	完卷	to finish an examination paper [V-O]
wánle	完了	to have expired; to be done; It's finished! 一切都完了! *Yíqiè dōu wánle!* an expression of despair after fire, flood, or defeat
wánmǎn	完滿	to be satisfactory, to be happy: 婚姻很完滿。*Hūnyīn hěn wánmǎn.* The marriage is satisfactory. [CC/SV]
wánměi	完美	to be happy; to be beautiful [CC/SV]
wánbǐ	完筆	to complete a written piece [V-O]
wánqīng	完清	to clear off (account) [VC]
wánquán	完全	to be complete [CC/SV]; completely [Adv]
wánrén	完人	a perfect person [SC/N]
wánshàn	完善	to be perfect, excellent [CC/SV]
wánshì(r)	完事(兒)	to be done, (work) is finished [V-O]
wánshuì	完稅	to pay tax [V-O]
wánzhěng	完整	(= 完好 *wánhǎo*) [CC/SV]

wán bǎxi	玩把戲	to play magic
wánfǎ	玩法	to juggle the law [V-O]
wánhào	玩好	favorite pastime, hobby [CC/N]
wánhū	玩忽	to ignore [CC/V]
wánxiàohuà	玩笑話	a joke, an empty promise [SC/N]
wánjù	玩具	toy [SC/N]
wánnòng	玩弄	to toy with, to play tricks on people: 玩弄人 *wánnòng rén* [CC/V]
wán'ǒu	玩偶	a toy figurine [SC/N]
wánr	玩兒	to play, to amuse oneself: 他是說着玩兒呢。你不要認真。 *Tā shi shuōzhe wánr ne. Nǐ búyào rènzhēn.* He was joking. Don't take it seriously.
wánr gǔpiào	玩兒股票	to buy stocks as a side investment
wánr huāyàngr	玩兒花樣兒	to play tricks: 別玩兒花樣兒。老老實實地做最好。 *Bié wánr huāyàngr. lǎolǎoshishīde zuò zuì hǎo.* Don't play tricks. It is best to do it honestly.
wánrhuǒ	玩兒火	to play with fire, to do something dangerous [V-O]
wánrmìng	玩兒命	to do something that endangers life [V-O]
wánr pái	玩兒牌	to play cards [V O]
wánshǎng	玩賞	to enjoy (flowers, moon, etc.) [CC/V]
wán shì bù gōng	玩世不恭	to live dangerously or in defiance of conventions
wánshǒuwàn	玩手腕	to play politics; to play tricks [V O]
wánshuǎ	玩耍	to play to relax [CC/V]; relaxation, pastime
wánwèi	玩味	to appreciate slowly (a profound saying, etc.) [CC/V]
wánwù	玩物	things for people to enjoy or play with [SC/N]
wánxiào	玩笑	something done for fun: 開玩笑。 *kāi wánxiào*, to play jokes upon (person) [CC/N]
wányìr	玩意兒	a toy, something interesting, a trifle

wǎngcháng	往常	usually, in the past: 往常他不喝酒。 *Wǎngcháng tā bùhējiǔ.* Usually he doesn't drink. [CC/Adv]
wǎngchū	往初	formerly [CC/Adv]
wàngdōng	往東	towards the east: 往東走 *wàngdōng zǒu*, to go towards the east [VO/Adv]
wǎngfǎn	往返	back and forth [CC/Adv]
wǎnghòu	往後	henceforth; *wànghòu*, backward: 往後走兩步 *wànghòu zǒu liǎng bù*, to go backward a couple of steps [VO/Adv]
wǎnglái	往來	to go and to come/to have social dealings [CC/V]; social intercourse: 我們沒有往來。 *Wǒmen méiyou wǎnglái.* We don't have any social intercourse.
wǎng liǎn shàng mǒhēi	往臉上抹黑	to make someone look bad
wǎngnián	往年	in former years [SC/TW]
wǎngrì	往日	in former days: 往日我有很多朋友。 *Wǎngrì wǒ yǒu hěn duō péngyou.* In the past I had many friends. [SC/TW]
wǎngshí	往時	formerly [SC/TW]
wǎngshì	往事	things of the past: 往事還提它做甚麼? *Wǎngshì hái tí ta zuò shénme?* Why do you still mention things of the past? [SC/N]
wǎngxī	往昔	in the past [N]
wǎngwǎng (r)	往往(兒)	oftentimes, frequently: 他往往兒把人記錯了。 *Tā wǎngwǎngr bǎ rén jìcuòle.* He often mixes people up. [Adv]
wǎngwǎng rú cǐ	往往如此	It is often like this.
gǔ wǎng jīn lái	古往今來	old go present come/all the time
jì wǎng bù jiū	既往不究	what is past do not blame/let bygones be bygones
láilái wǎngwǎng	來來往往	frequent social dealings; traffic is heavy: 這條路上來來往往的車子真多。 *Zhèitiáo lùshang láilái wǎngwǎngde chēzi zhēn duō.* This road has many cars driving back and forth.

wàng chén mō jí	望塵莫及	to see the dust but can't reach/to fall far behind
wàng'érquèbù	望而却步	to shrink back at the sight of (something dangerous or difficult); to flinch
wàng fēng dǎo	望風倒	to see the wind and fall/unable to maintain one's determination
wàng fēng zhuǎn duò	望風轉舵	to watch the wind and turn the rudder/to be an opportunist
wàngjian	望見	to see; to view 遠遠就望見了他。*Yuǎnyuǎn jiù wàngjianle tā.* I saw him when he was far away.
wàng méi zhǐ kě	望梅止渴	to look at plums to quench thirst/imagined satisfaction.
wàngxiāngtái	望鄉台	terrace in hell where deceased can see their homes in the distance
wàng yǎn yù chuān	望眼欲穿	wishing eyes about to bore through/to hope for something earnestly
wàng yáng xīng tàn	望洋興歎	to see the ocean and sigh/to view with despair something difficult to do
wàngyuǎnjìng	望遠鏡	telescope, binoculars
wàng zǐ chéng lóng	望子成龍	to hope one's son becomes a dragon/to hope one's son becomes a high official in the government
wàngzú	望族	respected clan [SC/N]
juéwàng	絕望	to despair, to give up hope [V-O]
míngwàng	名望	名譽 *míngyù*, reputation, and 人望 *rénwàng*, prestige [CC/N]
pànwàng	盼望	to long for, to hope for [CC/V]
qīwàng	期望	expectation [CC/N]
shēngwàng	聲望	名聲 *míngshēng*, reputation, and 人望 *rénwàng*, prestige [CC/N]
shīwàng	失望	to give up hope, to be disappointed [VO/SV]
wúwàng	無望	to be hopeless [VO]
xīwàng	希望	to hope [CC/V]
yuànwàng	願望	心願 *xīnyuàn*, wish, and 希望 *xīwàng*, hope [CC/N]

wěiguò	委過	to shift blame [VO]
wěijī	委積	to accumulate, to pile up [CC/V]
wěi juě bú xià	委決不下	to delay decision
wěi mí bú zhèn	委靡不振	to be weak
wěimìng	委命	to entrust to fate, to take fatalistic attitude [VO]
wěipài	委派	to appoint (someone): 政府委派誰去談判? *Zhèngfǔ wěipài shéi qu tánpàn?* Who is going to be sent by the government to negotiate? [CC/V]
wěiqì	委棄	to abandon, to cast away on the ground [CC/V]
wěiqū	委屈	to wrong (someone): 委屈你了 *wěiqū nǐ le*, to have wronged you [CC/V]; injustice, grievance: 你的委屈我知道。 *Nǐde wěiqū wǒ zhīdao.* I know your grievances.
wěiqū	委曲	to be winding; to be tortuous [S V]
wěi qū qiú quán	委曲求全	to stoop in order to accomplish something, to do the best possible under the circumstances.
wěirèn	委任	to appoint (someone to a post) [CC/V]; also used for a lower grade in Chinese civil service as in 委任官 *wěirèn guān* or 職 *zhí*, a post in the *wěirèn* grade
wěishí	委實	really (not bad): 委實不錯 *wěishí búcuò*; truthfully (confess): 委實招供 *wěishí zhāogōng* [Adv]
wěituō	委託	to entrust (person, task): 委託你替我做一件事。 *wěituō nǐ tì wǒ zuò yíjiàn shì* to entrust you to do one thing for me [CC/V]
wěiwǎn	委婉	to be tactful in telling the truth that may hurt: 他話說得很委婉，要不然怎麼吃得消? *Tā huà shuōde hěn wěiwǎn, yàoburán zěnme chīdexiāo.* He spoke very tactfully, otherwise how can the one spoken to have stood it? [CC/SV]
wěixiàn	委巷	isolated alley [N]
wěiyuán	委員	a committee member; 委員會 *wěiyuánhuì*, committee [SC/N]
wěizuì	委罪	to shift blame [VO]

wēnbao	溫飽	warm and full/to have enough to wear and eat [CC/N]
wēncún	溫存	to be kind and attentive: 溫存話兒 *wēncún huàr*, comforting words
wēndai	溫帶	temperate zone [SC/N]
wēndù	溫度	degree of temperature: 溫度計 *wēndùjì*, thermometer [SC/N]
wēn gù zhī xīn	溫故知新	to review the old and learn something new
wēnhé	溫和	mild (weather): 氣候溫和 *qìhou wēnhé*; gentle (temperament): 脾氣溫和 *píqi wēnhé* [CC/SV]
wēnhòu	溫厚	溫和 *wēnhé*, gentle, and 厚道 *hòudao*, generous [CC/SV]
wēn jiùqíng	溫舊情	to renew old friendship, to talk over old times
wēnkè	溫課	to review lessons, from 溫習功課 *wēnxí gōngkè* [V-O]
wēnliáng	溫良	溫和 *wēnhé*, gentle, and 善良 *shànliáng*, good [CC/SV]
wēnnuǎn	溫暖	warm (sun, fellowship) [CC/SV]; warmth: 人間溫暖 *rénjiān wēnnuǎn*, warmth between people
wēnqíng	溫情	warm feeling [SC/N]
wēnquán	溫泉	hot springs [SC/N]
wēnróu	溫柔	溫順 *wēnshùn*, obedient, and 柔和 *róuhé*, gentle/gentle and affectionate (particularly between lovers) [CC/SV]
wēnróuxiāng	溫柔鄉	love nest, a brothel
wēnshì	溫室	hothouse [SC/N]
wēnshū	溫書	to review lessons (in a book) [V-O]
wēnshùn	溫順	溫和 *wēnhé*, gentle, and 孝順 *xiàoshùn*, filial/filial, obedient [CC/SV]
wēnwén	溫文	溫和 *wēnhé*, gentle, and 文雅 *wényǎ*, cultured/cultured in manners [CC/SV]
wēnxí	溫習	to review [CC/V]
wēnxīn	溫馨	to be gentle and fragrant; to be warm [SV]
wēnyǎ	溫雅	to be refined [CC/SV]
chóng wēn jiù mèng	重溫舊夢	to relive an old dream/to have a reunion with lover

wèn'ān	問安	to ask about health, to give greeting: 他要我向你問安。 *Tā yào wǒ xiàng nǐ wèn'ān.* He asked me to remember him to you. [V-O]
wèn cháng wèn duǎn	問長問短	to ask all sorts of questions
wèndá	問答	dialogue: 問答題 *wèndá tí*, question and answer topics in examination [CC/N]
wèndǎo	問倒	to stymie someone in questions: 你把我問倒了。 *Nǐ bǎ wǒ wèndǎole.* Your question stymied me. [VC]
wèn dào yú máng	問道於盲	to ask the way from a blind person/to approach the wrong person
wènhǎo	問好	to give greeting (= 問安 *wèn'ān*) [V-O]
wènhou	問候	to greet people: 他要我問候你。 *Tā yào wǒ wènhou nǐ.* He asked me to remember him to you. [CC/V]
wènhuà	問話	to ask questions [V-O]; a question
wènmíng	問明	to find: 這件事一定得問明是誰搞的? *Zhèijiàn shì yídìng děi wènmíng shì shéi gǎo de.* We must find out who did this. [VC]
wènshì	問世	to be published: 你的書甚麼時候問世? *Nǐde shū shénme shíhòu wènshì?* When is your book going to be published? [V-O]
wèntí	問題	questions, problems [SC/N]
wèn xīn wú kuì	問心無愧	to have no regrets upon self-examination/to feel at ease
wènxùn	問訊	to inquire [VO]; 問訊處 *wènxùnchù*, information desk
wènzhu	問住	(= 問倒 *wèndǎo*) [VC]
wènzuì	問罪	to condemn, to sentence [V-O]
bù chǐ xià wèn	不恥下問	(Confucius) was not ashamed to ask from common people
bù wén bú wèn	不聞不問	neither ask nor hear/to show no interest in
bú wèn hǎo dǎi	不問好歹	without first asking about what happened
fǎngwèn	訪問	to interview and study (person, country)
rù jìng wèn jìn	入境問禁	to ask about taboos and bans upon entering a foreign country

xǐbǐ	洗筆	to wash the brush [V O]; a small water container for painting, also 筆洗 *bǐxǐ*
xǐchē	洗車	to wash a car; to have a car washed
xǐchén	洗塵	to wash off the dust/to give a welcome dinner to friend on return from a trip [VO]
xǐ ěr bùwén	洗耳不聞	to wash one's ears not to listen/to shut one's ears to happenings around him
xǐ ěr gōng tīng	洗耳恭聽	to wash one's ears to listen respectfully/to listen respectfully
xǐlǐ	洗禮	baptism: 他今天受洗(禮)了。 *Tā jīntiān shòu xǐ(lǐ) le.* He received baptism today. [SC/N]
xǐ'nǎo	洗腦	to wash brain/to brainwash: 他被洗腦了。 *Tā bèi xǐ'nǎo le.* He was brainwashed. [V-O]; brainwash
xǐpái	洗牌	to wash the cards/to shuffle the cards [V-O]
xǐ shǒu	洗手	to wash hands; to leave the gang and reform: 他洗手不幹了。 *Tā xǐ shǒu bú gàn le.* He has reformed himself and doesn't do that anymore. To go to the toilet [V O]
xǐshǒujiān	洗手間	restrooms, lavatory [N]
xǐshuā	洗刷	to wash and brush; to clear one's name of criminal charges [CC/V]
xǐtóu	洗頭	to wash head/to shampoo [V O]
xǐ xīn gé miàn	洗心革面	to wash one's heart and to change one's face/to reform: 他已經洗心革面不再做壞事了。 *Tā yǐjing xǐ xīn gé miàn búzài zuò huài shì le.* He has reformed and does not do anything bad anymore.
xǐxuě	洗雪	to right a wrong, to clear charges [CC/V]
xǐyī	洗衣	to wash clothes: 洗衣店 *xǐyīdiàn* laundry; 洗衣粉 *xǐyīfěn* washing powder; 洗衣機 *xǐyījī* washing machine [VO/N]
xǐyuān	洗冤	to right a wrong [V-O]
xǐzǎo	洗澡	to shower; [V]
tiào dào Huáng Hé xǐbùqīng	跳到黃河洗不清	to jump into the Yellow River and not be able to wash oneself clean/impossible to clear oneself of charges even with the water of the Yellow River

xǐài	喜愛	to like, to love (children, swimming, detective stories, etc.) [CC/V]
xǐbìng	喜病	joy sickness/pregnancy [SC/N]
xǐ chū wàng wài	喜出望外	to be pleased beyond expectation
xǐguǒ	喜果	eggs painted red to be presented to friends and relatives on birth of a child or on wedding [SC/N]
xǐhào	喜好	to love (sports, etc.) [CC/V]
xǐjiǔ	喜酒	wine served at wedding: 甚麼時候吃你的喜酒? *Shénme shíhou chī nǐde xǐjiǔ?* When (can we) drink your wedding wine?/When are you going to get married? [SC/N]
xǐ nù wú cháng	喜怒無常	joy and anger have no norm/to be unpredictable in mood: 這個人喜怒無常，不是哭就是笑。 *Zhèige rén xǐ nù wú cháng, búshì kū jiù shì xiào.* This person's mood is unpredictable. If he doesn't cry, he laughs.
xǐ qì yáng yáng	喜氣洋洋	to be filled with gayety
xǐshì	喜事	happy occasions (birthdays, weddings, etc.) [SC/N]
xǐ xīn yàn jiù	喜新厭舊	to like the new and dislike the old/to abandon the old for the new
xǐyuè	喜悅	to be happy and joyous [SV]
xǐ zhú yán kāi	喜逐顏開	to beam with happy smiles
xǐzīzī	喜滋滋	to feel pleased [SV]
bàoxǐ	報喜	to report on birth of a son, getting a degree, promotion, etc. [V-O]
dàoxǐ	道喜	to congratulate: 他升官的事，你給他道過喜了沒有? *Tā shēngguān de shì, nǐ gěi tā dàoguoxǐle meiyou?* Concerning his promotion, have you congratulated him? [V-O]
gōngxǐ	恭喜	to congratulate [VO/TV]; Congratulations! (usually in reduplicated form: 恭喜! 恭喜! *gōngxǐ! gōngxǐ!*
hàixǐ	害喜	to show symptoms of pregnancy (morning sickness) [V-O]
huān tiān xǐ dì	歡天喜地	to be overjoyed

xiàbǐ	下筆	to set down pen on paper/to write [V-O]
xià bān	下班	to get off work; to finish work [VO]
xià běnqián	下本錢	to put up capital
xià bù liǎo tái	下不了台	cannot find a way out of an embarrassing situation: 他當着那麼多人開我的玩笑。 真叫我下不了台。 *Tā dāngzhe nàme duō rén kāi wǒde wánxiào. Zhēn jiào wǒ xià bù liǎo tái.* He made fun of me in front of so many people, it caused unending embarrassment for me.
xiàchē	下車	to get off (a car, bus, train . . .) [VO]
xiàdàn	下蛋	to lay eggs [V-O]
xià dìngyì	下定義	to give a definition: 請你給民主下個定義。 *Qǐng nǐ gěi mínzhǔ xià ge dìngyì.* Please define democracy.
xiàfàng	下放	to reassign from urban to rural areas (PRC) [SC/V]
xià fēijī	下飛機	to disembark a plane
xià gōngfu	下功夫	to put forth effort: 不管做甚麼事都得下功夫。 *Bùguǎn zuò shénme shì dōu děi xià gōngfu.* No matter what one does, he has to put forth effort.
xiàguō	下鍋	to put raw food into cooking pan [V-O]
xiàhǎi	下海	to put out to sea; to get into a profession from status as amateur [V-O]
xiàhuò	下貨	to unload the goods [V-O]
xiàjiǔ	下酒	to go with wine: 這些都是下酒的好菜。 *Zhèixie dōu shì xiàjiǔ de hǎo cài.* These are all good dishes with wine. [V-O]
xià juéxīn	下決心	to take a firm resolve
xiàkè	下課	to finish class [VO]
xiàlèi	下淚	to shed tears: 我難過得都下淚了。 *Wǒ nánguòde dōu xiàlèi le.* I felt so bad that I cried. [V-O]
xià pìnshū	下聘書	to send a letter of appointment
xiàqí	下棋	to play chess [V-O]
xiàshǒu	下手	to start (work, to take action) [V-O]
xiàtái	下台	to get off stage (theatrical or political): 我們的州長甚麼時候下台? *Wǒmende zhōuzhǎng shénme shíhòu xiàtái?* When does our governor get off the stage (leave office)? [V-O]
xià xiāng	下鄉	to go to the country [V O]
xiàzuo	下作	to be low and contemptible [SC/SV]

xiànchǎng	現場	location of what actually happened: 出了事千萬別改變現場。 *Chūle shì qiānwàn bié gǎibiàn xiànchǎng.* When something happened, by all means, don't change anything on the spot. [SC/N]
xiànchéng(r)	現成(兒)	ready-made, immediately available: 吃現成兒飯。 *chī xiànchéngr fàn*, to have a living without doing any work; 說現成兒話。 *shuō xiànchéngr huà*, to speak with stock phrases [SC/Adj]
xiàn chī xiàn zuò	現吃現做	to prepare food as it is ordered (col. pron. *xuan*)
xiànchu(lai)	現出(來)	to show, to reveal: 毛病現出來了。 *Máobìng xiànchulaile.* The defects have been revealed. [VC]
xiànkuǎn	現款	cash: 你有多少現款? *Nǐ yǒu duōshǎo xiànkuǎn?* How much cash do you have? [SC/N]
xiànnòng	現弄	to show off [CC/V]
xiànrèn	現任	incumbent: 誰是現任市長? *Shéi shì xiànrèn shìzhǎng?* Who is the incumbent mayor? [SC/Adj]
xiàn shēn shuō fǎ	現身說法	to set an example by one's own conduct, to appear personally (at meetings, etc.)
xiànshí	現實	practical, realistic: 這個人真現實啊。 *Zhè ge rén zhēn xiànshí a.* This person is really practical. [CC/SV]
xiànxià	現下	= 現在 *xiànzài* [SC/TW]
xiànxíng	現形	to show one's true colors; to show the cloven hoof [V]
xiànxíng	現行	to be currently in effect; to be in force 現行價格 *xiànxíng jiàgé* the current price
xiànyǎn	現眼	to make a fool of oneself: 你請回去吧。 別再現眼了。 *Nǐ qǐng huíqu ba. Bié zài xiànyǎn le.* Please go back. Don't make a fool of yourself any longer [V-O]
xiàn yòng xiàn mǎi	現用現買	to buy as one needs for the day (col. pron. *xuàn*)
xiànzài	現在	at present, the present: 到現在為止，我還沒看見他呢。 *Dào xiànzài wéi zhǐ, wǒ hái méi kànjian tā ne.* Up to the present, I have not seen him [SC/TW]
xiànzhuàng	現狀	status quo: 維持現狀 *wéichí xiànzhuàng*, to maintain status quo [SC/N]

xiànbǎo	獻寶	to present valuables/to show off one's valuables [V O]
xiàncè	獻策	to offer a plan or strategy (= 獻計 *xiànjì*) [V-O]
xiàncí	獻辭	to offer a dedication speech [V-O]; a dedication speech, a written dedication
xiànchǒu	獻醜	(self-depreciating) to reveal awkwardness/to present a show or performance [V-O]
xiàngōng	獻功	to report one's accomplishment, contributions, etc. [V-O]
xiànhuā	獻花	to present fresh flowers [VO]
xiànjì	獻計	to present a plan or strategy [V-O]
xiàn jìcè	獻計策	to offer a plan or strategy (= 獻計 *xiànjì*, 獻策 *xiàncè*)
xiànjiǔ	獻酒	to offer wine [V-O]
xiànmèi	獻媚	to curry favor, to fawn upon, to cater to: 她就會向上司獻媚。 *Tā jiù huì xiàng shàngsī xiànmèi.* The only thing he knows how to do is to curry favor from his superior. [VO]
xiànshēn	獻身	to dedicate oneself to (cause, career, etc.): 中山先生獻身革命人人佩服。 *Zhōng Shān Xiānsheng xiànshēn gémìng rénrén pèifu.* Dr. Sun Yat-sen dedicated himself to the revolution. Everyone admires him. [V-O]
xiànyǎn	獻眼	to make a spectacle of oneself [V-O]
xiàn yīnqin	獻殷勤	to offer attentive hospitality to a superior: 有些人不靠本事靠獻殷勤升官。 *Yǒu xie rén búkào běnshi kào xiàn yīnqin shēngguān.* Some people depend on offering attentive hospitality rather than their ability to get promotions.
xiànyì	獻藝	to show one's skill [VO]
xiànzèng	獻贈	a contribution (of gift or ideas): 這是我對國家的獻贈。 *Zhè shì wǒ duì guójiā de xiànzèng.* This is my contribution to the country [CC/N]
xiànzhuō	獻拙	= 獻醜 *xiànchǒu* [V-O]
fèngxiàn	奉獻	to offer, to contribute (to church, superior) [CC/V]
gòngxiàn	貢獻	to contribute: 請你貢獻一點兒意見。 *Qǐng nǐ gòngxiàn yìdianr yìjiàn.* Please offer some suggestions. [CC/V]; contribution: 他做了很多對國家有貢獻的事情。 *Tā zuòle hěn duō duì guójia yǒu gòngxiàn de shìqing.* He has done a lot of things which were beneficial (a contribution) to the country. [CC/N]

xiǎngbìshi	想必是	probably it is that . . . : 想必是他病了。 *Xiǎngbìshi tā bìng le.* Probably it is that he is sick.
xiǎngdào	想到	to think of: 想得到，做得到 *Xiǎngdedào, zuòdedào.* If one can think of it, one can do it. [VC]
xiǎng fázi	想法子	to figure out a way: 我們得想法子救他。 *Wǒmen děi xiǎng fázi jiù tā.* We have to figure out a way to rescue him.
xiǎngjiā	想家	to think of home, to be homesick [V-O]
xiǎngjiàn	想見	to visualize: 他辛苦的情形可以想見。 *Tā xīnkǔde qíngxing kéyi xiǎngjiàn.* His difficult situation may be visualized; *xiǎng jiàn*, want to see (somebody) [CC/V]
xiǎngkāi	想開	to put something out of mind: 你想開了就不難過了。 *Nǐ xiǎngkāile jiù bùnánguò le.* If you have put that matter out of your mind, you won't feel bad anymore. [VC]
xiǎnglái	想來	I suppose: 想來我真不應該。 *Xiǎnglái wǒ zhēn bùyīnggāi.* I suppose I shouldn't have done it; 想來 *xiǎng lái*, want to come
xiǎng lái xiǎng qù	想來想去	to turn over and over in one's mind: 他想來想去也想不出個法子來。 *Tā xiǎng lái xiǎng qù yě xiǎngbuchū ge fázi lai.* He has thought it over and over, but still can't figure out a way.
xiǎngniàn	想念	to long for, to miss: 他很想念他哥哥。 *Tā hěn xiǎngniàn tā gēge.* He misses his brother every much. [CC/V]
xiǎngqilai	想起來	to think of, to recollect: 想起那件事來就傷心。 *Xiǎngqi nèijiàn shì lai jiù shāngxīn.* Whenever I think of that matter, I feel sad. [VC]
xiǎngsībìng	想思病	lovesick
xiǎngsǐle	想死了	to be dying for (something) [VC]
xiǎng tōng	想通	to think through, to realize (what the matter is) [VC]
xiǎngtou	想頭	worth thinking about: 那種事還有甚麼想頭呢？ *Nèizhong shì hái yǒu shénme xiǎngtou ne?* Is that kind of business worth thinking about?
xiǎngxiàng	想像	to imagine: 他那種窘迫的情形是可以想像得到的。 *Tā nèizhǒng jiòngpòde qíngxing shì kéyi xiǎngxiàngde dào de.* His embarrassment may be imagined. [CC/V]; imagination, an idea: 這是一個不可思議的想像。 *Zhè shì yíge bùkěsīyìde xiǎngxiàng.* This is an unthinkable idea; 想像力 *xiǎngxiànglì*, power of imagination
yì xiǎng tiān kāi	異想天開	a sudden fanciful thought: 他是異想天開，一點兒都不實際。 *Tā shì yì xiǎng tiān kāi, yìdiǎnr dōu bùshíjì.* Those are only fanciful thoughts, not a bit practical.

xiàngbèi	向背	toward or away from/for or against: 人心的向背 *rénxīnde xiàngbèi*, the public attitude for or against (a regime) [CC/N]
xiàngdǎo	向導	guide [N]
xiànglái	向來	hitherto: 他向來是這樣的。 *Tā xiànglái shì zhè yang de.* He is like this all the time [Adv]
xiàngqián	向前	to press forward: 向前走 *xiàngqián zǒu*, to go forward [VO/Adv]
xiàngrìkuí	向日葵	sunflower
xiàngshàn	向善	to seek the good [VO]
xiàngshàng	向上	to strive upwards: 不向上就會倒退的。 *Bú xiàngshàng jiù huì dàotuì de.* If one does not strive upwards, he will go backward. [VO]
xiàng tā	向他	to take his side (in an argument): 你可別老向着他說話。 *Nǐ kě bié lǎo xiàngzhe tā shuōhuà.* You shouldn't speak in his favor all the time. [V O]
xiàngwǎn	向晚	toward evening [VO/TW]
xiàngwǎng	向往	to look forward to: 向往幸福的新生活 *xiàngwǎng xìngfú de xīn shēnghuó* to look forward to a new happy life
xiàngxīn cí	向心詞	endocentric words
xiàngxīnlì	向心力	centripetal force
xiàngyáng	向陽	to face south or the sunny side [VO]
xiàngyú	向隅	facing a corner or dead end/to be left out: 以免向隅 *yǐmiǎn xiàngyú*, (hurry to buy) so that you will not miss the great chance
fāngxiàng	方向	direction [CC/N]
nèixiàng	內向	introvert [SC/SV]
xīn xīn xiàng róng	欣欣向榮	to be prosperous, (of plants) grow luxuriantly
yíxiàng	一向	= *xiànglái* [Adv]
yìxiàng	意向	meaning or intention [CC/N]
zhìxiàng	志向	ambition [N]

xiàngfa	相法	the art of face reading in fortune-telling [SC/N]
xiàng fu jiao zi	相夫教子	to assist husband and bring up children.
xiānggān	相干	to have something to do with: 這事與你毫不相干。 *Zhè shì yú nǐ háo bùxiānggān.* This has nothing to do with you. [SC/V]
xiàng jī ér dòng	相機而動	to watch for the right moment for action
xiàngmao	相貌	looks, personal appearance (also 像貌) [CC/N]
xiàngmiàn	相面	to practice physiognomy, to consult a physiognomist [V-O]
xiàngmìng	相命	to tell fortune [V-O]
xiàng nǔxu	相女婿	to look at prospective son-in-law for approval
xiàngpiàn	相片	photograph (also 像片) [SC/N]
xiàngqīn	相親	to look over prospective bride [V-O]
xiāng qīn xiāng ài	相親相愛	to love each other dearly
xiàngshēngr	相聲兒	act of two performers with a witty dialogue: 說相聲兒的 *shuō xiàngshēngrde*, one who does this kind of act [VO/N]
xiàngshi	相士	a fortune-teller [SC/N]
xiàngxiázi	相匣子	a camera (also 照相機 *zhàoxiàngjī*)
guàixiàng	怪相	strange, disgusting looks [SC/N]
jí rén tiān xiàng	吉人天相	God protects good people
nán rén běi xiàng	南人北相	a southerner with the looks of a northerner (considered a feature of a good person)
xiōngxiàng	兇相	face indicating violence, ill luck, or violent accidental death [SC/N]
zhàoxiàng	照相	to take pictures, to have picture taken: 天氣這麼好，我們出去照相去。 *Tiānqi zhème hǎo, wǒmen chūqu zhàoxiàng qu.* The weather is so good, we're going out to take some pictures. 我今天到照相館去照相。 *Wǒ jīntiān dào zhàoxiàngguǎn qù zhàoxiàng.* I am going to the photo studio to have my picture taken today. [V-O]
zhēnxiàng	真相	real situation, the truth: 真相大明 *Zhēnxiàng dà míng.* The truth is completely revealed. [SC/N]

xiàngmào	像貌	a person's looks (also 相貌): 相貌非凡 *xiàngmào fēi fán*, to have a distinguished appearance [CC/N]
xiàng mú xiàng yàng	像模像樣	to be with airs of importance
xiàngpiàn	像片	photographs (also 相片) [SC/N]
xiàng shà yǒu jiè shì	像煞有介事	to be with airs of importance: 別像煞有介事的樣子。 那不是甚麼了不起的事情。 *Bié xiàng shā yǒu jiè shì de yàngzi. Nà búshì shénme liǎobuqǐ de shìqing.* Don't put on airs of importance. It's not anything important.
xiàng shénme	像甚麼	What does it look like/What kind of business is this? 穿這樣的奇裝異服像甚麼？ *Chuān zhèyang de qí zhuāng yì fú xiàng shénme?* What is it to wear such strange clothes!
(hǎo)xiàngshì	(好)像是	It looks like, it seems: 他像是沒聽見。 *Tā xiàngshi méitīngjian.* It seems as if he didn't hear it. [Adv]
xiàngyàngr	像樣兒	to be presentable: 你今天可得穿得像樣兒點兒。 *Nǐ jīntiān kě děi chuānde xiàngyàngr diǎnr.* You must dress properly today. 這樣做還像樣兒。 *Zhèyang zuò hái xiàngyàngr.* It is presentable to do this way. [VO/SV]
búdà xiàng	不大像	not likely: 那件事聽著不大像，他做不出來。 *Nèijiàn shì tīngzhe búdà xiàng. Tā zuòbuchūlai.* That matter does not sound likely. He can't do that.
búxiànghuà	不像話	does not resemble language/to go too far, beyond the limit: 連父母都不管。真太不像話。 *Lián fùmǔ dōu bù guǎn. Zhēn tài búxiànghuà.* (He) doesn't even take care of his parents. It's really too preposterous.
búxiàng rén	不像人	not like a person (derogatory expression): 你看他。 三分不像人，七分倒像鬼。 *Nǐ kàn tā. Sānfēn búxiàng rén, qīfēn dào xiàng guǐ.* Look at him. He is more like a ghost than a human being.
diāoxiàng	雕像	statuary [N]
hǎoxiàng . . . (shide)	好像 . . . 似的	it seems: 他好像病了似的。 *Tā hǎoxiàng bìngle shide.* It seems he is sick.
xiāoxiàng	肖像	portrait [N]
yíxiàng	遺像	a portrait of a deceased person: 總理遺像 *Zǒnglǐ yíxiàng*, a portrait of the late Director General (Dr. Sun Yat-sen) [SC/N]

xiāochú	消除	to abolish, to do away with (obstacles); to remove (prejudice, bad habits, etc.) [CC/V]
xiāodú	消毒	to sterilize, to disinfect [V-O]
xiāofángduì	消防隊	fire brigade
xiāofèi	消費	to consume [CC/V]; expenditure: 物價高，消費跟着增加。 *Wùjià gāo, xiāofèi gēnzhe zēngjiā.* Prices to up; expenditures increase. 消費品 *xiāofèipǐn*, consumer goods.
xiāohào	消耗	to consume: 大汽車消耗汽油太多。 *Dà qìchē xiāohào qìyóu tài duō.* Big cars consume too much gasoline. [CC/V]; consumption.
xiāohuà	消化	to digest [CC/V]; digestion: 消化不良 *xiāohuà bùliáng*, indigestion
xiāohuǒqì	消火器	fire extinguisher =滅火器 *miè huǒqì*
xiāojí	消極	to be negative, pessimistic (opposite to 積極 *jījí*, positive, optimistic) [SC/SV]
xiāomiè	消滅	to exterminate, to destroy [CC/V]
xiāomó	消磨	to while away: 消磨歲月 *xiāomó suìyuè*, to while away the years [CC/V]
xiāoqiǎn	消遣	to relax: 忙了一年了，該消遣消遣啦。 *Mángle yìnián le, gāi xiāoqiǎnxiaoqian la.* Having been busy all year, we ought to relax a little now. [CC/V] relaxation, pastime
xiāoshì	消釋	to vanish, to be forgotten [CC/V]
xiāoshòu	消瘦	emaciated [CC/SV]
xiāowáng	消亡	to perish [CC/V]
xiāoxià	消夏	to take summer vacation: 你今年到哪兒去消夏? *Nǐ jīnnian dào nǎr qù xiāoxià?* Where are you going for summer vacation this year? [V-O]
xiāoxián	消閒	to be idol, to have leisure time [CC/SV]
xiāoyán	消炎	to decrease inflammation [V-O]
xiāoyè	消夜	to have a night snack [V-O]; night snack
xiāozhǒng	消腫	to decrease swelling [V-O]
chībùxiāo	吃不消	cannot take it: 工作太苦，吃不消。 *Gōngzuò tài kǔ, chībuxiāo.* The work is too hard, (I) can't take it. [VC]

xiàobǐng	笑柄	butt or target of laughter, a laughing-stock [SC/N]
xiào diào dà yá	笑掉大牙	to laugh one's teeth out/extremely laughable
xiàohāhā	笑哈哈	to roar with laughter
xiàohua	笑話	a joke, pleasantry: 給我們說個笑話。 *Gěi wǒmen shuō ge xiàohua.* Tell us a joke. [SC/N]; to laugh at: 我唱得不好，請別笑話。 *Wǒ chàngde bùhǎo, qǐng bié xiàohua.* My singing is not good. Please don't laugh at me. [SC/V]
xiào lǐ cáng dāo	笑裏藏刀	knife behind smile/smile of treachery
xiào mà yóu rén	笑罵由人	to let others say what they like
xiàomiànhǔ	笑面虎	tiger with a smiling face/a wicked person: 他是個笑面虎，你可得小心點兒。 *Tā shì ge xiàomiànhǔ. Nǐ kě děi xiǎoxīn diǎnr.* He is a wicked person. You really must be a little more careful.
xiàoróng kě jū	笑容可掬	a face beaming with smile: 看他笑容可掬，實在可愛。 *Kàn tā xiàoróng kě jū, shízài kěài.* Look at him. Beaming with smile, he is really lovable.
xiàosǐrén	笑死人	to shame one to death; to die from laughing [VC]
xiàotou	笑頭	something to laugh at
xiàoxīxī	笑嘻嘻	to smile happily
hāhādàxiào	哈哈大笑	to roar with laughter
jīxiào	譏笑	to deride, to make sarcastic remarks at [CC/V]
kāi wánxiào	開玩笑	to make fun of: 別老開他的玩笑。 *Bié lǎo kāi tāde wánxiào.* Don't make fun of him all the time. 這個玩笑可開大了。 *Zhèige wánxiào kě kāi dà le.* You went too far in making fun of him this time.
kěxiào	可笑	to be funny [SV]
kuángxiào	狂笑	to howl with laughter [SC/V]
kǔxiào	苦笑	to give a wry smile [SC/V]
lěngxiào	冷笑	to give a cold smile [SC/V]
qǔxiào	取笑	to make a laughing-stock of (someone): 請求你，別取笑我了，好嗎? *Qǐngqiú nǐ. Bié qǔxiào wǒ le, hǎo ma?* I beg you. Don't make a laughing-stock of me, O.K.? [VO/TV]
wéixiào	微笑	to give a smile [SC/V]; a smile

xiě
to write, to sketch 寫

xiěbudé	寫不得	cannot be written, should not be written [VC]
xiěfǎ	寫法	style of handwriting, penmanship [SC/N]
xiěgǎo	寫稿	to compose a draft [V-O]
xiěmíng	寫明	to write plainly, to set forth clearly [VC]
xiěshēng	寫生	to draw after a model [VO]
xiěshípài	寫實派	realistic school (as contrasted with romantic school)
xiěxialai	寫下來	to write it down [VC]
xiěshī	寫詩	to compose poem [VO]
xiě xìn	寫信	to write a letter [V O]
xiěyì	寫意	Impressionist outlines [VO]; to be pleased in spirit, relaxed, contented [SV]
xiězhào	寫照	a portrait, a portrayal (of conditions)
xiězhēn	寫真	to portray (a person, character) [VO]
xiě zì	寫字	to write (characters) [V O]
xiězuò	寫作	to write; to compose [V]
chāoxiě	抄寫	to copy by hand [CC/V]
jìzhàng	記賬	to make entry in bookkeeping [V-O]
miáoxiě	描寫	to describe [CC/V]; a description
shǒuxiě	手寫	to write by hand [SC/V]
shǒuxiěběn	手寫本	a draft manuscript
shūxiě	書寫	to write [CC/V]
sùxiě	速寫	to sketch [SC/V]; a sketch

xìn bǐ zhí shū	信筆直書	to write freely without hesitation
xìn bù sàn yóu	信步散遊	to roam about wherever the feet take one
xìncóng	信從	to believe and obey (God, His teachings, etc.) [CC/V]
xìnde	信得	to be believable: 他的話信得。 *Tāde huà xìnde.* His words are believable.
xìfèng	信奉	to believe in and worship: 你信奉甚麼教? *Nǐ xìnfèng shénme jiào?* What religion do you believe in? [CC/V]
xìnkào	信靠	to trust, to rely on (God) [CC/V]
xìn kǒu cí huáng	信口雌黃	to make thoughtless criticisms or accusations
xìn kǒu hú shuō	信口胡說	to talk nonsense
xìn kǒu kāi hé	信口開河	to say whatever comes to one's mind, to make careless remarks
xìnniàn	信念	faith [CC/N]
xìnrèn	信任	to trust, to place confidence in: 信任狀 *xìnrènzhuàng*, credentials
xìn shǎng bì fá	信賞必罰	awards and punishments rigorously carried out: 這個政府是信賞必罰。犯罪的一個也逃不了。 *Zhèige zhèngfǔ shì xìn shǎng bì fá. Fànzuìde yíge yě táobuliǎo.* This government carries out its awards and punishments rigorously. No criminal can escape punishment.
xìntú	信徒	follower, believer: 紅衛兵都是毛澤東的信徒。 *Hóngwèibīng dōu shì Máo Zédōng de xìntú.* The red guards are all followers of Mao Tze-tung. [SC/N]
xìntuō	信託	to entrust [CC/V]
xìnxīn	信心	faith, confidence: 他對你一點兒信心也沒有。 *Tā duì nǐ yìdiǎnr xìnxīn yě méiyou.* He doesn't have any confidence in you. [SC/N]
xìnyǎng	信仰	to believe in and worship [CC/V]; faith, belief
xìnyòng	信用	a person's trustworthiness, credit: 不守信用 *bùshǒu xìnyòng*, does not keep one's word [CC/N]
qīngxìn	輕信	to believe in whatever one is told [SC/V]
xiāngxìn	相信	to believe: 我相信你對。 *Wǒ xiāngxìn nǐ duì.* I believe you are right. to believe in: 我相信你。 *Wǒ xiāngxìn nǐ.* I believe in you. [SC/V]
zìxìn xīn	自信心	self-confidence

xíngbutōng	行不通	cannot be carried out [VC]
xíng buxíng	行不行	Is it all right?
xíngchéng	行程	itinerary [SC/N]
xíngchuán	行船	to sail a boat [V-O]
xíngfáng	行房	to have sexual intercourse [V-O]
xínghǎo	行好	to do a good deed [V-O]
xínghuì	行賄	to commit bribery [V-O]
xínglè	行樂	to enjoy oneself: 及時行樂 *jí shí xínglè*, make merry while possible [V-O]
xínglù	行路	to walk [V-O]
xíngqī	行期	date of departure [SC/N]
xíngrén	行人	pedestrians [SC/N]
xíng rénqíng	行人情	to fulfill social obligations (to give gifts, etc.), to return visits
xíngshàn	行善	to do a good deed [V-O]
xíng shī zǒu ròu	行屍走肉	walking corpse (used figuratively)
xíngwéi	行為	behavior: 行為科學 *xíngwéi kēxué*, behavior science [CC/N]
xíngxiào	行孝	to practice filial piety [V-O]
xíngxiōng	行兇	to commit violence [V-O]
xíngzǒu	行走	to go about [CC/V]
bùxíng	步行	to go on foot [SC/V]
fēngxíng	風行	to be well received (books): 風行全國 *fēngxíng quánguó*, well received all over the country [SC/V]
hángxíng	航行	to travel by plane or boat [SC/V]
lìxíng	力行	to proceed with determination [SC/V]
lǚxíng	旅行	travel: 旅行社 *lǚxíngshè*, travel service [CC/V, N]

xiūguài	休怪	don't blame somebody for: 休怪他不幫忙。 *Xiūguài tā bù bāngmáng*. Don't blame him for not helping you.
xiūhuì	休會	to adjourn a meeting [V-O]
xiūjià	休假	to take leave, to have a holiday, vacation [V-O]
xiūjiào tā pǎo le	休叫他跑了	Don't let him run away.
xiūkān	休刊	to discontinue publication (of a magazine, etc.) [V-O]
xiūkè	休克	(medical) shock [Transliteration]
xiūlǎo	休老	to retire from old age [VO]
xiūpà	休怕	don't be afraid
xiūqī	休妻	to divorce wife [V-O]
xiūxi	休息	to rest: 你累了吧? 好好兒休息休息。 *Nǐ lèi le ba? Hǎohāor xiūxixiuxi*. You must be tired. Take a good rest. [CC/V]
xiūxiá	休暇	holiday, days of rest
xiūxiǎng	休想	don't expect that: 休想他會回心轉意。 *Xiūxiǎng tā huì huí xīn zhuǎn yì*. Don't expect that he will change his mind.
xiūxué	休學	to withdraw from school [V-O]
xiūyǎng	休養	to rest and nourish [CC/V]
xiūyǎng shēng xí	休養生息	to nourish the people
xiū yào zhèyang	休要這樣	Don't be like this.
xiūyè	休業	to close up business, to have a recess [V-O]
xiūzhàn	休戰	to cease fire, armistice [V-O]
bàxiū	罷休	to forget it, to let off: 那件事他還不肯罷休。 *Nèijiàn shì tā hái bùkěn bàxiū*. Concerning that matter, he still won't forget it. [CC/V]
bùmián bùxiū	不眠不休	to go without sleep and rest
tuìxiū	退休	to retire from office: 退而不休 *tuì ér bùxiū*, retired but not rest/ work after retirement [CC/V]

xǔ buxǔ	許不許	Permit it or not?
xǔhūn	許婚	to pledge daughter's hand in marriage [V-O]
xǔjià	許嫁	to pledge daughter in marriage [V-O]
xǔkě	許可	to permit [CC/V]; permission
xǔkězhèng	許可證	license
xǔle rénjia	許了人家	to have been engaged to someone
xǔnuò	許諾	a promise [CC/N]
xǔpèi	許配	= 許婚 *xǔhūn* [VO]
xǔpìng	許聘	= 許婚 *xǔhūn* [VO]
xǔqīn	許親	to accept a proposal of marriage
xǔ shēn bào guó	許身報國	以身報國 *yǐ shēn bào guó* to dedicate oneself to country's cause
xǔyuàn	許願	to give pledge before God [V-O]
xǔzì	許字	= 許婚 *xǔhūn* [VO]
jiāxǔ	嘉許	to praise, to show appreciation (for an inferior's work) [CC/V]
mòxǔ	默許	to give silent consent [SC/V]
xīnxǔ	心許	to give her heart to someone [SC/V]
yǐ shēn xǔ guó	以身許國	to dedicate oneself to country's cause
yìngxǔ	應許	to promise, to assent to [CC/V]
yǔnxǔ	允許	to allow: 爸爸不允許你去。 *Bàba bùyǔnxǔ nǐ qù.* Father won't allow you to go. [CC/V]
zànxǔ	讚許	to praise (by a superior): 他工作努力。上司對他大加讚許。 *Tā gōngzuò hěn nǔlì. Shàngsi duì tā dàjiā zànxǔ.* He works hard. His superior greatly praised him. [CC/V]
zìxǔ	自許	to make promise to oneself to become somebody: 以救國救民的大人自許 *yǐ jiù guó jiù mín de dà rèn zìxǔ*, to make a promise to oneself to take the great responsibility to save the country and the people.

xuǎnbá	選拔	to select someone for promotion or special assignment [CC/V]
xuǎnchū	選出	to select, to elect [VC]
xuǎndú	選讀	to take an elective course: 我這個學期選讀英文。 *Wǒ zhèige xuéqī xuǎndú Yīngwén.* This term I'm taking English as an elective. [CC/V]
xuǎngòu	選購	to purchase selectively [CC/V]
xuǎnjǔ	選舉	to elect [CC/V]; election: 選舉權 *xuǎnjǔ quán*, right to vote
xuǎnměi	選美	to elect beauty/beauty contest [V-O]
xuǎnpài	選派	to select and appoint, to select and send: 選派留學生 *xuǎnpài liúxuéshēng*, to select and send students to study abroad [CC/V]
xuǎnshǒu	選手	champion, chosen members (of athletic team) [SC/N]
xuǎnxiū	選修	to take an elective course (= 選讀 *xuǎndú*) [CC/V]
xuǎnyòng	選用	to select and appoint to post: 現在的政府多喜歡選用青年。 *Xiànzàide zhèngfǔ duō xǐhuan xuǎnyòng qīngnián.* Governments now mostly prefer to select youth for appointments. [CC/V]
xuǎnzé	選擇	to pick out, to choose: 買東西當然要選擇好的。 *Mǎi dōngxi dāngran yào xuǎnzé hǎode.* When buying things, one naturally picks the good ones. [CC/V]: choice: 這家公司的貨太少，沒甚麼選擇。 *Zhèi jiā gōngsī de huò tài shǎo, méi shénme xuǎnzé.* This company doesn't have many things. There isn't any choice.
xuǎnzhǒng	選種	to select seeds [V-O]; selected breeds, select quality (of tea, etc.) [SC/N]
xuǎnzhòng	選中	to pick out someone by choice or examination, to succeed in such examinations [VC]
hòuxuǎnrén	候選人	candidate for election
jìngxuǎn	競選	to run for elective office [VO]
kǎoxuǎn	考選	to select by examinations: 公務員多半是考選來的。 *Gōngwùyuán duōbàn shì kǎoxuǎn lái de.* Civil servants are mostly recruited by examination. [CC/V]
luòxuǎn	落選	to fail in election: 競選的人多，落選的人也多。 *Jìngxuǎnde rén duō, luòxuǎnde rén yě duō.* Many ran for election, and many lost in the election. [VO]
tiāoxuǎn	挑選	to pick [CC/V]
tuīxuǎn	推選	to recommend or elect for post: 大家推選老張做代表。 *Dàjiā tuīxuǎn Lǎo Zhāng zuò dàibiǎo.* All elected Old Chang to be the representative [CC/V]

xuébushànglai	學不上來	cannot imitate, cannot learn [VC]
xué ér bújuàn	學而不倦	to enjoy learning without getting tired
xué ér búyàn	學而不厭	to enjoy learning without getting bored
xuéfēn	學分	credit hours: 這個學期你選了幾個學分的課? *Zhèige xuéqī nǐ xuǎnle jǐge xuéfēn de kè?* This term, how many credit hours are you taking? [SC/N]
xuéfǔ	學府	institution of higher learning: 最高學府 *zuìgāo xuéfǔ*, highest institution of learning [SC/N]
xué guāi le	學乖了	to learn how to behave
xué huài le	學壞了	to learn from bad examples: 這孩子最近學壞了。 *Zhè háizi zuìjìn xué huài le.* This child has been spoiled by bad examples recently.
xuéhuì	學會	a learned society: 亞洲學會 *Yǎzhōu Xuéhuì*, Association for Asian Studies [SC/N]; to master, to learn well [VC]
xuékē	學科	branch of study, discipline of study [CC/N]
xué lǐmào	學禮貌	to learn good manners
xuéqī	學期	school term (semester, quarter, etc.) [SC/N]
xuéshé	學舌	to repeat gossip, to carry tales (= 學嘴 *xuézuǐ*) [V-O]
xuéwèn	學問	knowledge, scholarship: 有學問 *yǒu xuéwèn*, to be learned [CC/N]
xué wú zhǐ jìng	學無止境	Learning has no end.
xuéxí	學習	to learn (a subject), to learn from models: 我們都應當向老李學習。 *Wǒmen dōu yīngdāng xiàng Lǎo Lǐ xuéxí.* We all ought to learn from Old Li. [CC/V]
xuézhě	學者	a scholar
xuézuǐ	學嘴	to repeat gossip, to carry tales (= 學舌 *xuéshé*) [V-O]
bùxué wúshù	不學無術	not learned and unskilled
bùxué yǒu shù	不學有術	not learned but skilled (know how to get favor from superior)
kēxué	科學	science, to be scientific [SV]
qínxué	勤學	to be studious: 這孩子勤學得不得了。 *Zhè háizi qínxuéde bùdeliǎo.* This child is awfully studious. [SC/SV]

yǎnbiàn	演變	to develop: 將來怎麼演變，誰也不敢說。 *Jiānglai zěnme yǎnbiàn, shéi yě bùgǎn shuō.* No one dares to say how it will develop in the future. [CC/V]; development, change
yǎnchàng	演唱	to give a singing performance [CC/V]
yǎnchū	演出	to give a performance [VC]; a performance: 這場演出很叫座。 *Zhèichǎng yǎnchū hěn jiàozuò.* This performance is very well received.
yǎnhuà	演化	to evolve, to develop [CC/V]; evolution, development: 演化論 *yǎnhuà lùn*, theory of evolution = 進化論 *jìnhuàlùn*
yǎnjiǎng	演講	to give a lecture [V-O]; a lecture, also 講演 *jiǎngyǎn*
yǎnjìn	演進	to make progress [CC/V]
yǎnhuàjù	演話劇	to give a stage performance [V-O]
yǎnshuō	演說	to give a lecture, to address the public [V-O]; a lecture, address
yǎnsuàn	演算	to do exercise in mathematics [CC/V]
yǎnxí	演習	to hold a military drill, to rehearse: 實彈演習 *shídàn yǎnxí*, to hold a military drill with live bullets [CC/V]; a military drill
yǎnxì	演戲	to play on a stage [V-O]
yǎnyì	演義	a historical fiction: 三國之演義 *Sānguó Zhì Yǎnyì*, The Romance of the Three Kingdoms
yǎnyìfǎ	演繹法	deductive method (opposite 歸納法 *guīnàfǎ*, inductive method)
yǎnyuán	演員	actor, performer [SC/N]
yǎnzòu	演奏	to give a recital [CC/V]; 演奏會 *yǎnzòuhuì*, a concert
bànyǎn	扮演	to play (a certain role) [CC/V]
biǎoyǎn	表演	to perform on stage [CC/V]
cāoyǎn	操演	to do military exercise [CC/V]
dǎoyǎn	導演	to direct (movie, play, etc.) [VO]; director
gōngyǎn	公演	public performance [SC/N]
shàngyǎn	上演	to present a performance [V-O]

yàobude	要不得	to be extremely bad: 這孩子真要不得。 *Zhè háizi zhēn yàobude.* This child is really very bad.
yàoburán	要不然	if not, otherwise: 今天下雨了。要不然我就去了。 *Jīntiān xiàyǔ le. Yàoburán wǒ jiù qù le.* It is raining today. If not, I would have gone.
yàodào	要道	main route: 交通要道 *jiāotōng yàodào*, important route for transportation [SC/N]
yàodiǎn	要點	important points [SC/N]
yàofàn	要飯	to beg for food: 要飯的 *yàofànde*, a beggar [V-O]
yàohài	要害	vital part of the body, vital area of defense: 國防要害 *guófáng yàohài*
yàohǎo	要好	to be friendly to each other: 兩個人很要好。 *Liǎngge rén hěn yàohǎo.* The two are very friendly to each other. [VO/SV]
yàojǐn	要緊	to be important [CC/SV]
yàoliǎn	要臉	to care for "face" [VO/SV]
yàolǐng	要領	main themes, points of discussion: 不得要領 *bùdé yàolǐng*, unlucid [CC/N]
yàomìng	要命	to be terrible: 吵得要命 *Chǎode yàomìng.* The noise is terrible. [V-O/SV]
yàoqián	要錢	to charge 這個不要錢。 *Zhèi ge bú yàoqián.* This is free. [V O]
yàoqiáng	要強	to want to be successful, to be ambitious [VO/SV]
yāoqiú	要求	to demand [CC/V]; a demand
yàoren	要人	important person, V.I.P. [SC/N]; 要人 *yào rén*, to demand the return of a criminal or hostage [V O]
yāogōng	要功	to take credit for someone's achievements [V O]
yāoxié	要脅	to coerce by threat of force or other pressure: 你總是這樣要脅人。真要命。 *Nǐ zǒngshì zhèyang yāoxié rén. Zhēn yàomìng.* You coerce people (me) like this all the time. It kills me.
yàozhàng	要賬	to ask for repayment [V-O]
yàozuǐchī	要嘴吃	to ask for food like a glutton

yǎngbìng	養病	to recuperate [V-O]
yǎngchéng	養成	to form (good habits, etc.): 習慣養成了就不好改了。 *Xíguàn yǎngchéngle jiù bùhǎo gǎile.* When a habit has been formed, it will be hard to change. [VC]
yǎng háizi	養孩子	to give birth to, and to raise, children [VO]
yǎng hàn	養漢	(woman) to keep a lover [V-O]
yǎng hǔ yí huàn	養虎貽患	to raise a tiger cub and regret it later
yǎnghuo	養活	to feed (a family): 靠薪水養活家 *kào xīnshuǐ yǎnghuo jiā*, to depend on salary to feed the family [VC]
yǎngjiā	養家	to support a family [V-O]
yǎnglǎo	養老	to support the old/to live on pension: 養老金 *yǎnglǎo jīn*, old age pension
yǎngliào	養料	nutrition, feed for animals [SC/N]
yǎnglù	養路	to maintain roads [VO]
yǎngqīn	養親	to support and serve parents [V-O]
yǎngshēn	養身	to nourish the body: 他養身有道，總是那麼健康。 *Tā yǎngshēn yǒu dào, zǒngshì nàme jiànkāng.* He was a way to nourish his body and is always so healthy. [VO]
yǎngshén	養神	to refresh by keeping quiet for a little while [V-O]
yǎng xiǎo lǎopó	養小老婆	to keep a mistress
yǎngxīn	養心	to cultivate mental calmness [V-O]
yǎngxìng	養性	to cultivate mental poise [V-O]
yǎngyù	養育	to bring up (children): 不忘父母養育之恩。 *Búwàng fùmǔ yǎngyù zhī ēn.* Don't forget parents' kindness in bringing up one from childhood. [CC/V]
yǎngzǐ	養子	foster son [SC/N]
yǎng zūn chǔ yōu	養尊處優	to live a comfortable, well-fed life
fúyǎng	扶養	to take care of (the aged, sick) [CC/V]
péiyǎng	培養	to train (personnel): 培養人材 *péiyǎng réncái*, to train personnel [CC/V]

yìnfā	印發	to print and distribute 印發廣告 *yìnfā guǎnggào* to print and distribute advertisements [V]
yìnjiàn	印鑑	copy of seal, name chop for verification [CC/N]
yìnmó	印模	metal dice used for marking (trademarks, etc.) [CC/N]
yìnní	印泥	Chinese ink pad (containing cinnabar and oil) [SC/N]
yìnr	印兒	a trace, a scratch: 桌子上有很多印兒。 *Zhuōzishang yǒu hěn duō yìnr.* On the table there are many scratches.
yìnsè	印色	= 印泥 *yìnní* [SC/N]
yìnshuā	印刷	to print: 印刷品 *yìnshuāpǐn*, printed materials [CC/V]
yìnxiàng	印象	impressions or reactions: 你對他的印象好不好？ *Nǐ duì tā de yìnxiàng hǎo buhǎo?* Is your impression of him good? 別給人壞印象 *Bié gěi rén huài yìnxiàng.* Don't give people bad impressions.
yìnxiàngpài	印象派	impressionist
yìnxìn	印信	official seal [CC/N]
yìnzhāng	印章	a seal, name chop [CC/N]
yìnzhèng	印證	to corroborate: 互相印證 *hùxiāng yìnzhèng*, to corroborate each other [CC/N]
chóngyìn	重印	to make reprints [SC/V]
fùyìn	複印	to duplicate [SC/V]
gàiyìn	蓋印	to stamp seal on paper [V-O]
jiǎoyìn	腳印	footprint [SC/N]
shuǐyìn	水印	watermark [SC/N]
xīn xīn xiāng yìn	心心相印	hearts and feelings find perfect response (of two lovers)
zhǐyìn	指印	fingerprint [SC/N]

yìngbiàn	應變	to respond to changing situation [VO]
yìngcheng	應承	to promise [CC/V]
yìngchou	應酬	to socialize, to engage in social parties [CC/V]; social parties
yìngdá	應答	to reply; to respond; to echo; to answer [V]
yìngdí	應敵	to meet an enemy attack [V O]
yìng duì rú liú	應對如流	to respond fluently
yìngfu	應付	to deal with (situation, person, etc.): 這種局面真難應付。 *Zhèi zhǒng júmiàn zhēn nán yìngfu.* This kind of situation is really difficult to deal with. [CC/V]
yìngjí	應急	to meet an emergency: 先給你點兒錢應個急。 *Xiān gěi ni diǎnr qián yìng ge jí.* (I'll) give you a little money first to meet your urgent need [V-O]
yìngjiē bùxiá	應接不暇	too many (affairs, visitors) to attend to
yìngkǎo	應考	to register or take part in an examination [V-O]
yìng shēng chóng	應聲蟲	a yes man
yìngshì	應試	= 應考 *yìngkǎo* [V-O]
yìngxǔ	應許	to promise, to approve [CC/V]
yìngyāo	應邀	upon invitation to; at someone's invitation [V]
yìngyòng	應用	to apply: 應用科學 *yìngyòng kēxué*, applied science
yìngyuán	應援	to make move to help an ally (in battle) [VO]
yìngyǔn	應允	to promise, to consent [CC/V]
yìngzhàn	應戰	to meet challenge to battle [V-O]
yìng zhāo nǚláng	應召女郎	call girl
fǎnyìng	反應	to react [SC/V]; reaction
yǒu qiú bì yìng	有求必應	requests always granted

yòngbuzháo	用不着	there is no need to: 你用不着去。 *Nǐ yòngbuzháo qù.* You don't have to go. 今天你用不着這本書吧? *Jīntian nǐ yòngbuzháo zhèiběn shū ba?* You're not going to use this book today, are you? [VC]
yòng chá	用茶	to drink tea (more elegant than 喝茶 *hē chá*) [V O]
yòngchǎng	用場	usefulness [SC/N]
yòngchu	用處	use, practical application [SC/N]
yòngdù	用度	habit of spending money [SC/N]
yòngfǎ	用法	instructions (included in appliances, etc.) [SC/N]
yòngfèi	用費	expenses, fees [SC/N]
yònggōng	用功	to work hard (esp. at studies) [V–O]; to be studious, diligent [SV]
yòng gōngfu	用功夫	to practice hard, to spend time on practice, also 下功夫 *xià gōngfu*: 對學問他真肯用功夫。 *Duì xuéwèn tā zhēn kěn yòng gōngfu.* As for knowledge, he is really willing to spend time on it.
yòngjì	用計	to adopt strategy, to play trick [V–O]
yòngjìn	用盡	to exhaust (efforts, etc.): 雖然我用盡了力量幫他的忙，可是他還是不滿意。 *Suīrán wǒ yòngjìnle lìliang bāng tā de máng, kěshì tā háishi bùmǎnyì.* Although I did everything to help him, he is still not satisfied. [VC]
yònglì	用力	to apply effort, to try best at [V–O]
yòng qián	用錢	to spend money [V O]
yòng qíng bùzhuān	用情不專	cannot concentrate one's love on one person
yòng rén	用人	to handle personnel: 不會用人，就做不好行政工作。 *Búhuì yòng rén, jiù zuòbuhǎo xíngzhèng gōngzuò.* If one doesn't know how to handle personnel, he can't do well in administrative work. [V O]
yòngxīn	用心	to be attentive, to pay attention: 用心做事 *yòngxīn zuòshì*, to work attentively [VO]
yòngyì	用意	intention: 用意很好，可是結果反而把朋友給得罪了。 *Yòngyì hěn hǎo, kěshì jiéguǒ fǎn'ér bǎ péngyou gěi dézuì le.* His intentions were good, but the result was that he offended his friend instead. [VO/N]
búyòng	不用	don't have to, there is no need to: 不用客氣 *Búyòng kèqi.* There is no need to be polite.
yòngwǔ	用武	to use force; to display one's abilities or talents: 大有用武之地 *dàyǒu yòngwǔ zhī dì* to have good opportunity to display one's talent

yóudàng	遊蕩	to loaf, to indulge in pleasure [CC/V]
yóuguàng	遊逛	to take a stroll, to visit (temples, fairs, etc.) [CC/V]
yóuhún	遊魂	a homeless spirit; (fig.) somebody with a departing spirit, a listless person [SC/N]
yóujiē	遊街	to hold a street demonstration, to parade a criminal on the street [V O]
yóukè	遊客	a tourist [SC/N]
yóulǎn	遊覽	to tour: 遊覽車 *yóulǎn chē*, a tourist car or bus [CC/V]
yóuláng	遊廊	a covered corridor (in a Chinese garden) [SC/N]
yóulè	遊樂	to have fun: 遊樂場 *yóulèchǎng*, amusement park [CC/V]
yóulì	遊歷	to travel, to visit (particularly foreign countries) [CC/V]
yóu shǒu hào xián	遊手好閒	to be lazy
yóutíng	遊艇	yacht, pleasure boat for hire [SC/N]
yóuwán	遊玩	to play [CC/V]
yóuxì	遊戲	to play [CC/V]; amusement, games
yóuxì rénjiān	遊戲人間	fairies descending to earth and worldly pleasures; (fig.) world of fun and frolic
yóushǎng	遊賞	to travel and enjoy sightseeing [V]
yóuxíng	遊行	to hold a street demonstration [CC/V]; a demonstration: 愛國遊行 *àiguó yóuxíng*, patriotic demonstration
yóuxìng	遊興	interest in sightseeing and travel: 遊興大發 *Yóuxìng dà fā*. Interest in sightseeing becomes very strong. [SC/N]
yóuxué	遊學	to study abroad [V–O]
yóuyìhuì	遊藝會	funfest [N]
yóuyuánhuì	遊園會	a fun party
yóuzōng	遊蹤	places one has traveled [SC/N]

yǒu bǎn yǒu yǎn	有板有眼	to be methodical, to be orderly
yǒu biānr le	有邊兒了	to take shape, to be hopeful: 那件事已經說得有邊兒了。 *Nèijiàn shì yǐjing shuōde yǒu biānr le.* The discussion on that matter is taking shape.
yǒude	有的	some: 有的去，有的不去。 *Yǒude qù, yǒude búqù.* Some go, some don't. *yǒude rén*, some people; 有的時候 *yǒude shíhou*, sometimes
yǒude shi	有的是	to have plenty of: 他有的是錢。 *Tā yǒude shi qián.* He has plenty of money
yǒu dú	有毒	to be poisonous: 小心！ 這個東西有毒。 *Xiǎoxīn! Zhèige dōngxi yǒu dú.* Be careful! This thing is poisonous. [V O]
yǒufèn	有分	to have proper share [V–O]
yǒuhéng	有恆	to have persistence, to be persistent [VO/SV]
yǒuhòu	有後	to have progeny after death, opposite 無後 *wúhòu* without progeny [V–O]
yǒujìn	有勁	to be strong, energetic [VO/SV]
yǒujiù	有救	can be saved [V]
yǒukǒuwúxīn	有口無心	to be sharp-tongued but not malicious
yǒulǐ	有理	to have reason, to be reasonable, to be justifiable: 革命有理 *Gémìng yǒulǐ.* Revolution is justifiable. [VO/SV]
yǒuliǎngxiàzi	有兩下子	to have real skill; to be really something: 你真有兩下子。 *Nǐ zhēn yǒu liǎngxiàzi.* You are really something.
yǒuliǎn	有臉	to have honor (face): 有臉的人 *yǒuliǎnde rén*, person with good social status [V–O]
yǒu ménr	有門兒	to have door/to know the ropes, to be on the right track [VO/SV]
yǒuqíng rén	有情人	person who has affection/lover
yǒuqùr	有趣兒	to be interesting [VO/SV]
yǒuxīn	有心	to have the intention to: 有心人 *yǒuxīn rén*, a good hearted person; a considerate person [V–O]
yǒu xīnxiōng	有心胸	to have ambition
yǒu xīnyǎnr	有心眼兒	to be calculating
yǒuzhǔnr	有準兒	to be sure: 你有準兒能成功嗎？ *Nǐ yǒuzhǔnr néng chénggōng ma?* Are you sure you can succeed? [V–O/SV]

yuēdìng	約定	to agree (on date, meeting): 我們約定明天開會。 *Wǒmen yuēdìng míngtian kāihuì.* We agree to hold the meeting tomorrow. [VC]
yuē dìng sú chéng	約定俗成	(of language) something conventional, customary: 語言是一種約定俗成的東西。 *Yǔyán shì yìzhǒng yuēdìng sú chéng de dōngxi.* Language is a kind of conventional thing.
yuē fǎ sān zhāng	約法三章	to have a simple agreement with the people by a new government
yuēhuì	約會	an appointment: 你們有沒有約會? *Nǐmen yǒu méiyou yuēhuì?* Do you have an appointment? [CC/N]
yuējì	約計	to reckon roughly: 這次旅行約計得十天。 *Zhèicì lǚxíng yuējì děi shí tiān.* This trip, to reckon roughly, needs ten days. [SC/V]
yuējiàn	約見	to arrange an interview [V]
yuējù	約據	written agreement [SC/N]
yuēmo	約莫	= 大約 *dàyuē* [Adv]
yuēqǐng	約請	to invite: 約請朋友來吃飯。 *yuēqǐng péngyou lái chīfàn*, to invite friends for dinner [CC/V]
yuēshù	約束	to restrain, to control [CC/V]; discipline: 他們家的小孩兒一點兒約束都沒有。 *Tāmen jiā de xiǎoháir, yìdiǎnr yuēshù dōu méiyou.* So far as the children of their family are concerned, there is no discipline at all.
dàyuē	大約	roughly: 大約這個時候 *dàyuē zhèige shíhòu*, about this time; 大約半年的時間 *dàyuē bànnián de shíjiān*, roughly half a year's time [CC/Adv]
héyuē	合約	peace treaty [SC/N]
hūnyuē	婚約	marriage agreement [SC/N]
jiùyuē	舊約	the Old Testament [SC/N]
lìyuē	立約	to make an agreement [V–O]
méngyuē	盟約	treaty of alliance [SC/N]
qìyuē	契約	deeds, commercial agreement [CC/N]
tiáoyuē	條約	treaty: 不平等條約 *bùpíngděng tiáoyuē*, unequal treaties [CC/N]
xīnyuē	新約	the New Testament [SC/N]

yuèchū	越出	to exceed: 越出範圍 *yuèchū fànwéi*, to exceed the limits [VC]
yuè duō yuè hǎo	越多越好	the more the better
yuèfā	越發	more and more: 她長得越發好看了。 *Tā zhǎngde yuèfa hǎokàn le.* She grows prettier and prettier. [Adv]
yuèguǐ	越軌	to be out of bounds: 越軌行為 *yuèguǐ xíngwéi*, rude behavior [V–O]
yuèguò	越過	to surpass, to cross over, to cross
yuèjí	越級	to bypass the immediate leadership; to skip a grade or rank
yuèjiè	越界	to cross the border (= 越境 *yuèjìng*) [V–O]
yuèjìng	越境	to cross the border (= 越界 *yuèjiè*) [V–O]
yuè lái yuè máng	越來越忙	to get busier and busier
yuèlǐ	越禮	to overstep propriety, indecorous [V–O]
yueqı	越期	to pass the time limit: 借書越期要罰錢的。 *Jiè shū yuèqī yào fá qián de.* When borrowed books are overdue, there will be a fine. [V–O]
yuèquán	越權	to exceed one's power [V–O]
yuèxí	越席	to away from one's seat
yuèyě sàipǎo	越野賽跑	crosscountry race
yuèyù	越獄	to escape from prison [V–O]
chāoyuè	超越	to stand above: 他的成績超越任何人。 *Tāde chéngjī chāoyuè rènhé rén.* His achievement stands above all others'. [CC/V]
chāozhòng	超重	to exceed the weight limit, from 超過重量 *chāoguò zhòngliang* [V–O]
yuè zǒu yuè kuài	越走越快	the more one walks, the faster one gets
yuè zǔ dài páo	越俎代庖	kitchen assistant taking the place of the chef/to do what is not in one's department

zàicháo	在朝	(of politicians) to be in power: 在朝黨 *zàicháo dǎng*, party in power [VO]
zàiháng	在行	to be an expert in some field: 她對管家真在行。 *Tā duì guǎnjiā zhēn zàiháng.* She is an expert in housekeeping. [VO/SV]
zàihu	在乎	to attach importance to: 他說我甚麼也不在乎。 *Tā shuō wǒ shénme wǒ yě búzàihu.* I don't care what he says about me.
zàijiā	在家	to be at home
zàilǐ	在理	to be reasonable/right/sensible
zài nǐ shēnshang	在你身上	to be on your body/to depend on you: 這件事能不能成功完全在你身上了。 *Zhèijiàn shì néngbuneng chénggōng wánquán zài nǐ shēnshang le.* It depends completely on you whether this matter will succeed or not.
zàishì	在世	to be alive: 我父母都還在世。 *Wǒ fùmǔ dōu hái zàishì.* My parents are both alive. [VO]
zài suǒ bùmiǎn	在所不免	to be unavoidable (one of those things)
zàitáo	在逃	to be at large [VO]
zàiwài	在外	to be away from home: 出門在外 *chūmén zài wài*; to be excluded: 小費在外。 *Xiǎofèi zàiwài.* Tips are not included.
zàiwàng	在望	to be within sight, within reach [VO]
zài wǒ kàn(lái)	在我看(來)	in my opinion: 在我看，肯定不行。 *Zài wǒ kàn, kěndìng bùxíng.* In my opinion, it is definitely unsatisfactory.
zàixiān	在先	to be first, formerly [VO]
zàiyě	在野	(of politicians) to be in opposition: 在野黨 *zàiyě dǎng*, opposition party [VO]
zàiyì	在意	to be careful, to be attentive, to mind [VO]
zàizhí	在職	to be in active service [VO]
búzàiyì	不在意	to be unconcerned: 你說了半天，他一點兒也不在意。 *Nǐ shuōle bàntiān, tā yìdiǎnr yě búzàiyì.* Although you talked for a long time, he didn't pay any attention to it.
móu shì zài rén, chéng shì zài tiān	謀事在人， 成事在天	Plan as one may, success depends on luck.

zàobàobiǎo	造報表	to compile report on funds expended [V–O]
zàochéng	造成	to create; to cause
zàofǎn	造反	to revolt, to rebel: 造反無罪 *Zàofǎn wúzuì*. To rebel is not a crime; (of children) to be noisy: 孩子造反了 *Háizi zàofǎnle*. The children are too noisy. [V–O]
zàofǎng	造訪	to pay a visit to [CC/V]
zàofú rénlèi	造福人類	to benefit the human beings
zàohuà	造化	fortune, blessings: 你的造化可不小。*Nǐde zàohuà kě bùxiǎo.* Your blessings are many.
zàojiù	造就	to help somebody to succeed in life: 造就人材 *zàojiù réncái*, to help train personnel [CC/V]; accomplishments
zàojù	造句	to make sentences [V–O]
zàolín	造林	to afforest [V–O]
zàoniè	造孽	to do evil, to do something detestable [V–O]
zàoyáo	造謠	to start a rumor [V]
zàoyì	造詣	to visit with, to call on [CC/V]; scholastic attainments: 王先生在數學方面的造詣很高。*Wáng Xiānsheng zài shùxué fāngmiàn de zàoyì hěn gāo.* Mr Wang's attainments in mathematics are very high.
zàozuì	造罪	to sin (against gods) [V–O]
chuàngzào	創造	to create [CC/V]
gǎizào	改造	to reform, to reshape, to remodel [CC/V]
jiànzào	建造	to construct [CC/V]
niēzào	捏造	to fabricate, to invent (stories, alibi) [CC/V]
rénzào sī	人造絲	artificial silk
wěizào	偽造	to falsify, to forge [SC/V]
xiūzào	修造	to repair [CC/V]
zhìzào	製造	to manufacture [CC/V]

zēngbīng	增兵	to reinforce, to send more troops [V O]
zēngchǎn	增產	to increase production [V-O]
zēngdà	增大	to enlarge, to swell [VC]
zēngduō	增多	to become more [VC]
zēngfáng	增防	to increase the defense: 敵人在哪兒增防? *Díren zài nǎr zēngfáng?* Where is the enemy increasing its defense? [V-O]
zēngguāng	增光	to add honor, luster: 你的前言給我的書增光不少。 *Nǐde qiányán gěi wǒde shū zēngguāng bùshǎo.* Your foreword adds much luster to my book. [V-O]
zēnghuī	增輝	to add luster, brightness of the presence of a person [VO]
zēngjiā	增加	to increase, to add to: 增加負擔 *zēngjiā fùdān*, to increase burden; 人口增加 *rénkǒu zēngjiā*, population increases [CC/V]
zēngjiǎn	增減	increase and decrease, fluctuation [CC/N]
zēngjìn	增進	to develop (skills, technical knowledge, etc.), to cultivate (friendship), to improve (relations, mutual understanding, etc.) [CC/V]
jiājù	加劇	to increase in severity: 病情加劇 *bìngqíng jiàjù*. The illness becomes more severe. [VO]
zēngqiáng	增強	to reinforce, to become stronger [VC]
zēngshān	增刪	to edit, to emendate: 編輯有增刪權 *Biānjí yǒu zēngshān quán.* The editor has the right to emendate. [CC/V]
zēngshōu	增收	to increase income [V]
zēngsǔn	增損	increase or decrease, fluctuation [CC/N]
zēngtiān	增添	= *zēngjiā* [CC/V]
zēngyí	增益	to add something to the original stock [VO]
zēngyuán	增援	to reinforce [V-O]
zēngzhǎng	增長	to grow, to increase: 增長知識 *zēngzhǎng zhīshi*, to increase knowledge [CC/V]
zēngzhí	增值	to increase in value: 土地增值稅 *tǔdì zēngzhí shuì*, land increment tax [V-O]

zhǎnbài	展拜	to kowtow [SC/V]
zhǎnchì	展翅	to open wings [V-O]
zhǎnhuǎn	展緩	to postpone [CC/V]
zhǎnjì	展技	to show one's skill [V-O]
zhǎn juàn yǒu yì	展卷有益	It is beneficial to read (open a book)
zhǎnkāi	展開	to open up [VC]
zhǎnlǎn	展覽	to exhibit, exhibition [CC/V, N]
zhǎnméi	展眉	to look pleasant [V-O]
zhǎnqī	展期	the exhibition period (展覽的時間) 展期延長了。 *Zhǎnqī yáncháng le.* The exhibition has been extended. [N]
zhǎnshì	展示	to exhibit, to show [V]
zhǎnsuō	展縮	flexibility [CC/N]
zhǎnwàng	展望	to look into the future; prospect, hope
zhǎnxiàn	展限	to extend time limit [VO]
zhǎnzhuǎn	展轉	to proceed amidst setbacks or by circuitous route; to wander aimlessly or restlessly [CC/V]
dà zhǎn hóng tú	大展鴻圖	to put one's talents to use
dà zhǎn shēn shǒu	大展身手	to show one's capabilities
fāzhǎn	發展	to develop: 發展中國家 *fāzhǎnzhōng guójiā*, developing countries [CC/V]; development: 這是一種新的發展。 *Zhè shi yìzhǒng xīnde fāzhǎn.* This is a new development.
jìnzhǎn	進展	to make progress: 沒甚麼進展 *Méi shénme jìnzhǎn.* There has not been any progress. [CC/V]
kāizhǎn	開展	to be open-minded [CC/SV]; to develop [V]

zhànbuzhù	站不住	cannot hold position: 這樣做下去是站不住的。 *Zhèyang zuòxiaqu shì zhànbúzhù de.* If this continues, (we) can't hold our position. [VC]
zhàndezhù jiǎo	站得住腳	to be able to stand on one's feet/to be tenable, convincing
zhànduì	站隊	to line up: 買東西得站隊，受不了。 *Mǎi dōngxi děi zhànduì, Shòubuliǎo.* One has to stand in line when buying things. It is unbearable. [V-O]
zhàngǎng	站崗	to stand guard at a post: 今天晚上輪誰站崗? *Jīntiān wǎnshàng lún shéi zhàngǎng?* Whose turn is it to stand guard tonight? [V-O]
zhànkāi	站開	to stand aside, to move on: 汽車來了，請站開點兒。 *Qìchē lái le. Qǐng zhànkāi diǎnr.* A car is coming. Please stand aside. [VC]
zhàntái	站臺	railway platform [SC/N]
zhànwěn	站穩	to stand firmly: 站穩，小心摔下來。 *Zhànwěn, xiǎoxīn shuāixiàlai.* Stand firmly. Be careful, you may fall. [VC]
zhànzhǎng	站長	stationmaster [SC/N]
zhànzhu	站住	to stand still; "Stop!" [VC]
búpà màn jiù pà zhàn	不怕慢就怕站	Don't be afraid of being slow, but fear standing still. 不怕慢，就怕站。每天多少做一點兒，總有做完的時候。 *Búpà màn jiù pà zhàn. Měitiān duōshǎo zuò yìdiǎnr, zǒng yǒu zuòwán de shíhòu.* Don't be afraid of being slow. If you do a little every day, one day you will finish.
chēzhàn	車站	railway or bus station [SC/N]
gōngyìngzhàn	供應站	supply station [SC/N]
jiāyóuzhàn	加油站	filling station [SC/N]
qǐdiǎnzhàn	起點站	start station [N]
zhōngdiǎnzhàn	終點站	last station [N]

zhāngdà	張大	to open wide: 張大嘴 *zhāngdà zuǐ*, to open mouth wider [RC]
zhāngdà qí cí	張大其詞	to exaggerate: 說話別張大其詞 *Shuōhuà bié zhāngdà qí cí*. When talking don't exaggerate.
zhāng dēng jié cǎi	張燈結彩	to hang up lanterns and silk festoons
zhānghuáng shī cuò	張皇失措	to be nervous, to lose mental control
zhāngkāi	張開	to open up or wide: 張開手臂 *zhāngkāi shǒu bì*, to open arms wide [VC]
zhāngkuáng	張狂	to be unruly, insolent [CC/SV]
zhāngkǒu	張口	to open mouth: 錢來伸手，飯來張口。 *Qián lái shēn shǒu, fàn lái zhāngkǒu*. When money comes, just extend your hands; when food comes, just open your mouth/to lead a very easy life. [V-O]
zhāng kǒu jié shé	張口結舌	tongue tied
zhāngluo	張羅	to try to get (money, etc.) [CC/V]
zhāngshè	張設	to set up (tables, decorations, etc.) for occasions [CC/V]
zhāngtiē	張貼	to post (bills): 不準張貼 *Bùzhǔn zhāngtiē*, Post no bills [CC/V]
zhāngwàng	張望	to look about or watch for (signs of enemy, etc.) [CC/V]
zhāngyáng	張揚	to make widely known: 這件事情別張揚出去。 *Zhèijiàn shì qing bié zhāngyángchuqu*. Please keep this matter to yourself. [CC/V]
zhāng yá wǔ zǎo	張牙舞爪	to show one's fangs and claws/ready to fight
zhāngzuǐ	張嘴	to open mouth, to speak up: 不好意思張嘴 *bùhǎoyìsi zhāngzuǐ*, to feel embarrassed to speak up [V-O]
kāizhāng	開張	to open (shop): 大開張 *dà kāizhāng*, grand opening [CC/V]
kuāzhāng	誇張	to boast [CC/V]
pūzhāng	鋪張	to embellish for showing off [CC/V]
xiāozhāng	囂張	to be unruly [CC/SV]
zhǔzhāng	主張	to advocate: 他主張男女平等。 *Tā zhǔzhāng nán nǚ píngděng.* He advocates that men and women should be equal. [CC/V]

zhǎobúzìzài	找不自在	to ask for trouble
zhǎochár	找碴兒	to pick quarrel: 別老是找我的碴兒。 *Bié lǎoshi zhǎo wǒde chár.* Don't pick quarrels with me all the time. [V-O]
zhǎochàzi	找岔子	to be fussy [V O]
zhǎo chūlù	找出路	to look for a way out or for a job with a future
zhǎocuòr	找錯兒	to find fault [VO]
zhǎofèngzi	找縫子	to look for a crack/to look for an opening for attack, to look for a pretext [VO]
zhǎomà	找罵	to ask for scolding: 好好做，免得找罵。 *Hǎohāo zuò, miǎnde zhǎomà.* Be careful with your work, or you will be asking for a scolding. [VO]
zhǎo máfan	找麻煩	to ask for unnecessary trouble: 你理他就是自找麻煩。 *Nǐ lǐ tā jiù shì zì zhǎo máfan.* Your bothering with him is to ask for unnecessary trouble for yourself.
zhǎo máobìng	找毛病	to find fault: 他專喜歡找人的毛病。 *Tā zhuān xǐhuan zhǎo rénde máobìng.* He particularly enjoys finding fault with people.
zhǎo ménlù	找門路	to look for approach to an important person.
zhǎo miànzi	找面子	to try to save face [V O]
zhǎo qián	找錢	to give change: 你給我找錢。 *Nǐ gěi wǒ zhǎo qián.* You give me change. 我找給你錢。 *Wǒ zhǎogei nǐ qián.* I give you change [VO]
zhǎo shìr	找事兒	to look for job; to look for trouble [V O]
zhǎosǐ	找死	to look for death (contemptuous remark): 你來找死。 *Nǐ lái zhǎosǐ.* This is your end (I warn you). [VO]
zhǎo tìshēn	找替身	to look for a substitute
zhǎotou	找頭	change due at a purchase
zhǎoxún	找尋	to search for, to look for [CC/V]
dōng zhǎo xī zhǎo	東找西找	to look for in all directions
yǒu shì zhǎo wǒ	有事找我	If anything happens, look for me (I shall be responsible).

zhuó (zhāo, zháo, zhe)
to send, to put on, to put one's hand on

著(着)

zhāohuāng	著慌	to become nervous, tense: *línshí zhāohuāng*, to become nervous at the last moment. [V-O]
zháohuǒ	著火	to catch fire [V-O]
zhāojí	著急	to become anxious, agitated: 為了孩子的事著急。 *wèile háizi de shì zhāojí*, to become agitated on account of children [V-O]
zhuóliáng	著凉	to catch cold
zhuólìng	著令	to order [CC/V]
zhuólù	著陸	to land
zhuóluò	著落	whereabouts: 著落不明 *Zhuóluò bùmíng.* Whereabouts are not known; settlement: 那件事還一點著落都沒有呢。 *Nèijian shì, hái yìdiǎnr zhuóluò dōu méiyou ne.* So far as that matter is concerned, there has not been any settlement. [CC/N]
zhuómí	著迷	to be fascinated
zhuó rén qù bàn	著人去辦	to send someone to do it: 那件事快著人去辦吧。 *Nèijiàn shì kuài zhuó rén qù bàn ba.* Send someone to do that right away, won't you?
zhuósè	著色	to apply color: 你的畫兒著色了沒有? *Nǐde huàr zhuósè le meiyou?* Have you applied color on your painting? [V-O]
zhuóshí	著實	really, in earnest: 這張畫著實畫得不錯。 *Zhèizhāng huà zhuóshí huàde búcuò.* This picture is really well done. [Adv]
zhuóshǒu	著手	to begin to (write, build, etc.): 我那本書還得著手寫呢。 *Wǒ nèiběn shū hái méi zhuóshǒu xiě ne.* I haven't started writing that book of mine yet. [VO]
zhuóxiǎng	著想	to consider; to think about
cāizháole	猜著了	to have guessed correctly [VC]
dǎzháo	打著	to succeed in hitting, to light (a match, lighter) [VC]
huǒ zháole	火著了	the fire begins to burn
qízhe lǘ xún lǘ	騎著驢尋驢	to find a donkey by riding one/before locating a new job, hold on to the present one.
shuìzháo	睡著	to fall asleep [VC]

zhàobàn	照辦	to do accordingly: 你吩咐下來，我們一定照辦。*Nǐ fēnfu xialai, wǒmen yídìng zhàobàn.* You tell us, and we will act accordingly. [CC/V]
zhàocháng	照常	as usual: 週末，商店照常營業 During the weekend, the store opens as usual. [VO/Adv]
zhàogu	照顧	to look after another's welfare, to attend to (patient, child, etc.) [CC/V]
zhàoguǎn	照管	to look after (house, children, etc.) [CC/V]
zhàohuì	照會	official communication, diplomatic note
zhàojìngzi	照鏡子	to look into the mirror [V-O]
zhàojiù	照舊	to be as before: 照舊有效 *zhàojiù yǒuxiào*, to be valid as usual [VO/Adv]
zhàokàn	照看	= 照顧 *zhàogu* [CC/V]
zhàolì	照例	according to precedence, regulations, etc.: 照例免費 *zhàolì miǎnfèi*, fees exempted according to regulations [VO/Adv]
zhàoliào	照料	to look after [CC/V]
zhàomiànr	照面兒	to meet face to face: 我跟他沒照個面兒就走了。*Wǒ gēn tā méizhào ge miànr jiù zǒu le.* I left without seeing him face to face. [V-O]
zhàopiàn	照片	a photograph [SC/N]
zhàoshè	照射	to project light upon, to illuminate [CC/V]
zhàoxiàng	照相	to photograph [V-O]; a photograph: 照相機 *zhàoxiàngjī*, camera
zhàoyàngr	照樣兒	to follow the pattern [V-O]; in the same manner [Adv]
zhàoyào	照耀	to illuminate, to shine in glory [CC/V]
zhàoyāojìng	照妖鏡	a mirror which reveals disguise of monster or demon
zhàoying	照應	to look after; to fit with (prophecy, original) [CC/V]
guānzhào	關照	to look after [CC/V]

zhēngbà	爭霸	to compete for hegemony among states [V-O]
zhēngbiàn	爭辯	to argue: 跟他爭辯了半天 *gēn tā zhēngbiànle bàntiān*, argued with him for a long time [CC/V]
zhēngchǎo	爭吵	to squabble, to quarrel [CC/V]
zhēngchí	爭持	to wrangle, to contend: 爭持不讓 *zhēngchí búràng*, to contend without yielding [CC/V]
zhēngduó	爭奪	to fight for possession (of land, power, woman, etc.) [CC/V]
zhēngdòu	爭鬥	to fight [CC/V]
zhēng fēng chī cù	爭風吃醋	fight for love, to quarrel for jealousy
zhēnggōng	爭功	to fight for recognition of merit [V-O]
zhēngguāng	爭光	to vie for honor: 替國家爭光 *tì guójiā zhēngguāng*, to win honor for the country [V O]
zhēnglùn	爭論	to argue [CC/V]; argument
zhēngmíng	爭名	to fight for fame [V-O]
zhēngqì	爭氣	to fight for emotional reasons, to be honor conscious: 這孩子真不爭氣。 *Zhè háizi zhēn buzhēngqì.* This child is really disappointing; 爭口氣 *zhēng kǒu qì*, to win some honor [V-O]
zhēngqiáng	爭強	to compete for supremacy [VO]
zhēngqǔ	爭取	to strive for, to fight for: 爭取最後勝利 *zhēngqǔ zuìhòu shènglì*, to fight for final victory; 爭取朋友 *zhēngqǔ péngyou*, to win friends [CC/V]
zhēng quán duó lì	爭權奪利	to struggle for power and money
zhēng xiān kǒng hòu	爭先恐後	in a mad rush to be first
zhēngzhí	爭執	= 爭持 *zhēngchí* [CC/V]
zhēngzuǐ	爭嘴	to bicker, to squabble [V-O]
dòuzhēng	鬥爭	to struggle [CC/V]; a struggle: 階級鬥爭 *jiējí dòuzhēng*, class struggle (PRC)
jìngzhēng	競爭	to compete, to contest [CC/V]; a competition, a contest

zhěngbiān	整編	to reorganize, to regroup (military) [CC/V]
zhěngdùn	整頓	to put to order, to restore to good shape: 整頓學風 *zhěngdùn xuéfēng*, to restore good order in the school [CC/V]
zhěngfēng	整風	to rectify atmosphere (of schools, party, etc.), to restore morale [VO]
zhěnggèr	整個兒	whole piece [SC/N]; completely: 整個兒垮了 *zhěnggèr kuǎle*, completely collapsed [Adv]
zhěngjié	整潔	to be clean and neat [CC/SV]
zhěnglǐ	整理	to put to order, to tidy up, to revise, to sort out (material for manuscript): 把材料整理一下寫篇文章 *bǎ cáiliao zhěnglǐ yixia xiě piān wénzhāng*. To sort out the material for writing an article. [CC/V]
zhěngqí	整齊	to be tidy, orderly, to be complete [CC/SV]; 整整齊齊 *zhěngzhengqíqi*, reduplication of 整齊 *zhěngqí*
zhěng rì zhěng yè	整日整夜	whole day and night
zhěngróng	整容	to do plastic surgery [V-O]
zhěngshù	整數	a whole number, integral [SC/N]
zhěngsù	整肅	to purge [CC/V]
xiū zhěng	修整	to repair and maintain: 修整犁耙 *xiū zhěng lí ba* to repair the plow
zhěngtǐ	整體	the whole [SC/N]
zhěngtiān	整天	the whole day: 整天玩兒，一點兒事也不做。*Zhěngtiān wánr, yìdiǎnr shì yě búzuò*, to play all day, don't do any work [SC/TW]
zhěngzhěng	整整	exactly: 整整十塊錢 *zhěngzhēng shíkuài qián*, exactly ten dollars [Adv]
zhěngzhì	整治	to put to order, to teach a lesson, to punish: 整治整治他 *zhěngzhìzhengzhi tā*, to teach him a lesson [CC/V]

zhīchǐ	知恥	to have a sense of shame or of honor:不知恥 *bùzhīchǐ*, to be shameless [VO]
zhī fǎ fàn fǎ	知法犯法	to flout the law deliberately
zhīgēnr	知根兒	to know the root/to be an expert [VO]
zhī guò gǎi guò	知過改過	to realize one's mistake and correct it
zhījǐ	知己	a bosom friend [VO/N]
zhī jǐ zhī běi	知己知彼	to know one's own and enemy's strength
zhījué	知覺	to perceive; perception [CC/V]
zhīmíng	知名	to be well-known [VO/SV]
zhī mìng zhī nián	知命之年	the year when one knows the decrees of Heaven fifty years of age
zhīqùr	知趣兒	to be tactful, to have a sense of the situation (know what is right for the situation): 那個人不知趣兒。 *Nèige ren bùzhīqùr.* That person is insensible. [VO/SV]
zhī rén zhī miàn bùzhī xīn	知人知面不知心	to know a man's exterior but not his heart
zhī rén zhī míng	知人之明	capacity to judge a person's qualities
zhīshi	知識	knowledge: 知識分子 *zhīshi fènzǐ*, intellectuals [CC/N]
zhīxīn huà	知心話	heart to heart talk: 他說的都是知心話。 *Tā shuōde dōu shi zhīxīn huà.* What he said are all heartfelt words.
zhīyīn	知音	a good understanding friend [VO/N]
zhīyǒu	知友	a bosom friend [SC/N]
zhī yù zhī ēn	知遇之恩	gratitude for a superior's recognition and encouragement
zhīzú	知足	to be contented: 知足常樂 *Zhī zú cháng lè.* One who is contented is always happy. [VO/SV]
wú suǒ bùzhī	無所不知	to know everything
yì wú suǒ zhī	一無所知	to know nothing
yì zhī bàn jiě	一知半解	to have superficial knowledge

zhǐbù	止步	don't go further: 請止步 *Qǐng zhǐbù*. Please don't go any further (used by a departing guest when a host is accompanying him to the door.) 遊人止步 *yóu rén zhǐbù*, visitors stop here/no admittance (sign in park) [V-O]
zhǐ tòng	止痛	to relieve pain: 甚麼藥止痛最有效? *Shénme yào zhǐ tòng zuì yǒuxiào?* What drug relieves pain most effectively? [V O]
zhǐtòngjì	止痛劑	pain reliever: 阿司匹林是最普通的止痛劑。*Asīpīlín shì zuì pǔtōngde zhǐtòngjì*. Aspirin is the most common pain reliever.
zhǐ xuě	止血	to stop bleeding [VO]
zhǐzhù	止住	stopped: 血止住了嗎? *Xuě zhǐzhùle ma?* Has the bleeding been stopped? 止住了。*Zhǐzhùle*. Yes, it has. [VC]
jiézhǐ	截止	to expire: 報名後天截止。*bàomíng hòutiān jiézhǐ*. Registration expires day after tomorrow. [CC/V]
jìnzhǐ	禁止	to forbid: 禁止抽煙 *jìnzhǐ chōuyān*, no smoking [CC/V]
liú ge bùzhǐ	流個不止	to flow without stopping
shì kě ér zhǐ	適可而止	not to overdo it: 凡事適可而止，不要做得太過份了。*Fán shì shì kě ér zhǐ, búyào zuòde tài guòfèn le*. For anything, play it just right. Don't overdo it too much.
wàng méi zhǐ kě	望梅止渴	to stoop the thirst by looking at the plums/wishful thinking
xīn rú zhǐ shuǐ	心如止水	mind as tranquil as still water/to refuse to be affected: 她心如止水，不管你怎麼挑逗也不會打動她的。*Tā xīn rú zhǐ shuǐ, bùguǎn nǐ zěnme tiǎodòu yě búhuì dǎdòng tā de*. Her mind is so tranquil that you simply can't arouse her no matter how hard you try.
xué wú zhǐ jìng	學無止境	There is no end to learning.
zhōngzhǐ	中止	to stop halfway [SC/V]
zǔzhǐ	阻止	to obstruct: 阻止前進 *zǔzhǐ qiánjìn*, to obstruct the advance [CC/V]

zhǐbiāo	指標	an index sign; (mathematics) characteristic [SC/N]
zhǐchì	指斥	to censure, blame [CC/V]
zhǐdǎo	指導	to guide, to advise: 指導教授 *zhǐdǎo jiàoshòu*, major professor (adviser) [CC/V]
zhǐdiǎn	指點	to point out (mistakes, pitfalls), to advise [CC/V]
zhǐdìng	指定	to assign (date, person, etc.): 主任指定誰就是誰。*Zhǔrèn zhǐdìng shéi jiù shi shéi.* The person will be whoever the chairman assigns. [CC/V]
zhǐhuà	指畫	finger painting [SC/N]; to gesticulate with fingers [CC/V]
zhǐhuī	指揮	to direct (a choir, a battle, etc.), to conduct (a performance), to command (army) [CC/V]
zhǐjiào	指教	to instruct, to advise, to offer suggestions for revision (used courteously for opinion): 請多多指教 *Qǐng duōduō zhǐjiào.* Please offer suggestions for improvement. [CC/V]
zhǐ jī mà gǒu	指雞罵狗	to point to the chicken while scolding the dog/ to scold one by ostensibly pointing to the other
zhǐmíng	指名	to mention names (in accusations): 指名責罵 *zhǐmíng zé mà*, to mention names in scolding [V-O]
zhǐnán	指南	a guide book [VO/N]
zhǐnánzhēn	指南針	a compass
zhǐ sāng mà huái	指桑罵槐	to point to the mulberry tree while scolding the locust tree/to scold one by ostensibly pointing to the other
zhǐshì	指示	to advise (inferior), to instruct [CC/V]
zhǐ shǒu huà jiǎo	指手畫腳	to gesticulate wildly
zhǐwàng	指望	to hope: 指望成功 *zhǐwàng chénggōng*, to look forward to success [CC/V]; hope: 有沒有點兒指望 *yǒu meiyou diǎnr zhǐwàng?* Is there any hope?
zhǐyǐn	指引	to guide: 指引你走上大路 *zhǐyǐn nǐ zǒushang dà lù*, to guide you to get on the highway [CC/V]; guidance
zhǐzé	指責	to scold; to blame (fault) [CC/V]
shí shǒu suǒ zhǐ	十手所指	that which ten hands point to/target of public accusation

zhìān	治安	public security: 這個地方的治安好不好? *Zhèige dìfangde zhìān hǎo buhao?* Is the public security here good? [CC/N]
zhìběn	治本	to effect basic reform, to give basic cure in medicine [V-O]
zhìbiāo	治標	to alleviate symptoms of disease or social ills without thorough cure [V-O]
zhìbìng	治病	to treat a patient [V-O]
zhìchǎn	治產	to manage property: 他這幾年置了不少產。 *Tā zhè jǐ nián zhìle bùshǎo chǎn.* These few years he has acquired quite a bit of property. [V-O]
zhìguó	治國	to rule a country [V-O]
zhìjiā	治家	to run a family [V-O]
zhìjīng	治經	to study classics [V-O]
zhìjūn	治軍	to train and command military forces [V-O]
zhìlǐ	治理	to rule, manage, put in order [CC/V]
zhìliáo	治療	to cure [CC/V]; a therapy: 精神治療 *jīngshen zhìliáo*, psychotherapy
zhìsāng	治喪	to manage, set up a funeral [V-O]
zhì wénxué	治文學	to do research on literature
zhìxué	治學	to study: 專心治學 *zhuānxīn zhìxué*, to concentrate on studies [VO]
zhìzhuāng	治裝	to buy clothing and other things for a journey: 治裝費 *zhìzhuāngfèi*, allowance for purchasing clothing, etc. for foreign assignment [V-O]
zhìzuì	治罪	to punish: 治他的罪 *zhì tāde zuì*, to punish him [V-O]
chǔzhì	處治	to dispose: 他的請求應當如何處治? *Tāde qǐngqiú yīngdāng rúhé chǔzhì?* How should his request be dealt with? to deal punishment to: *chǔzhì bùliáng shàonián*, to deal punishment to juvenile delinquents [CC/V]
tǒngzhì	統治	to rule (a country) [CC/V]
zìzhì	自治	self-governing, self-government; 地方自治 *dìfāng zìzhì*, local autonomy [SC/N]

zhìcái	制裁	to impose sanction on (aggressor), to bring under control: 制裁侵略者 *zhìcái qīnlüè zhě*, to impose sanction on aggressors [CC/V]; sanction: 法律制裁 *fǎlǜ zhìcái*, legal sanction
zhìdí	制敵	to subdue the enemy [VO]
zhìdìng	制定	to set up (rules, rites, etc.) [CC/V]
zhìfú	制伏	to subdue: 他力大如牛，很不容易制伏。*Tā lì dà rú niú, hěn bùróngyi zhìfú*. He is strong like a cow, not easy to subdue. [CC/V]
zhìshèng	制勝	to overcome, to come out victorious [VO]
zhìxiàn	制憲	to write, establish constitution [V-O]
zhìyù	制慾	to restrain the passions [VO]
zhìzhǐ	制止	to stop (riot, strike, etc.): 無理的罷工一定要制止。*Wúlǐde bàgōng yídìng yào zhìzhǐ*. Unreasonable strikes must be stopped. [CC/V]
zhìzuò	制作	creation (of art, music, etc.) [CC/N]
dǐzhì	抵制	to boycott: 抵制洋貨 *dǐzhì yánghuò*, to boycott foreign goods [CC/V]
guǎnzhì	管制	to control: 管制交通 *guǎnzhì jiāotōng*, to control traffic [CC/V]; control: 交通管制 *jiāotōng guǎnzhì*, traffic control
jiézhì	節制	to control: 節制生育 *jiézhì shēngyù*, to practice birth control [CC/V]
jìnzhì	禁制	to forbid, to prohibit [CC/V]
xiànzhì	限制	to limit: 限制行動 *xiànzhì xíngdòng*, to limit activities [CC/V]; limits, restrictions: 學校的限制太多。*Xuéxiàode xiànzhì tài duō*. The school has too many restrictions.
zhuānzhì	專制	to be tyrannical [SC/SV]
zìzhì	自制	self-restraint: 自制能力 *zìzhì nénglì*, ability to control oneself [SC/V]

zhùcí	助詞	(grammar) an auxiliary, grammatical particles [SC/N]
zhùchǎnshì	助產士	a midwife
zhùdòngcí	助動詞	(grammar) auxiliary verb
zhùjiào	助教	an assistant at college [SC/N]
zhùlǐ	助理	to assist [CC/V]; an assistant: 他是我的助理。*Tā shì wǒde zhùlǐ.* He is my assistant.
zhùrén	助人	to help others: 助人為快樂之本。*Zhùrén wéi kuàilè zhī běn.* To help others is the source of happiness. [VO]
zhùrénwéilè	助人為樂	to get pleasure from helping others
zhùshǒu	助手	an assistant [SC/N]
zhùtīngqì	助聽器	hearing aid [N]
zhùwēi	助威	to give oral or moral support [V-O]
zhùxìng	助興	to liven things up; to add to the fun [V]
zhùxuéjīn	助學金	scholarship
bá miáo zhù zhǎng	拔苗助長	to help a plant grow by pulling/wrong approach to do anything
bāngzhù	幫助	to help [CC/V]
bǔzhù	補助	to subsidize [CC/V]; subsidy
nèizhù	內助	inside help/wife [SC/N]
tiān zhù zì zhù	天助自助	Heaven helps those who help themselves
xiāngzhù	相助	to help each other [SC/V]
zīzhù	資助	to help with money: 資助他出國 *zīzhù tā chūguó*, to help him financially to go abroad
zìzhùcān	自助餐	self-help meal/buffer or cafeteria style meal

zhùbuxià	住不下	cannot accommodate: 屋子太小，住不下這麼多人。*Wūzi tài xiǎo, zhùbuxià zhème duō rén.* The room is too small to accommodate so many people. [VC]
zhùchù	住處	place where one lives [SC/N]
zhùhù	住戶	inhabitant, house [SC/N]
zhùjiā	住家	to stay at home, same as 住在家裏 *zhùzai jiāli*; [V-O]
zhùkôu	住口	stop mouth/shut up! [V-O]
zhùrén	住人	to accommodate people: 這個地方能住人嗎? *Zhèige dìfang néng zhùrén ma?* Is this place suitable for people to live in? [V-O]
zhùshǒu	住手	stop hand/stop! [V-O]
zhùsuǒ	住所	place where one lives (= 住處 *zhùchù*) [SC/N]
zhùxia	住下	to lodge: 天晚了，我們住下再說。*Tiān wǎn le. Wǒmen zhùxia zài shuō.* It is getting late. Let's lodge here and then talk about it [VC]
zhùxiào	住校	to live in a dormitory: 學生有的住家，有的住校。*Xuésheng yǒude zhùjiā, yǒude zhùxiào.* Some of the students stay home, some stay in the dormitory. [V-O]
zhùzái	住宅	residence, house [SC/N]
zhùzhǐ	住址	address (location of residence) [SC/N]
zhùzuǐ	住嘴	Shut up! (= 住口 *zhùkôu*) [V-O]
jūzhù	居住	to live: 你在哪兒居住? *Nǐ zài nǎr jūzhù?* Where do you live? [CC/V]
kàobuzhù	靠不住	to be unreliable: 他的話靠不住。*Tāde huà kàobúzhù.* His words are not reliable. [VC]
liúzhù	留住	to ask guest to stay longer: 他今天一定要走。我怎麼也留不住。*Tā jīntiān yídìng yào zǒu. Wǒ zěnme yě liúbúzhù.* He insists on leaving today. No matter what, I cannot get him to stay longer. [VC]
rěnzhù	忍住	to bear: 這種委屈，你要是忍得住就別告訴他。*Zhèizhǒng wěiqū, nǐ yàoshi rěndezhù jiù bié gàosu ta.* Concerning the grievance, if you can bear it, don't tell him. [VC]
zhūazhu	抓住	to hold fast: 魚太滑，我簡直抓不住。*Yú tài huá, wǒ jiǎnzhí zhuābúzhù.* The fish is too slippery; I simply cannot hold it.

zhuābiànzi	抓辮子	to capitalize on someone's vulnerable point = 抓小辮子 *zhuā xiǎo biànzi* [VO]
zhuā dàtóu	抓大頭	a game of picking lines leading to covered numbers (for pooling money), in which the 大頭 *dàtóu* pays more than others; to make a fool of someone: 別抓我的大頭。*Bié zhuā wǒde dàtóu.* Don't make a fool of me.
zhuājiūr	抓鬮兒	to draw lots [V-O]
zhuākōng	抓空	to fail in an attempt [V-O]
zhuā kuáng	抓狂	to be nuts; to get crazy
zhuāpò liǎn	抓破臉	to scratch the face so that it bleeds, (figuratively) don't care about the matter of face: 抓破了臉，甚麼都不在乎。*Zhuāpòle liǎn, shénme dōu búzàihu.* Without considering face, nothing matters.
zhuā rén	抓人	to arrest people: 警察進來抓了不少的人。*Jǐngchá jìnlai zhuāle bùshǎode rén.* The police arrested many people recently. [V O]
zhuā shēngchǎn	抓生產	to catch up with production (PRC)
zhuāxiā	抓瞎	to find oneself at a loss
zhuāyǎng	抓癢	to scratch an itchy spot [V-O]
zhuā yào	抓藥	to fill a prescription (particularly in a Chinese herb shop) [V O]
zhuāzhōur	抓週兒	to test a child on his first birthday by placing different things around him. The item he grabs will indicate his future. [V-O]
zhuāzhu jīhuì	抓住機會	to grab the opportunity

zhuǎnbiàn	轉變	to change: 轉變方向 zhuǎnbiàn fāngxiàng, to change direction [CC/V]; a change: 沒有甚麼轉變 Méiyou shénme zhuǎnbiàn. There is no change.
zhuǎndòng	轉動	to revolve (machine), to turn about (body) [SC/V]
zhuǎnhuán	轉圜	to go around, to save a situation by going about or speaking to someone: 這件事簡直沒有轉圜的余地。Zhèjian shì jiǎnzhí méiyou zhuǎnhuánde yúdì. About this matter, there is simply no way to do anything about it.
zhuǎnjī	轉機	a change for the better: 他的病有點兒轉機了。Tāde bìng yǒu diǎnr zhuǎnjī le. His condition (physical) shows some improvement.
zhuǎnlù	轉錄	to reprint [SC/V]
zhuǎnmài	轉賣	to resell to a third party [SC/V]
zhuǎnniànjiān	轉念間	in a short while, before you know it [Adv]
zhuǎnràng	轉讓	to sell out, to transfer [SC/V]
zhuǎnshēng	轉生	to be born in next incarnation (as dog, donkey, another human being, etc.) [SC/V]
zhuǎnshǒu	轉手	to change hands, to pass on to another [V-O]; in a moment: 他轉手就變卦了。Tā zhuǎnshǒu jiù biànguà le. He changes his mind so quickly. [Adv]
zhuǎnshùnjiān	轉瞬間	in the twinkling of an eye, quickly [Adv]
zhuǎntuō	轉託	to request through a third person [SC/V]
zhuǎnwān(r)	轉彎兒	to turn a corner, to make a turn, to drive around: 轉了一個大彎兒 zhuǎnle yíge dà wānr, to make a big round [V-O]
zhuǎnwānzi	轉彎子	to beat about the bush: 別轉彎子罵人 Bié zhuǎnwānzi mà rén. Don't make oblique remarks. [V-O]
zhuǎnxiàng	轉向	to change directions [V-O]
zhuǎnxué	轉學	to transfer to another school: 轉學生 zhuǎnxué shēng, transfer students (from 轉學的學生 zhuǎnxuéde xuésheng)
zhuǎnyǎn	轉眼	in the twinkling of an eye: 他轉眼就不見了。Tā zhuǎnyǎn jiù bújiàn le. In the twinkling of an eye; he is nowhere. [VO/Adv]
zhuǎnyí	轉移	to change, to shift: 轉移陣地 zhuǎnyí zhèndì, to shift battlefield [SC/V]

zhòngdà	重大	to be important, to be serious: 責任重大 *Zérèn zhòngdà*. The responsibility is great. [CC/SV]
zhòngdì	重地	place of strategic importance: 軍事重地，遊人止步 *Jūnshì zhòngdì, yóu rén zhǐ bù*. Place of military importance, please don't enter. [SC/N]
zhòngdiǎn	重點	important point: 說話要抓得住重點 *Shuōhuà yào zhuādezhù zhòngdiǎn*. To speak, one must be able to grasp the important points. [SC/N]
zhòngfàn	重犯	key criminal, a person convicted of grave crime [SC/N]
zhòng gōngyè	重工業	heavy industry
zhònglì	重力	gravitation [SC/N]
zhònglì	重利	to place value on money [VO/SV]; big profit [SC/N]
zhòngliàng	重量	weight, substance: 這篇東西有重量。*Zhèipiān dōngxi yǒu zhòngliàng*. This article has real substance. [SC/N]
zhòngmíng	重名	great reputation [SC/N]; to place value on reputation [VO]
zhòngshēnzi	重身子	to be pregnant: 她現在重身子出不了門。*Tā xiànzài zhòngshēnzi chūbuliǎo mén*. She is now pregnant, cannot go out. [SC/SV]
zhòngshì	重視	to value (friendship, money, etc.) [SC/SV]
zhòngtīng	重聽	to be hard of hearing [SC/SV]
zhòngtóu xì	重頭戲	an opera that is difficult to perform: 那是一出重頭戲。*Nà shì yìchū zhòngtóu xì*. That is an opera difficult to perform.
zhòngxiào	重孝	deep mourning for parents [SC/N]
zhòngxīn	重心	center for gravity [SC/N]
zhòngyā	重壓	heavy pressure [SC/N]
zhòngyào	重要	to be important [CC/SV]
zhòngyīn	重音	stress (of words) [SC/N]
zhòngzhèn	重鎮	important military base [SC/N]
zhòngzuì	重罪	a grave crime [SC/N]
zhēnzhòng	珍重	to take good care of one's health [CC/V]
zìzhòng	自重	to have self-respect [SC/V]

zhuāngbāo	裝包	to pack [V-O]
zhuāngbìng	裝病	to malinger [V-O]
zhuāngdìng	裝訂	to bind a book [CC/V]
zhuānghuáng	裝潢	to furnish and decorate [CC/V]; furniture and decorations, handsome book-binding: 這本書的裝潢不錯。*Zhèiběn shū de zhuānghuang hěn búcuò.* The binding of this book is really good.
zhuānghuǎngzi	裝幌子	to put up a false front, to put up a show to deceive [V-O]
zhuāngjiǎ	裝甲	to armor: 裝甲部隊 *zhuāngjiǎ bùduì*, armored unit [VO]
zhuāngjiǎ	裝假	to pretend: 他就喜歡裝假。誰知道他心裏想的是甚麼。*Tā jiù xǐhuan zhuāngjiǎ. Shéi zhīdao tā xīnli xiǎng de shi shénme.* He enjoys to pretend. Who knows what is in his mind. [V-O]
zhuānglǎo	裝老	to pretend to be old [V-O]
zhuāng ménmiàn	裝門面	to put up a front
zhuāngpèi	裝配	to provide with accessories, to decorate [CC/V]
zhuāngqiāng	裝腔	to affect certain airs: 裝腔作勢 *zhuāngqiāng zuòshì*, to assume airs of importance [V-O]
zhuāngshǎ	裝傻	to pretend to be stupid: 他心裏明白表面兒裝傻。*Tā xīnli míngbai biǎomiànr zhuāngshǎ.* He knows it but pretends to be ignorant. [V-O]
zhuāngshi	裝飾	to decorate [CC/V]; 裝飾品 *zhuāngshipǐn*, jewelry and ornaments
zhuāngshù	裝束	attire [CC/N]
zhuāngsuàn	裝蒜	to assume airs, to put up a false show: 他是水仙不開花，裝蒜。*Tā shi shuǐxiān bùkāihuā, zhuāngsuàn.* He is like an unblooming narcissus, pretending to be garlic/He is just putting up a false show. [V-O]
zhuāngxiāng	裝箱	to pack the box (for shipping) [V-O]
zhuāngxiū	裝修	to repair and install [CC/V]
zhuāngyùn	裝運	to transport, to ship [CC/V]
zhuāngzài	裝載	to load [CC/V]
zhuāngzhì	裝置	to arrange, to set up, to install: 裝置一個電話 *zhuāngzhì yíge diànhuà*, to install a telephone [CC/V]

zhuībǔ	追捕	to search and arrest (thief, deserter, etc.) [CC/V]
zhuīdào	追悼	to grieve for the dead: 追悼會 *zhuīdàohuì*, memorial service for the dead [CC/V]
zhuīdaoshǒu	追到手	to succeed in chasing (girl friend): 女朋友一追到手，他就不要了。*Nǚ péngyou yì zhuīdaoshǒu, tā jiù búyào le.* As soon as he wins a girl's heart, he will give her up.
zhuīgǎn	追趕	to chase after: 賊跑了，快點兒追趕。*Zéi pǎole, kuàidianr zhuīgǎn.* The theif ran away. Chase after him quickly. [CC/V]
zhuīhuán jiù zhài	追還舊債	to demand payment on old debt
zhuīhuí	追回	to recover (debt, lost property) [VC]
zhuīhuǐ	追悔	to regret [CC/V]
zhuījiā yùsuàn	追加預算	to pass addition to budget
zhuījiù	追究	to pursue investigation of origin, cause, sources of event, etc. [CC/V]
zhuīná	追拿	to pursue and apprehend: 追拿逃犯 *zhuīná táo fàn*, to pursue and apprehend a criminal at large [CC/V]
zhuīniàn	追念	to remember with fond regret [CC/V]
zhuīqiú	追求	to seek after (truth, progress, girl friend) [CC/V]
zhuīrèn	追認	to approve, admit retroactively [CC/V]
zhuīshang	追上	to catch up in chasing: 他跑得真快，居然能追上那條狗。*Tā pǎode zhēn kuài, jūrán néng zhuīshang nèitiáo gǒu.* He runs really fast, he can even catch up with that dog. [VC]
zhuīsuí	追隨	to follow (a leader, master): 他追隨我好多年了。*Tā zhuīsuí wǒ hǎoduō nián le.* He has followed me for many years. [CC/V]
zhuīwèn	追問	to cross-examine, to examine with thoroughness [CC/V]
zhuīxiǎng	追想	to think back (upon old days, etc.) [CC/V]
zhuīyì	追憶	to think back (past events) [CC/V]
zhuīzāng	追贓	to recover thief's booty [V-O]
zhuīzōng	追蹤	to follow in the steps of those who have gone before [V-O]

zǒudiào	走調	to be out of tune: 他唱走調了。 *Tā chàng zǒudiàole.*
zǒubukāi	走不開	to be unable to tear oneself away, to be too narrow to allow easy passage: 胡同太窄，汽車走不開。 *Hútong tài zhǎi, qìchē zǒubukāi.* The alley is too narrow for the car to go through. [VC]
zǒudòng	走動	to be able to walk: 他老得走不動了。 *Tā lǎode zǒubudòng le.* He is too old to walk. [VC]; to have social intercourse with friends: 他常到張家走動。 *Tā cháng dào Zhāngjiā zǒudòng.* He has social intercourse with the Zhangs; to take a stroll [CCV]
zǒugǒu	走狗	a running dog/a lacky [SC/N]
zǒuhóng	走紅	to have good luck, to be more popular [VO/SV]
zǒuhuǒ	走火	to have a short circuit, to fire accidentally [V-O]
zǒu jiānghú	走江湖	to go from place to place to stage show for a living (acrobats, magicians, singers, etc.)
zǒulòu	走漏	to leak out: 走漏風聲 *zǒulòu fēngsheng*, leak a secret [CC/V]
zǒulù	走路	to walk [VO]
zǒu mǎ kàn huā	走馬看花	to view the flowers on horseback/to go over things quickly
zǒusī	走私	to smuggle: 走私貨 *zǒusī huò*, smuggled goods [V-O]
zǒu xiédàor	走斜道兒	to approach through devious means; to patronize brothels
zǒuyàngr	走樣兒	to be out of shape, to fail to conform to the norm [V-O]
zǒuyùn	走運	to have luck: 他這幾年走好運。 *Tā zhèi jǐnián zǒu hǎoyùn.* He has had good luck in recent years; *zǒu bèiyùn*, to have bad luck [V-O]
zǒuzhe qiáo	走着瞧	Let's see that will happen later: 你現在先別得意。我們走着瞧。 *Nǐ xiànzài xiān bié déyì. Wǒmen zǒuzhe qiáo.* Don't you be so happy now. Let's see what will happen to you later.
zǒuzīpài	走資派	capitalist routers (PRC)

bānzǒu	搬走	to move away [VC]
zuòbān	坐班	to work in one's office during office time
zuòchán	坐禪	to sit in meditation
zuò dì fēn zāng	坐地分贓	to divide the booty on the spot
zuòfǎ	坐法	to be punished for crime [V-O]
zuògōng	坐功	(Taoism) the practice of sitting in silence to meditate [SC/N]
zuòjiāngshān	坐江山	to rule the country: 打江山難，坐江山更難 *dǎ jiāngshān nán, zuòjiāngshān gèng nán.*
zuòjìnbì	坐禁閉	to be placed in confinement as a disciplinary measure
dǎzuò	打坐	to sit quietly for meditation [V-O]
zuò jǐng guān tiān	坐井觀天	to see the sky by sitting in a well/to take a narrow view of things
zuòkè	坐客	a passenger on a boat, etc. [SC/N]
zuò lì bù ān	坐立不安	to feel uneasy, restless whether sitting or standing
zuò lěng bǎndèng	坐冷板凳	to sit on a cold stool/to be given the cold shoulder
zuò shī liáng jī	坐失良機	to let a golden opportunity slip by
zuò chī shān kōng	坐吃山空	to remain at home and eat away a whole future
zuòtáng	坐堂	to sit as a judge or magistrate [V-O]
zuòxí	坐席	to take seat at a banquet [V-O]
zuòyuèzǐ	坐月子	to be confined for a month after childbirth [VO]
zuòzhèn	坐鎮	to garrison (a city, area, etc.) [CC/V]
zuòzhuāng	坐莊	to be the banker in games of chance [V-O]

zuòbà	作罷	to dismiss as not worth further discussion or action: 這件事既然大家都沒有興趣就作罷。 *Zhèijiàn shì jìrán dàjiā dōu méiyou xìngqu jiù zuòbà.* Since nobody is interested in this matter, no further discussion is needed. [VO]
zuòbàn(r)	作伴(兒)	to serve as companion, to keep company: 誰給你作伴兒? *Shéi gěi nǐ zuòbànr?* Who keeps you company? [V-O]
zuòbǎo	作保	to be guarantor: 我給你作保。 *Wǒ gěi nǐ zuòbǎo.* I will be your guarantor. [V-O]
zuòbì	作弊	to practice irregularities (fraud), to cheat (in examinations, etc.): 作弊的人遲早會被人發現的。 *Zuòbìde rén chízǎo huì bèi rén fāxiàn de.* Those who cheat will be discovered sooner or later. [V-O]
zuòbié	作別	to bid goodbye [V-O]
zuòdǎi	作歹	to do evil [V-O]
zuòduì	作對	to set against, to be opposed to: 他跟我作對。 *Tā gēn wǒ zuòduì.* He is opposed to me. [V-O]
zuòfǎ	作法	method of making, doing things, course of action [SC/N]
zuòfēng	作風	way of doing things, manner in which one does things [SC/N]
zuòguài	作怪	to cause trouble, to play tricks, to act in a strange way: 他近來不知道在作甚麼怪。 *Tā jìnlai bùzhīdao zài zuò shénme guài.* Nobody knows what tricks he is playing lately. [V-O]
zuòhuó(r)	作活(兒)	to do work: 你這幾天作些甚麼活兒? *Nǐ zhèijǐtiān zuò xie shénme huór?* What kind of work have you been doing these few days? [V-O]
zuòkè	作客	to be a guest at a friend's; to travel in a foreign country [V-O]
zuònán	作難	to find oneself in a predicament, to be put on the spot [V-O]
zuòshēng	作聲	to break silence, to begin to speak: 你為甚麼不作聲呢? *Nǐ wèi shénme bú zuò shēng ne?* Why don't you say something? [V-O]
zuòzhǔ	作主	to make decision: 你們家誰作主? *Nǐmen jiā shéi zuòzhǔ?* Who makes the decisions in your family? [V-O]
dàngzuò	當作	to treat as: 把他當作好人看待 *bǎ ta dàngzuò hǎorén kàndài*, to treat him as a good person

zuòcài	做菜	to cook (dishes) [V O]
zuòdeliǎo	做得了	can be done: 那件事做得了 *Nèi jiàn shì zuòdeliǎo.* That matter can be done.
zuòdōng	做東	to be host, to pay the bill: 今天我做東。 *Jīntiān wǒ zuòdōng.* Today I am the host. [V-O]
zuò'è rén	做惡人	to act the part of a villain
zuòguān	做官	to be in an official position [V O]
zuòguǐr	做鬼兒	to play tricks, to practice irregularities [V-O]
zuò hǎorén	做好人	to act the part of a sympathizer
zuò hǎoshì	做好事	to do good deeds
zuòjiǎo	做脚	to serve to pass secret messages [V-O]
zuòkuò	做闊	to show off one's riches [V-O]
zuò liǎn(r)	做臉(兒)	to do something for the sake of appearance [V-O]
zuònòng	做弄	to manipulate for selfish ends, to take someone as a sucker: 做弄人 *zuònòng rén* [CC/V]
zuòmèng	做夢	to dream, to attempt something unpractical: 你簡直是做夢。 *Nǐ jiǎnzhí shì zuòmèng!* You are simply dreaming/You are attempting the impossible! [V-O]
zuòqīn	做親	to make marriage arrangements for one's child [V-O]
zuò rénqíng	做人情	to do someone a favor
zuò shēngrì	做生日	to hold a birthday party
zuòshòu	做壽	to give a birthday in honor of an elder [V-O]
zuò shǒujiǎo	做手脚	to resort to irregular practices, to make secret arrangements
zuòtou	做頭	expected results: 這件事沒甚麼做頭。 *Zhèijiàn shì méi shénme zuòtou.* You cannot expect any results from doing this.
zuòxiànren	做線人	to serve to pass secret messages [V-O]
zuòxiǎo	做小	to be someone's concubine [V-O]
zuòyǎnxiàn	做眼線	to gather information [V-O]
zuò zéi xīn xū	做賊心虛	to have a guilty conscience

APPENDIX I

CONVERSION FROM REGULAR TO SIMPLIFIED CHARACTERS

7笔

〔車〕车
〔夾〕夹
〔貝〕贝
〔見〕见
〔壯〕壮
〔妝〕妆

8笔

【一】

〔長〕长
〔亞〕亚
〔軋〕轧
〔東〕东
〔兩〕两
〔協〕协
〔來〕来
〔戔〕戋

【丨】

〔門〕门
〔岡〕冈

【丿】

〔侖〕仑
〔兒〕儿

【一】

〔狀〕状
〔糾〕纠

9笔

【一】

〔剋〕克
〔軌〕轨
〔庫〕库

〔頁〕页
〔郟〕郏
〔剄〕刭
〔勁〕劲

【丨】

〔貞〕贞
〔則〕则
〔閂〕闩
〔迴〕回

【丿】

〔俠〕侠
〔係〕系
〔鳧〕凫
〔帥〕帅
〔後〕后
〔釓〕钆
〔釔〕钇
〔負〕负
〔風〕风

【丶】

〔訂〕订
〔計〕计
〔訃〕讣
〔軍〕军
〔祇〕只

【一】

〔陣〕阵
〔韋〕韦
〔陝〕陕
〔陘〕陉
〔飛〕飞
〔紆〕纡
〔紅〕红
〔紂〕纣

〔紈〕纨
〔級〕级
〔約〕约
〔紇〕纥
〔紀〕纪
〔紉〕纫

10笔

【一】

〔馬〕马
〔挾〕挟
〔貢〕贡
〔華〕华
〔莢〕荚
〔莖〕茎
〔莧〕苋
〔莊〕庄
〔軒〕轩
〔連〕连
〔軔〕轫
〔劃〕划

【丨】

〔鬥〕斗
〔時〕时
〔畢〕毕
〔財〕财
〔盰〕眍
〔閃〕闪
〔唄〕呗
〔員〕员
〔豈〕岂
〔峽〕峡
〔峴〕岘
〔剛〕刚
〔剮〕剐

【丿】

〔氣〕气
〔郵〕邮
〔倀〕伥
〔倆〕俩
〔條〕条
〔們〕们
〔個〕个
〔倫〕伦
〔隻〕只
〔島〕岛
〔烏〕乌
〔師〕师
〔徑〕径
〔釘〕钉
〔針〕针
〔釗〕钊
〔釙〕钋
〔殺〕杀
〔倉〕仓
〔脅〕胁
〔狹〕狭
〔狽〕狈
〔芻〕刍

【丶】

〔訐〕讦
〔訌〕讧
〔討〕讨
〔訕〕讪
〔訖〕讫
〔訓〕训
〔這〕这
〔訊〕讯
〔記〕记

〔凍〕冻
〔畝〕亩
〔庫〕库
〔浹〕浃
〔涇〕泾

【一】

〔書〕书
〔陸〕陆
〔陳〕陈
〔孫〕孙
〔陰〕阴
〔務〕务
〔紜〕纭
〔純〕纯
〔紕〕纰
〔紗〕纱
〔納〕纳
〔紝〕纴
〔紛〕纷
〔紙〕纸
〔紋〕纹
〔紡〕纺
〔紖〕纼
〔紐〕纽
〔紓〕纾

11笔

【一】

〔責〕责
〔現〕现
〔匭〕匦
〔規〕规
〔殼〕壳
〔埡〕垭
〔掗〕挜

〔捨〕舍
〔捫〕扪
〔掆〕㧏
〔堝〕埚
〔頂〕顶
〔掄〕抡
〔執〕执
〔捲〕卷
〔掃〕扫
〔堊〕垩
〔萊〕莱
〔萵〕莴
〔幹〕干
〔梘〕枧
〔軛〕轭
〔斬〕斩
〔軟〕软
〔專〕专
〔區〕区
〔堅〕坚
〔帶〕带
〔廁〕厕
〔硃〕朱
〔麥〕麦
〔頃〕顷

【丨】

〔鹵〕卤
〔處〕处
〔敗〕败
〔販〕贩
〔貶〕贬
〔啞〕哑
〔閉〕闭
〔問〕问
〔婁〕娄
〔啢〕唡

〔國〕国
〔喎〕㖞
〔帳〕帐
〔崬〕崬
〔峽〕峡
〔崗〕岗
〔圇〕囵
〔過〕过

【丿】
〔氫〕氢
〔動〕动
〔偵〕侦
〔側〕侧
〔貨〕货
〔進〕进
〔梟〕枭
〔鳥〕鸟
〔偉〕伟
〔徠〕徕
〔術〕术
〔從〕从
〔鉈〕铊
〔釬〕釬
〔釧〕钏
〔釤〕钐
〔釣〕钓
〔釩〕钒
〔釹〕钕
〔釵〕钗
〔貪〕贪
〔覓〕觅
〔飥〕饦
〔貧〕贫
〔脛〕胫
〔魚〕鱼

【丶】
〔詎〕讵
〔訝〕讶
〔訥〕讷
〔許〕许
〔訛〕讹

〔訢〕䜣
〔訩〕讻
〔訟〕讼
〔設〕设
〔訪〕访
〔訣〕诀
〔產〕产
〔牽〕牵
〔烴〕烃
〔淶〕涞
〔淺〕浅
〔渦〕涡
〔淪〕沦
〔悵〕怅
〔啟〕启
〔視〕视

【一】
〔將〕将
〔晝〕昼
〔張〕张
〔階〕阶
〔陽〕阳
〔隊〕队
〔婭〕娅
〔媧〕娲
〔婦〕妇
〔習〕习
〔參〕参
〔紺〕绀
〔紲〕绁
〔綏〕绥
〔組〕组
〔紳〕绅
〔紬〕䌷
〔細〕细
〔終〕终
〔絆〕绊
〔紼〕绋
〔絀〕绌
〔紹〕绍

〔給〕给
〔貫〕贯
〔鄉〕乡

12 笔

【一】
〔貳〕贰
〔頇〕顸
〔堯〕尧
〔揀〕拣
〔馭〕驭
〔項〕项
〔賁〕贲
〔場〕场
〔揚〕扬
〔塊〕块
〔達〕达
〔報〕报
〔揮〕挥
〔壺〕壶
〔惡〕恶
〔葉〕叶
〔貫〕贯
〔萬〕万
〔葦〕苇
〔喪〕丧
〔葷〕荤
〔葒〕荭
〔葤〕荮
〔棖〕枨
〔棟〕栋
〔棧〕栈
〔棡〕㭎
〔極〕极
〔軲〕轱
〔軻〕轲
〔軸〕轴
〔軼〕轶
〔軫〕轸
〔軺〕轺
〔畫〕画

〔腎〕肾
〔棗〕枣
〔硨〕砗
〔硤〕硖
〔硯〕砚
〔殘〕残
〔雲〕云

【丨】
〔覘〕觇
〔睏〕困
〔貼〕贴
〔貺〕贶
〔貯〕贮
〔貽〕贻
〔閏〕闰
〔開〕开
〔閑〕闲
〔間〕间
〔閔〕闵
〔悶〕闷
〔貴〕贵
〔鄖〕郧
〔勛〕勋
〔單〕单
〔喲〕哟
〔買〕买
〔剴〕剀
〔凱〕凯
〔幀〕帧
〔嵐〕岚
〔幃〕帏
〔圍〕围

【丿】
〔無〕无
〔氬〕氩
〔喬〕乔
〔筆〕笔
〔備〕备
〔貸〕贷
〔順〕顺

〔傖〕伧
〔傯〕傯
〔傢〕家
〔鄔〕邬
〔眾〕众
〔復〕复
〔須〕须
〔鈃〕钘
〔鈣〕钙
〔鈈〕钚
〔鈦〕钛
〔鈑〕钣
〔鈍〕钝
〔鈔〕钞
〔鈉〕钠
〔鈴〕铃
〔欽〕钦
〔鈞〕钧
〔鈎〕钩
〔鈧〕钪
〔鈁〕钫
〔鈥〕钬
〔鈄〕钭
〔鈕〕钮
〔鈀〕钯
〔傘〕伞
〔爺〕爷
〔創〕创
〔飩〕饨
〔飪〕饪
〔飫〕饫
〔飭〕饬
〔飯〕饭
〔飲〕饮
〔為〕为
〔脹〕胀
〔腖〕胨
〔腡〕脶
〔勝〕胜
〔猶〕犹
〔貿〕贸
〔鄒〕邹

【丶】
〔詁〕诂
〔詞〕词
〔評〕评
〔詛〕诅
〔詗〕诇
〔詐〕诈
〔訴〕诉
〔診〕诊
〔詆〕诋
〔詞〕词
〔詘〕诎
〔詔〕诏
〔詒〕诒
〔馮〕冯
〔痙〕痉
〔勞〕劳
〔湞〕浈
〔測〕测
〔湯〕汤
〔淵〕渊
〔渢〕沨
〔渾〕浑
〔愜〕惬
〔惻〕恻
〔惲〕恽
〔惱〕恼
〔運〕运
〔補〕补
〔禍〕祸

【一】
〔尋〕寻
〔費〕费
〔違〕违
〔韌〕韧
〔隕〕陨
〔賀〕贺
〔發〕发
〔綁〕绑
〔絨〕绒
〔結〕结

〔綺〕绮
〔經〕经
〔絎〕绗
〔給〕给
〔絢〕绚
〔絳〕绛
〔絡〕络
〔絞〕绞
〔統〕统
〔絕〕绝
〔絲〕丝
〔幾〕几

13 笔

【一】

〔項〕项
〔琿〕珲
〔瑋〕玮
〔頑〕顽
〔載〕载
〔馱〕驮
〔馴〕驯
〔馳〕驰
〔塒〕埘
〔塤〕埙
〔損〕损
〔遠〕远
〔塏〕垲
〔勢〕势
〔搶〕抢
〔搗〕捣
〔塢〕坞
〔壺〕壶
〔聖〕圣
〔蓋〕盖
〔蓮〕莲
〔蒔〕莳
〔蓽〕荜
〔夢〕梦
〔蒼〕苍
〔幹〕干
〔蓀〕荪

〔蔭〕荫
〔蒓〕莼
〔楨〕桢
〔楊〕杨
〔嗇〕啬
〔楓〕枫
〔軾〕轼
〔輕〕轻
〔輅〕辂
〔較〕较
〔豎〕竖
〔賈〕贾
〔匯〕汇
〔電〕电
〔頓〕顿
〔盞〕盏

【丨】

〔歲〕岁
〔虜〕虏
〔業〕业
〔當〕当
〔睞〕睐
〔賊〕贼
〔賄〕贿
〔賂〕赂
〔賅〕赅
〔嗎〕吗
〔嘩〕哗
〔嗊〕唝
〔暘〕旸
〔閘〕闸
〔黽〕黾
〔暈〕晕
〔號〕号
〔園〕园
〔蛺〕蛱
〔蜆〕蚬
〔農〕农
〔嗩〕唢
〔嗶〕哔
〔鳴〕鸣

〔嗆〕呛
〔圓〕圆
〔骯〕肮

【丿】

〔筧〕笕
〔節〕节
〔與〕与
〔債〕债
〔僅〕仅
〔傳〕传
〔傴〕伛
〔傾〕倾
〔僂〕偻
〔賃〕赁
〔傷〕伤
〔傭〕佣
〔裊〕袅
〔頎〕颀
〔鈺〕钰
〔鉦〕钲
〔鉗〕钳
〔鈷〕钴
〔鉢〕钵
〔鉅〕钜
〔鈳〕钶
〔鈸〕钹
〔鉞〕钺
〔鉬〕钼
〔鉭〕钽
〔鉀〕钾
〔鈾〕铀
〔鈿〕钿
〔鉑〕铂
〔鈴〕铃
〔鉛〕铅
〔鉚〕铆
〔鈰〕铈
〔鉉〕铉
〔鉈〕铊
〔鉍〕铋
〔鈮〕铌

〔鈹〕铍
〔斂〕敛
〔會〕会
〔亂〕乱
〔愛〕爱
〔飾〕饰
〔飽〕饱
〔飼〕饲
〔飴〕饴
〔頒〕颁
〔頌〕颂
〔腸〕肠
〔腫〕肿
〔腦〕脑
〔魛〕鱽
〔像〕象
〔獁〕犸
〔鳩〕鸠
〔獅〕狮
〔猻〕狲

【丶】

〔誆〕诓
〔誄〕诔
〔試〕试
〔詿〕诖
〔詩〕诗
〔詰〕诘
〔誇〕夸
〔詼〕诙
〔誠〕诚
〔誅〕诛
〔話〕话
〔誕〕诞
〔詬〕诟
〔詮〕诠
〔詭〕诡
〔詢〕询
〔詣〕诣
〔靜〕净
〔該〕该

〔詳〕详
〔詫〕诧
〔詡〕诩
〔裏〕里
〔準〕准
〔頏〕颃
〔資〕资
〔羥〕羟
〔義〕义
〔煉〕炼
〔煩〕烦
〔煬〕炀
〔塋〕茔
〔熒〕荧
〔煒〕炜
〔遞〕递
〔溝〕沟
〔漣〕涟
〔滅〕灭
〔湞〕浈
〔滌〕涤
〔溮〕浉
〔塗〕涂
〔滄〕沧
〔愷〕恺
〔愾〕忾
〔愴〕怆
〔惻〕恻
〔窩〕窝
〔禎〕祯
〔禕〕祎

【一】

〔肅〕肃
〔裝〕装
〔遜〕逊
〔際〕际
〔媽〕妈
〔預〕预
〔疊〕迭
〔綆〕绠
〔經〕经

〔綃〕绡
〔絹〕绢
〔綉〕绣
〔綏〕绥
〔綈〕绨
〔彙〕汇

14 笔

【一】

〔瑪〕玛
〔璉〕琏
〔瑣〕琐
〔駁〕驳
〔摶〕抟
〔摳〕抠
〔趙〕赵
〔趕〕赶
〔摟〕搂
〔摑〕掴
〔臺〕台
〔撾〕挝
〔墊〕垫
〔壽〕寿
〔摺〕折
〔摻〕掺
〔摜〕掼
〔勩〕勚
〔蔞〕蒌
〔蔦〕茑
〔蓯〕苁
〔蔔〕卜
〔蔣〕蒋
〔薌〕芗
〔構〕构
〔樺〕桦
〔榿〕桤
〔覡〕觋
〔槍〕枪
〔輒〕辄
〔輔〕辅
〔輕〕轻

〔塹〕堑
〔匱〕匮
〔監〕监
〔緊〕紧
〔厲〕厉
〔厭〕厌
〔碩〕硕
〔碭〕砀
〔碸〕砜
〔奩〕奁
〔爾〕尔
〔奪〕夺
〔殞〕殒
〔鳶〕鸢
〔巰〕巯

【丨】

〔對〕对
〔幣〕币
〔彆〕别
〔嘗〕尝
〔嘖〕啧
〔曄〕晔
〔夥〕伙
〔賑〕赈
〔賒〕赊
〔嘆〕叹
〔暢〕畅
〔嗩〕唢
〔閨〕闺
〔聞〕闻
〔閩〕闽
〔閭〕闾
〔閥〕阀
〔閤〕合
〔閣〕阁
〔閡〕阂
〔閱〕阅
〔嘔〕呕
〔蝸〕蜗
〔團〕团
〔嘍〕喽

〔鄲〕郸
〔鳴〕鸣
〔幘〕帻
〔嶄〕崭
〔嶇〕岖
〔罰〕罚
〔嶁〕嵝
〔幗〕帼
〔圖〕图

【丿】

〔製〕制
〔種〕种
〔稱〕称
〔箋〕笺
〔僥〕侥
〔債〕债
〔僕〕仆
〔僑〕侨
〔偽〕伪
〔銜〕衔
〔釧〕钏
〔銬〕铐
〔銠〕铑
〔鉺〕铒
〔鋩〕铓
〔鋁〕铝
〔銅〕铜
〔錦〕锦
〔錮〕锢
〔銖〕铢
〔銑〕铣
〔銛〕铦
〔鋌〕铤
〔銓〕铨
〔鉿〕铪
〔銚〕铫
〔銘〕铭
〔鉻〕铬
〔錚〕铮
〔銫〕铯

〔鉸〕铰
〔銥〕铱
〔銃〕铳
〔銨〕铵
〔銀〕银
〔鉶〕铏
〔餞〕饯
〔餌〕饵
〔蝕〕蚀
〔餉〕饷
〔餄〕饸
〔餎〕饹
〔餃〕饺
〔餅〕饼
〔領〕领
〔鳳〕凤
〔颱〕台
〔獄〕狱

【丶】

〔誠〕诚
〔誣〕诬
〔語〕语
〔誚〕诮
〔誤〕误
〔誥〕诰
〔誘〕诱
〔誨〕诲
〔誑〕诳
〔說〕说
〔認〕认
〔誦〕诵
〔誒〕诶
〔廣〕广
〔麼〕么
〔廎〕庼
〔瘧〕疟
〔瘍〕疡
〔瘋〕疯
〔塵〕尘
〔颯〕飒

〔適〕适
〔齊〕齐
〔養〕养
〔鄰〕邻
〔鄭〕郑
〔燁〕烨
〔熗〕炝
〔榮〕荣
〔滎〕荥
〔犖〕荦
〔熒〕荧
〔潰〕溃
〔漢〕汉
〔滿〕满
〔漸〕渐
〔漚〕沤
〔滯〕滞
〔滷〕卤
〔漊〕溇
〔漁〕渔
〔滸〕浒
〔滻〕浐
〔滬〕沪
〔漲〕涨
〔滲〕渗
〔慚〕惭
〔慪〕怄
〔慳〕悭
〔慟〕恸
〔慘〕惨
〔慣〕惯
〔寬〕宽
〔賓〕宾
〔窪〕洼
〔寧〕宁
〔寢〕寝
〔實〕实
〔皸〕皲
〔複〕复

【一】

〔劃〕划

〔盡〕尽
〔屢〕屡
〔獎〕奖
〔墮〕堕
〔隨〕随
〔韍〕韨
〔墜〕坠
〔嫗〕妪
〔頗〕颇
〔態〕态
〔鄧〕邓
〔緒〕绪
〔綾〕绫
〔綺〕绮
〔綫〕线
〔緋〕绯
〔綽〕绰
〔緄〕绲
〔綱〕纲
〔網〕网
〔維〕维
〔綿〕绵
〔綸〕纶
〔綬〕绶
〔綳〕绷
〔綢〕绸
〔綹〕绺
〔綣〕绻
〔綜〕综
〔綻〕绽
〔綰〕绾
〔綠〕绿
〔綴〕缀
〔緇〕缁

15 笔

【一】

〔鬧〕闹
〔璡〕琎
〔靚〕靓
〔輦〕辇
〔髮〕发

〔撓〕挠
〔墳〕坟
〔撻〕挞
〔駔〕驵
〔駛〕驶
〔駙〕驸
〔駒〕驹
〔駐〕驻
〔駝〕驼
〔駘〕骀
〔撲〕扑
〔頡〕颉
〔撣〕掸
〔賣〕卖
〔撫〕抚
〔撟〕挢
〔撳〕揿
〔熱〕热
〔鞏〕巩
〔摯〕挚
〔撈〕捞
〔穀〕谷
〔慤〕悫
〔㩳〕㧐
〔撥〕拨
〔蕘〕荛
〔蕆〕蒇
〔蕓〕芸
〔邁〕迈
〔蕒〕荬
〔蕢〕蒉
〔蕪〕芜
〔蕎〕荞
〔蕕〕莸
〔蕩〕荡
〔蕁〕荨
〔樁〕桩
〔樞〕枢
〔標〕标
〔樓〕楼
〔樅〕枞

〔麩〕麸
〔賁〕贲
〔橢〕椭
〔輛〕辆
〔輥〕辊
〔輞〕辋
〔槧〕椠
〔暫〕暂
〔輪〕轮
〔輟〕缀
〔輜〕辎
〔甌〕瓯
〔歐〕欧
〔毆〕殴
〔賢〕贤
〔遷〕迁
〔鴇〕鸨
〔憂〕忧
〔碼〕码
〔磖〕硆
〔確〕确
〔賚〕赉
〔遼〕辽
〔殤〕殇
〔鴉〕鸦

【丨】

〔輩〕辈
〔劌〕刿
〔齒〕齿
〔劇〕剧
〔膚〕肤
〔慮〕虑
〔鄲〕郸
〔輝〕辉
〔賞〕赏
〔賦〕赋
〔腈〕腈
〔賬〕账
〔賭〕赌
〔賤〕贱

〔賜〕赐
〔賙〕赒
〔賠〕赔
〔賧〕赕
〔嘵〕哓
〔噴〕喷
〔嘩〕哒
〔噁〕恶
〔闈〕闱
〔闉〕阓
〔閱〕阅
〔闋〕阆
〔數〕数
〔踐〕践
〔遺〕遗
〔蝦〕虾
〔嘸〕呒
〔嘮〕唠
〔噝〕咝
〔嘰〕叽
〔嶢〕峣
〔罷〕罢
〔嶠〕峤
〔嶔〕嵚
〔幟〕帜
〔嶗〕崂

【丿】

〔頲〕颋
〔篋〕箧
〔範〕范
〔價〕价
〔儂〕侬
〔儉〕俭
〔儈〕侩
〔億〕亿
〔儀〕仪
〔皚〕皑
〔樂〕乐
〔質〕质
〔徵〕征
〔衝〕冲

〔慫〕怂
〔徹〕彻
〔衛〕卫
〔盤〕盘
〔鋪〕铺
〔鋏〕铗
〔鋱〕铽
〔銷〕销
〔鋥〕锃
〔鋰〕锂
〔鋇〕钡
〔鋤〕锄
〔鋯〕锆
〔鋨〕锇
〔銹〕锈
〔銼〕锉
〔鋒〕锋
〔鋅〕锌
〔銳〕锐
〔銻〕锑
〔銀〕铔
〔鋟〕锓
〔鋼〕钢
〔鋦〕锔
〔頜〕颌
〔劍〕剑
〔劊〕刽
〔鄶〕郐
〔餑〕饽
〔餓〕饿
〔餘〕余
〔餒〕馁
〔膞〕膞
〔膕〕腘
〔膠〕胶
〔鴇〕鸹
〔魷〕鱿
〔魯〕鲁
〔魴〕鲂
〔潁〕颍
〔颳〕刮
〔劉〕刘

〔皺〕皱

【丶】

〔請〕请
〔諸〕诸
〔諏〕诹
〔諾〕诺
〔諑〕诼
〔誹〕诽
〔課〕课
〔諉〕诿
〔諛〕诿
〔誰〕谁
〔論〕论
〔諗〕谂
〔調〕调
〔諂〕谄
〔諒〕谅
〔諄〕谆
〔誶〕谇
〔談〕谈
〔誼〕谊
〔廟〕庙
〔廠〕厂
〔廡〕庑
〔瘞〕瘗
〔瘡〕疮
〔賡〕赓
〔慶〕庆
〔廢〕废
〔敵〕敌
〔頦〕颏
〔導〕导
〔瑩〕莹
〔潔〕洁
〔澆〕浇
〔潼〕汰
〔潤〕润
〔澗〕涧
〔潰〕溃
〔潿〕涠
〔漘〕浐

〔潙〕沩
〔澇〕涝
〔潯〕浔
〔潑〕泼
〔憤〕愤
〔憫〕悯
〔憒〕愦
〔憚〕惮
〔憮〕怃
〔憐〕怜
〔寫〕写
〔審〕审
〔窮〕穷
〔褳〕裢
〔褲〕裤
〔鳩〕鸠

【一】

〔遲〕迟
〔層〕层
〔彈〕弹
〔選〕选
〔槳〕桨
〔漿〕浆
〔險〕险
〔嬈〕娆
〔嫻〕娴
〔駕〕驾
〔嬋〕婵
〔嫵〕妩
〔嬌〕娇
〔嫿〕妫
〔嫒〕媛
〔驚〕惊
〔翬〕翚
〔鮊〕鲅
〔緙〕缂
〔緗〕缃
〔練〕练
〔緘〕缄
〔緬〕缅
〔緹〕缇

〔潣〕沩
〔澇〕涝
〔緲〕缈
〔緝〕缉
〔縕〕缊
〔緦〕缌
〔緞〕缎
〔緱〕缑
〔縋〕缒
〔緩〕缓
〔締〕缔
〔編〕编
〔緡〕缗
〔緯〕纬
〔緣〕缘

16笔
【一】

〔璣〕玑
〔墻〕墙
〔駱〕骆
〔駭〕骇
〔擁〕扤
〔駢〕骈
〔擄〕掳
〔擋〕挡
〔擇〕择
〔赬〕赪
〔撿〕捡
〔擔〕担
〔壇〕坛
〔擁〕拥
〔據〕据
〔薔〕蔷
〔薑〕姜
〔薈〕荟
〔薊〕蓟
〔薦〕存
〔蕭〕萧
〔頤〕颐
〔鴣〕鸪
〔薩〕萨
〔蕷〕蓣
〔橈〕桡

[樹] 树	[噸] 吨
[樸] 朴	[鴞] 鸮
[橋] 桥	[噦] 哕
[機] 机	[踴] 踊
[輳] 辏	[螞] 蚂
[輻] 辐	[螄] 蛳
[輯] 辑	[噹] 当
[輸] 输	[罵] 骂
[賴] 赖	[噥] 哝
[頭] 头	[戰] 战
[醞] 酝	[噲] 哙
[醜] 丑	[鴦] 鸯
[勵] 励	[噯] 嗳
[磧] 碛	[嘯] 啸
[磚] 砖	[還] 还
[磣] 碜	[嶧] 峄
[歷] 历	[嶼] 屿
[曆] 历	

【丿】

[奮] 奋	[積] 积
[頰] 颊	[頹] 颓
[殨] 㱮	[穆] 穆
[殫] 殚	[篤] 笃
[頸] 颈	[築] 筑

【丨】

[頻] 频	[篳] 筚
[盧] 卢	[篩] 筛
[曉] 晓	[舉] 举
[瞞] 瞒	[興] 兴
[縣] 县	[嶨] 峃
[瞘] 眍	[學] 学
[瞜] 䁖	[儔] 俦
[賵] 赗	[憊] 惫
[鴨] 鸭	[儕] 侪
[閾] 阈	[儐] 傧
[閫] 阃	[儘] 尽
[鬮] 阄	[鴕] 鸵
[閲] 阅	[艙] 舱
[閹] 阉	[錶] 表
[閻] 阎	[鍺] 锗
[閼] 阏	[錯] 错
[曇] 昙	[鍩] 锘
	[錨] 锚

[錛] 锛	[鮐] 鲐
[錸] 铼	[鴣] 鸪
[錢] 钱	[獲] 获
[鍀] 锝	[穎] 颖
[錁] 锞	[獨] 独
[錕] 锟	[獫] 猃
[錇] 锎	[獪] 狯
[錫] 锡	[鴛] 鸳
[錮] 锢	

【丶】

[鋼] 钢	[謀] 谋
[鍋] 锅	[諶] 谌
[錘] 锤	[諜] 谍
[錐] 锥	[謊] 谎
[錦] 锦	[諫] 谏
[鍁] 锨	[諧] 谐
[鋯] 锆	[謔] 谑
[錠] 锭	[謁] 谒
[鍵] 键	[謂] 谓
[錄] 录	[諤] 谔
[鋸] 锯	[諭] 谕
[錳] 锰	[諼] 谖
[錙] 锱	[諷] 讽
[艦] 舰	[諮] 谘
[墾] 垦	[諳] 谙
[餞] 饯	[諺] 谚
[餜] 馃	[諦] 谛
[餛] 馄	[謎] 谜
[餡] 馅	[諢] 诨
[館] 馆	[諞] 谝
[鴒] 鸰	[諱] 讳
[膩] 腻	[諝] 谞
[鴟] 鸱	[憑] 凭
[鮁] 鲅	[廩] 廪
[鮃] 鲆	[瘻] 瘘
[鮎] 鲇	[瘮] 瘆
[鮓] 鲊	[瘥] 瘥
[穌] 稣	[親] 亲
[鮒] 鲋	[辦] 办
[卿] 卿	[龍] 龙
[鮑] 鲍	[劑] 剂
[鮍] 鲏	[燒] 烧
	[燜] 焖

[熾] 炽	**17 笔**
[螢] 萤	
[營] 营	【一】
[縈] 萦	[樓] 楼
[燈] 灯	[環] 环
[濛] 蒙	[贅] 赘
[燙] 烫	[璦] 瑷
[澠] 渑	[覯] 觏
[濃] 浓	[黿] 鼋
[澤] 泽	[幫] 帮
[濁] 浊	[騁] 骋
[澮] 浍	[駸] 骎
[澱] 淀	[駿] 骏
[懞] 蒙	[趨] 趋
[憚] 惮	[擱] 搁
[憶] 忆	[擬] 拟
[憲] 宪	[擴] 扩
[窺] 窥	[壙] 圹
[窶] 窭	[擠] 挤
[窩] 窝	[蟄] 蛰
[褸] 褛	[縶] 絷
[禪] 禅	[擲] 掷

【一】

[隱] 隐	[擯] 摈
[嬙] 嫱	[擰] 拧
[嬡] 嫒	[轂] 毂
[縉] 缙	[聲] 声
[縝] 缜	[藉] 借
[縛] 缚	[聰] 聪
[縟] 缛	[聯] 联
[緻] 致	[艱] 艰
[縧] 绦	[藍] 蓝
[縫] 缝	[舊] 旧
[縐] 绉	[薺] 荠
[繯] 缳	[藎] 荩
[縞] 缟	[韓] 韩
[縭] 缡	[隸] 隶
[縑] 缣	[檉] 柽
[縊] 缢	[檣] 樯
	[檟] 槚
	[檔] 档
	[櫛] 栉
	[檢] 检

〔檜〕桧	〔嚀〕咛	〔餳〕饧	〔鰲〕鳌		**18笔**	〔轆〕辘	
〔麯〕曲	〔嶺〕岭	〔餶〕饹	〔鷔〕鳌			〔覆〕复	
〔轅〕辕	〔嶺〕岭	〔鍛〕锻	〔糞〕粪		**【一】**	〔醫〕医	
〔轄〕辖	〔嵷〕嵘	〔餿〕馊	〔糝〕糁		〔鬆〕鬆	〔礎〕础	
〔輾〕辗	〔點〕点	〔斂〕敛	〔燦〕灿		〔鬪〕阅	〔殯〕殡	
〔擊〕击		〔鴿〕鸽	〔燭〕烛		〔瓊〕琼	〔霧〕雾	
〔臨〕临	**【丿】**	〔膿〕脓	〔燴〕烩		〔擡〕抬		
〔磽〕硗	〔矯〕矫	〔臉〕脸	〔鴻〕鸿		〔鬆〕松	**【丨】**	
〔壓〕压	〔鵠〕鹄	〔膾〕脍	〔濤〕涛		〔翹〕翘	〔豐〕丰	
〔礄〕硚	〔簀〕箦	〔膽〕胆	〔濫〕滥		〔擷〕撷	〔覷〕觑	
〔磯〕矶	〔篓〕篓	〔膳〕眷	〔濕〕湿		〔擾〕扰	〔懟〕怼	
〔鵃〕鸼	〔輿〕舆	〔鮭〕鲑	〔濟〕济		〔騏〕骐	〔叢〕丛	
〔邇〕迩	〔欼〕欤	〔鮚〕鲒	〔濱〕滨		〔騎〕骑	〔矇〕蒙	
〔尷〕尴	〔鵂〕鸺	〔鮪〕鲔	〔濘〕泞		〔騍〕骒	〔題〕题	
〔鵃〕鸯	〔龜〕龟	〔鮦〕鲖	〔濜〕浕		〔騅〕骓	〔韙〕韪	
〔殮〕殓	〔優〕优	〔鮫〕鲛	〔澀〕涩		〔據〕据	〔臉〕睑	
	〔償〕偿	〔鮮〕鲜	〔濰〕潍		〔擻〕擞	〔闖〕闯	
【丨】	〔儲〕储	〔颮〕飐	〔懨〕恹		〔甕〕冬	〔闔〕阖	
〔齔〕龀	〔魎〕魉	〔獷〕犷	〔賽〕赛		〔擺〕摆	〔闐〕阗	
〔戲〕戏	〔鵃〕鸻	〔獰〕狞	〔襇〕裥		〔贅〕赘	〔闓〕闿	
〔虧〕亏	〔禦〕御		〔禩〕禩		〔燾〕焘	〔闞〕阚	
〔斃〕毙	〔聳〕耸	**【丶】**	〔襖〕袄		〔聶〕聂	〔顓〕颛	
〔瞭〕了	〔鵃〕鹇	〔講〕讲	〔禮〕礼		〔職〕职	〔曠〕旷	
〔顆〕颗	〔鍥〕锲	〔謨〕谟			〔藝〕艺	〔蹣〕蹒	
〔購〕购	〔鐯〕锗	〔謖〕谡	**【一】**		〔覲〕觐	〔嚙〕啮	
〔賻〕赙	〔鍘〕铡	〔謝〕谢	〔屨〕屦		〔鞦〕秋	〔壘〕垒	
〔嬰〕婴	〔錫〕锡	〔謠〕谣	〔彌〕弥		〔藪〕薮	〔蟯〕蛲	
〔賺〕赚	〔鍶〕锶	〔謅〕诌	〔嬪〕嫔		〔蠆〕虿	〔蟲〕虫	
〔嚇〕吓	〔鍔〕锷	〔謗〕谤	〔績〕绩		〔繭〕茧	〔蟬〕蝉	
〔闌〕阑	〔錘〕锤	〔謚〕谥	〔縹〕缥		〔藥〕药	〔蟣〕虮	
〔闃〕阒	〔鐘〕钟	〔謙〕谦	〔縷〕缕		〔藭〕劳	〔鵑〕鹃	
〔闆〕板	〔鍛〕锻	〔謐〕谧	〔縵〕缦		〔躕〕蹰	〔嚕〕噜	
〔闊〕阔	〔鍍〕镀	〔褻〕亵	〔繆〕缪		〔蘊〕蕴	〔顒〕颙	
〔闈〕闱	〔鍬〕锹	〔氈〕毡	〔總〕总		〔檯〕台		
〔闋〕阕	〔鍰〕锾	〔應〕应	〔縱〕纵		〔櫃〕柜	**【丿】**	
〔曖〕暧	〔鎄〕锿	〔癘〕疬	〔縴〕纤		〔檻〕槛	〔鵠〕鹄	
〔蹕〕跸	〔鍍〕镀	〔療〕疗	〔縮〕缩		〔檸〕桐	〔鵝〕鹅	
〔蹌〕跄	〔鎂〕镁	〔癇〕痫	〔繅〕缫		〔檳〕槟	〔穫〕获	
〔蟎〕螨	〔鎇〕镅	〔癉〕瘅	〔繚〕缭		〔檸〕柠	〔穡〕穑	
〔螻〕蝼	〔鍋〕锅	〔癆〕痨	〔嚮〕向		〔鵓〕鹁	〔穢〕秽	
〔蟈〕蝈	〔懇〕恳	〔鵂〕鹇			〔轉〕转	〔簡〕简	
〔雖〕虽	〔餷〕馇	〔齋〕斋				〔簣〕篑	
						〔簞〕箪	

〔雙〕双
〔軀〕躯
〔邊〕边
〔歸〕归
〔鏵〕铧
〔鎮〕镇
〔鏈〕链
〔鎘〕镉
〔鎖〕锁
〔鎧〕铠
〔鎸〕镌
〔鎳〕镍
〔鎢〕钨
〔鏺〕铩
〔鎿〕镎
〔鎦〕镏
〔鎬〕镐
〔鎊〕镑
〔鎰〕镒
〔鎵〕镓
〔鎘〕镉
〔鵒〕鹆
〔饃〕馍
〔餺〕馎
〔餼〕饩
〔餾〕馏
〔饈〕馐
〔臍〕脐
〔鯁〕鲠
〔鯉〕鲤
〔鯀〕鲧
〔鯇〕鲩
〔卿〕卿
〔颺〕飏
〔颻〕飖
〔觴〕觞
〔獵〕猎
〔雛〕雏
〔臏〕膑

【丶】

〔謹〕谨

〔謳〕讴
〔謾〕谩
〔謫〕谪
〔譓〕谳
〔謬〕谬
〔癠〕疖
〔雜〕杂
〔離〕离
〔顏〕颜
〔糧〕粮
〔燼〕烬
〔鵜〕鹈
〔瀆〕渎
〔懣〕懑
〔濾〕滤
〔鯊〕鲨
〔濺〕溅
〔瀏〕浏
〔濼〕泺
〔瀉〕泻
〔瀋〕沈
〔竄〕窜
〔竅〕窍
〔額〕额
〔禰〕祢
〔襠〕裆
〔襝〕裣
〔禱〕祷

【一】

〔醬〕酱
〔韞〕韫
〔隴〕陇
〔嬸〕婶
〔繞〕绕
〔繚〕缭
〔織〕织
〔繕〕缮
〔繒〕缯
〔斷〕断

19笔

【一】

〔鵡〕鹉
〔鶿〕鹚
〔鬍〕胡
〔騙〕骗
〔騷〕骚
〔壢〕坜
〔壚〕垆
〔壞〕坏
〔攏〕拢
〔蕷〕蓣
〔難〕难
〔鵲〕鹊
〔藶〕苈
〔蘋〕苹
〔蘆〕芦
〔鶓〕鹋
〔藺〕蔺
〔躉〕趸
〔蘄〕蕲
〔勸〕劝
〔蘇〕苏
〔藹〕蔼
〔蘢〕茏
〔顛〕颠
〔櫝〕椟
〔櫟〕栎
〔櫓〕橹
〔櫧〕槠
〔櫞〕橼
〔轎〕轿
〔鏨〕錾
〔轍〕辙
〔轔〕辚
〔繫〕系
〔鶊〕鹒
〔麗〕丽
〔厴〕厣
〔礪〕砺
〔礙〕碍

〔礦〕矿
〔贗〕赝
〔願〕愿
〔鶘〕鹕
〔璽〕玺
〔豶〕豮

【丨】

〔贈〕赠
〔闞〕阚
〔關〕关
〔嚦〕呖
〔疇〕畴
〔蹺〕跷
〔蟶〕蛏
〔蠅〕蝇
〔蟻〕蚁
〔嚴〕严
〔獸〕兽
〔嚨〕咙
〔羆〕罴
〔羅〕罗

【丿】

〔氌〕氇
〔犢〕犊
〔贊〕赞
〔穩〕稳
〔簽〕签
〔簾〕帘
〔簫〕箫
〔牘〕牍
〔懲〕惩
〔鐯〕锗
〔鏗〕铿
〔鏢〕镖
〔鏜〕镗
〔鏤〕镂
〔鏝〕镘
〔鏰〕镚
〔鏞〕镛
〔鏡〕镜
〔鏟〕铲

〔鏑〕镝
〔鏃〕镞
〔鏇〕旋
〔鵮〕鹐
〔鏷〕镤
〔饉〕馑
〔饅〕馒
〔鵬〕鹏
〔臘〕腊
〔鯖〕鲭
〔鯪〕鲮
〔鯫〕鲰
〔鯡〕鲱
〔鯤〕鲲
〔鯧〕鲳
〔鯢〕鲵
〔鯰〕鲶
〔鯛〕鲷
〔鯨〕鲸
〔鯔〕鲻
〔獺〕獭
〔鶥〕鹛
〔颼〕飕

【丶】

〔譚〕谭
〔譖〕谮
〔譙〕谯
〔識〕识
〔譜〕谱
〔證〕证
〔譎〕谲
〔譏〕讥
〔鶉〕鹑
〔廬〕庐
〔癟〕瘪
〔癢〕痒
〔龐〕庞
〔壟〕垄
〔鵲〕鹝
〔類〕类
〔爍〕烁

〔瀟〕潇
〔瀨〕濑
〔瀝〕沥
〔瀕〕濒
〔瀘〕泸
〔瀧〕泷
〔懶〕懒
〔懷〕怀
〔寵〕宠
〔襪〕袜
〔襤〕褴

【一】

〔韜〕韬
〔騭〕骘
〔鶩〕鹜
〔顙〕颡
〔繮〕缰
〔繩〕绳
〔繾〕缱
〔繰〕缲
〔繹〕绎
〔繯〕缳
〔繳〕缴
〔繪〕绘

20笔

【一】

〔瓏〕珑
〔驁〕骜
〔驊〕骅
〔騮〕骝
〔騶〕驺
〔騸〕骟
〔攖〕撄
〔攔〕拦
〔攙〕搀
〔聹〕聍
〔顢〕颟
〔驀〕蓦
〔蘭〕兰
〔蘞〕蔹

〔蘚〕藓
〔鶘〕鹕
〔飄〕飘
〔櫪〕枥
〔櫨〕栌
〔櫸〕榉
〔礬〕矾
〔麵〕面
〔櫬〕榇
〔櫧〕槠
〔礫〕砾

【丨】
〔鹹〕咸
〔齟〕龃
〔齙〕龅
〔齡〕龄
〔齣〕出
〔鮑〕鲍
〔齠〕龆
〔獻〕献
〔黨〕党
〔懸〕悬
〔鷴〕鹇
〔罌〕罂
〔贍〕赡
〔闥〕闼
〔闡〕阐
〔鵑〕鹃
〔曨〕昽
〔蠣〕蛎
〔蠐〕蛴
〔蠑〕蝾
〔嚶〕嘤
〔鶚〕鹗
〔髏〕髅
〔鶻〕鹘

【丿】
〔犧〕牺
〔鶩〕鹜
〔籌〕筹
〔籃〕篮

〔譽〕誉
〔覺〕觉
〔謄〕誊
〔蕢〕蒉
〔艦〕舰
〔鐃〕铙
〔鐝〕镢
〔鎂〕镁
〔鐧〕锏
〔鐋〕铴
〔鐓〕镦
〔鐘〕钟
〔鐠〕镨
〔錯〕错
〔鑼〕锣
〔鐦〕锎
〔鎇〕镅
〔鐙〕镫
〔鏺〕钹
〔釋〕释
〔饒〕饶
〔黴〕霉
〔饋〕馈
〔饌〕馔
〔饑〕饥
〔臚〕胪
〔朧〕胧
〔騰〕腾
〔鯖〕鲭
〔鰈〕鲽
〔鰂〕鲗
〔鰥〕鳏
〔鰓〕鳃
〔鰐〕鳄
〔鰍〕鳅
〔鰒〕鳆
〔鰉〕鳇

【丶】
〔護〕护
〔譴〕谴
〔譯〕译
〔譫〕谵
〔議〕议
〔辯〕辩
〔龔〕龚
〔競〕竞
〔贏〕赢
〔糰〕团
〔鶘〕鹕
〔爐〕炉
〔瀾〕澜
〔瀲〕潋
〔彌〕弥
〔懺〕忏
〔寶〕宝
〔騫〕骞
〔竇〕窦
〔擺〕摆

【一】
〔鶼〕鹣
〔騖〕骛
〔纊〕纩
〔繽〕缤
〔繼〕继
〔饗〕飨
〔響〕响

21 笔
【一】
〔糲〕粝
〔瓔〕璎
〔鰲〕鳌
〔攝〕摄
〔騾〕骡
〔驅〕驱
〔驃〕骠

〔驄〕骢
〔驂〕骖
〔攛〕撺
〔韉〕鞯
〔轎〕轿
〔歡〕欢
〔權〕权
〔櫻〕樱
〔欄〕栏
〔轟〕轰
〔覽〕览
〔酈〕郦
〔飆〕飙
〔殲〕歼

【丨】
〔齜〕龇
〔齦〕龈
〔齬〕龉
〔贐〕赆
〔囁〕嗫
〔囈〕呓
〔闢〕辟
〔囀〕啭
〔顥〕颢
〔躊〕踌
〔躋〕跻
〔躑〕踯
〔躍〕跃
〔纍〕累
〔蠟〕蜡
〔囂〕嚣
〔歸〕归
〔髒〕脏

【丿】
〔儺〕傩
〔儷〕俪
〔儼〕俨
〔鵬〕鹏
〔鐵〕铁
〔鑊〕镬

〔鐳〕镭
〔鐺〕铛
〔鐸〕铎
〔鐶〕镮
〔鐲〕镯
〔鐮〕镰
〔鐿〕镱
〔鷉〕鹈
〔鶉〕鹑
〔鷁〕鹢
〔鷄〕鸡
〔臟〕脏
〔騰〕腾
〔鰭〕鳍
〔鰱〕鲢
〔鰨〕鳎
〔鰩〕鳐
〔鰟〕鳑
〔鰜〕鳒

【丶】
〔癩〕癞
〔癟〕瘪
〔癮〕瘾
〔斕〕斓
〔辯〕辩
〔鶼〕鹣
〔爛〕烂
〔鶯〕莺
〔灄〕滠
〔灃〕沣
〔灕〕漓
〔懾〕慑
〔懼〕惧
〔竈〕灶
〔顧〕顾
〔襯〕衬
〔鶴〕鹤

【一】
〔屬〕属
〔纈〕缬
〔續〕续
〔纏〕缠

22 笔
【一】
〔鬚〕须
〔驍〕骁
〔驕〕骄
〔攤〕摊
〔覿〕觌
〔攢〕攒
〔鷙〕鸷
〔聽〕听
〔蘿〕萝
〔驚〕惊
〔轢〕轹
〔鷗〕鸥
〔鑒〕鉴
〔邐〕逦
〔鷖〕鹥
〔霽〕霁

【丨】
〔齬〕龉
〔齪〕龊
〔鱉〕鳖
〔贖〕赎
〔躚〕跹
〔躓〕踬
〔蠨〕蟏
〔囌〕苏
〔囉〕罗
〔囑〕嘱
〔轡〕辔
〔巔〕巅
〔邏〕逻
〔體〕体

【丿】
〔罎〕坛
〔籜〕箨
〔籟〕籁
〔籙〕箓
〔籠〕笼
〔鱉〕鳖
〔儻〕傥
〔艫〕舻
〔鑄〕铸
〔鑌〕镔
〔鑔〕镲
〔龕〕龛
〔糴〕籴
〔鰳〕鳓
〔鰹〕鲣
〔鰾〕鳔
〔鱈〕鳕
〔鰻〕鳗
〔鱅〕鳙
〔鰷〕鲦
〔玃〕猡

【丶】丶
〔讀〕读
〔讅〕谉
〔巒〕峦
〔彎〕弯
〔孿〕孪
〔孌〕娈
〔顫〕颤
〔鷂〕鹞
〔癭〕瘿
〔癬〕癣
〔聾〕聋
〔龔〕龚
〔襲〕袭
〔灘〕滩
〔灑〕洒
〔竊〕窃

【一】
〔鷚〕鹨

〔鷯〕鹩

23 笔

【一】
〔瓚〕瓒
〔驛〕驿
〔驗〕验
〔攪〕搅
〔欏〕椤
〔轤〕轳
〔厴〕厣
〔魘〕魇
〔靨〕靥
〔鷯〕鹩
〔顬〕颥

【丨】
〔曬〕晒
〔鷳〕鹇
〔顯〕显
〔蠱〕蛊
〔髖〕髋
〔髕〕髌

【丿】
〔籤〕签
〔雛〕雏
〔鷦〕鹪
〔黴〕霉
〔鑠〕铄
〔鑕〕锧
〔鑥〕镥
〔鑣〕镳
〔鑞〕镴
〔臢〕臜
〔鱖〕鳜
〔鱗〕鳞
〔鱒〕鳟
〔鱘〕鲟

【丶】
〔讖〕谶
〔欒〕栾
〔攣〕挛
〔變〕变
〔戀〕恋
〔驚〕惊
〔癰〕痈
〔齏〕齑
〔讋〕詟

【一】
〔鷸〕鹬
〔纓〕缨
〔纖〕纤
〔纔〕才
〔鷥〕鸶

24 笔

【一】
〔鬢〕鬓
〔攬〕揽
〔驟〕骤
〔壩〕坝
〔韆〕千
〔觀〕观
〔鹽〕盐
〔釀〕酿
〔靂〕雳
〔靈〕灵
〔靄〕霭
〔蠶〕蚕

【丨】
〔艷〕艳
〔鼇〕鳌
〔齷〕龌
〔齪〕龊
〔鹼〕硷
〔贜〕赃
〔鷺〕鹭
〔囑〕嘱
〔羈〕羁

【丿】
〔籩〕笾
〔籬〕篱
〔籪〕簖
〔黌〕黉
〔鱟〕鲎
〔鱧〕鳢
〔鱠〕鲙
〔鱣〕鳣

【丶】
〔讕〕谰
〔讒〕谗
〔讓〕让
〔鸇〕鹯
〔鷹〕鹰
〔癱〕瘫
〔癲〕癫
〔贛〕赣
〔灝〕灏

【一】
〔鸏〕鹲

25 笔

【一】
〔韉〕鞯
〔欖〕榄
〔靉〕叆

【丨】
〔顱〕颅
〔躡〕蹑
〔躥〕蹿
〔鼉〕鼍

【丿】
〔籮〕箩
〔鑭〕镧
〔鑰〕钥
〔鑲〕镶
〔饞〕馋
〔鱨〕鲿
〔鱭〕鲚

【丶】
〔蠻〕蛮
〔臠〕脔
〔廳〕厅
〔灣〕湾

【一】
〔糶〕粜
〔纘〕缵

26 笔

【一】
〔驥〕骥
〔驢〕驴
〔趲〕趱
〔顴〕颧
〔黶〕黡
〔釃〕酾
〔釅〕酽

【丨】
〔矚〕瞩
〔躪〕躏
〔躦〕躜

【丿】
〔釁〕衅
〔鑷〕镊
〔鑹〕镩

【丶】
〔灤〕滦

27 笔

【一】
〔鬮〕阄
〔驤〕骧
〔顳〕颞

【丨】
〔鸕〕鸬
〔黷〕黩

【丿】
〔鑼〕锣
〔鑽〕钻
〔鱸〕鲈

【丶】
〔讜〕谠
〔讝〕谵
〔鑾〕銮
〔灩〕滟

【一】
〔纜〕缆

28 笔
〔鸛〕鹳
〔欞〕棂
〔鑿〕凿
〔鸚〕鹦
〔钂〕镋
〔戇〕戆

29 笔
〔驪〕骊
〔鬱〕郁

30 笔
〔鸝〕鹂
〔饢〕馕
〔鱺〕鲡
〔鸞〕鸾

32 笔
〔籲〕吁

APPENDIX II

INITIALS AND FINALS IN VARIOUS PHONETIC SYMBOLS

INITIALS IN PINYIN*

Place \ Manner	Unaspirated Stops	Aspirated Stops	Nasals	Fricatives	Voiced Continuants
Labials	b	p	m	f	
Dentals	d	t	n		l
Dental sibilants	z	c		s	
Retroflexes	zh	ch		sh	r
Palatals	j	q		x	
Gutturals	g	k		h	

Pinyin and Other Phonetic Symbols Compared @

PY	IPA	YALE	GR	W–G	ZYFH
b	ḅ	b	b	p	ㄅ
p	pʰ	p	p	p'	ㄆ
m	m	m	m	m	ㄇ
f	f	f	f	f	ㄈ
d	ḍ	d	d	t	ㄉ
t	tʰ	t	t	t'	ㄊ
n	n	n	n	n	ㄋ
l	l	l	l	l	ㄌ
z	ts	dz	tz	ts, tz	ㄗ
c	tsʰ	ts	ts	ts', tz'	ㄘ
s	s	s	s	s	ㄙ

PY	IPA	YALE	GR	W–G	ZYFH
zh	tʂ	j	j	ch	ㄓ
ch	tʂʰ	ch	ch	ch'	ㄔ
sh	ʂ	sh	sh	sh	ㄕ
r	ɹ	r	r	j	ㄖ
j	tɕ	j	j	ch	ㄐ
q	tɕʰ	ch	ch	ch'	ㄑ
x	ç	sy	sh	hs	ㄒ
g	ğ	g	g	k	ㄍ
k	kʰ	k	k	k'	ㄎ
h	x	h	h	h	ㄏ

* The tables for the initials and finals are adapted from Professor Chao's *A Grammar of Spoken Chinese*, p. 22 and p. 24.

@ The abbreviations for the different phonetic symbols are for pinyin (PY), International Phonetic Alphabet (IPA), Yale System (Yale), Gwoyeu Romatzyh (GR), Wade-Gilees (W-G), and Zhuyin Fuhao (ZYFH).

FINALS IN PINYIN

Ending Medial	Open			-i		-u		-n		-ng			-r
Row–a	i	a	e	ai	ei	ao	ou	an	en	ang	eng	ong	r
Row–i	i	ia	ie	iai		iao	iu	ian	in	iang	ing	iong	
Row–u	u	ua	uo	uai	ui			uan	un	uang	weng		
Row–ü	ü	üe						üan	ün				

Pinyin and Other Symbols Compared

PY	IPA	YALE	GR	W–G	ZYFH		PY	IPA	YALE	GR	W–G	ZYFH
i	ʐ, ɨ	z, r	y	ih,u			ian	iɛn	yan	ian	ien	ㄧㄢ
a	A	a	a	a	ㄚ		in	in	in	in	in	ㄧㄣ
e	ɤ	e	e	e,o	ㄜ,ㄛ		iang	iaŋ	yang	iang	iang	ㄧㄤ
ai	ai	ai	ai	ai	ㄞ		ing	iŋ	ing	ing	ing	ㄧㄥ
ei	ei	ei	ei	ei	ㄟ		iong	Iᵤŋ	yung	iong	iung	ㄩㄥ
ao	au	au	au	ao	ㄠ		u	u	(w)u	u	u	ㄨ
ou	ou	ou	ou	ou	ㄡ		ua	uA	wa	ua	ua	ㄨㄚ
an	an	an	an	a(e)n	ㄢ		uo	uɤ	wo	uo	uo	ㄨㄛ
en	ən	en	en	en	ㄣ		uai	uai	wai	uai	uai	ㄨㄞ
ang	aŋ	ang	ang	ang	ㄤ		ui	uei	wei	uei	u(e)i	ㄨㄟ
eng	ʌŋ	eng	eng	eng	ㄥ		uan	uan	wan	uan	uan	ㄨㄢ
ong	ʌŋ	ung	ong	ung	ㄨㄥ		un	uən	wu(e)n	uen	un	ㄨㄣ
er	ɚ	er	el	erh	ㄦ		uang	uaŋ	wang	uang	uang	ㄨㄤ
i	i	i(y)	i	i	ㄧ		weng	uəŋ	weng	ueng	weng	ㄨㄥ
ia	iA	ya	ia	ia	ㄧㄚ		ü(u)	y	yu	iu	ü	ㄩ
ie	iɛ	ye	ie	ieh	ㄧㄝ		üe	yɛ	ywe	iue	üeh	ㄩㄝ
iai	iai	yai	iai	iai	ㄧㄞ		üan	yan	ywan	iuan	üan	ㄩㄢ
iao	iau	yau	iau	iao	ㄧㄠ		ün	yn	yun	iun	ün	ㄩㄣ
iu	iou	you	iou	iu	ㄧㄡ							

APPENDIX III

COMPARATIVE TABLE OF PINYIN, YALE, WADE-GILES, YHUYIN FUHAO AND GWOYEU ROMATZYH (TONAL SPELLING) SYSTEMS

PY	YALE	WG	ZYFH	ROMATZYH 1	2	3	4
a	a	a	ㄚ	a	ar	aa	ah
ai	ai	ai	ㄞ	ai	air	ae	ay
an	an	an	ㄢ	an	arn	aan	ann
ang	ang	ang	ㄤ	ang	arng	aang	ang
ao	au	ao	ㄠ	au	aur	ao	aw
ba	ba	pa	ㄅㄚ	ba	bar	baa	bah
bai	bai	pai	ㄅㄞ	bai	bair	bae	bay
ban	ban	pan	ㄅㄢ	ban	barn	baan	bann
bang	bang	pang	ㄅㄤ	bang	barng	baang	banq
bao	bau	pao	ㄅㄠ	bau	baur	bao	baw
bei	bei	pei	ㄅㄟ	bei	beir	beei	bey
ben	ben	pen	ㄅㄣ	ben	bern	been	benn
beng	beng	peng	ㄅㄥ	beng	berng	beeng	benq
bi	bi	pi	ㄅㄧ	bi	byi	bii	bih
bian	byan	pien	ㄅㄧㄢ	bian	byan	bean	biann
biao	byau	piao	ㄅㄧㄠ	biau	byau	beau	biaw
bie	bye	pieh	ㄅㄧㄝ	bie	bye	biee	bieh
bin	bin	pin	ㄅㄧㄣ	bin	byn	biin	binn
bing	bing	ping	ㄅㄧㄥ	bing	byng	biing	binq
bo	bwo	po	ㄅㄛ	bo	bor	boo	boh
bu	bu	pu	ㄅㄨ	bu	bwu	buu	buh
ca	tsa	ts'a	ㄘㄚ	tsa	tsar	tsaa	tsah
cai	tsai	ts'ai	ㄘㄞ	tsai	tsair	tsae	tsay
can	tsan	ts'an	ㄘㄢ	tsan	tsarn	tsaan	tsann
cang	tsang	ts'ang	ㄘㄤ	tsang	tsarng	tsaang	tsanq
cao	tsau	ts'ao	ㄘㄠ	tsau	tsaur	tsao	tsaw
ce	tse	ts'e	ㄘㄜ	tse	tser	tsee	tseh
cen	tsen	ts'en	ㄘㄣ	tsen	tsern	tseen	tsenn
ceng	tseng	ts'eng	ㄘㄥ	tseng	tserng	tseeng	tsenq
cha	cha	ch'a	ㄔㄚ	cha	char	chaa	chah
chai	chai	ch'ai	ㄔㄞ	chai	chair	chae	chay
chan	chan	ch'an	ㄔㄢ	chan	charn	chaan	chann
chang	chang	ch'ang	ㄔㄤ	chang	charng	chaang	chanq
chao	chau	ch'ao	ㄔㄠ	chau	chaur	chao	chaw
che	che	ch'e	ㄔㄜ	che	cher	chee	cheh
chen	chen	ch'en	ㄔㄣ	chen	chern	cheen	chenn
cheng	cheng	ch'eng	ㄔㄥ	cheng	cherng	cheeng	chenq
chi	chr	ch'ih	ㄔ	chy	chyr	chyy	chyh
chong	chung	ch'ung	ㄔㄨㄥ	chong	chorng	choong	chonq
chou	chou	ch'ou	ㄔㄡ	chou	chour	choou	chow
chu	chu	ch'u	ㄔㄨ	chu	chwu	chuu	chuh
chua	chua	ch'ua	ㄔㄨㄚ	chua	chwa	choa	chuah
chuai	chwai	ch'uai	ㄔㄨㄞ	chuai	chwai	choai	chuay
chuan	chwan	ch'uan	ㄔㄨㄢ	chuan	chwan	choan	chuann

PY	YALE	WG	ZYFH	1	ROMATZYH 2	3	4
chuang	chwang	ch'uang	ㄔㄨㄤ	chuang	chwang	choang	chuanq
chui	chwei	ch'ui	ㄔㄨㄟ	chuei	chwei	choei	chuey
chun	chwun	ch'un	ㄔㄨㄣ	chuen	chwen	choen	chuenn
chuo	chwo	ch'o	ㄔㄨㄛ	chuo	chwo	chuoo	chuoh
ci	tsz	tz'u	ㄘ	tsy	tsyr	tsyy	tsyh
cong	tsung	ts'ung	ㄘㄨㄥ	tsong	tsorng	tsoong	tsonq
cou	tsou	ts'ou	ㄘㄡ	tsou	tsour	tsoou	tsow
cu	tsu	ts'u	ㄘㄨ	tsu	tswu	tsuu	tsuh
cuan	tswan	ts'uan	ㄘㄨㄢ	tsuan	tswan	tsoan	tsuann
cui	tswei	ts'ui	ㄘㄨㄟ	tsuei	tswei	tsoei	tsuey
cun	tswun	ts'un	ㄘㄨㄣ	tsuen	tswen	tsoen	tsuenn
cuo	tswo	ts'o	ㄘㄨㄛ	tsuo	tswo	tsuoo	tsuoh
da	da	ta	ㄉㄚ	da	dar	daa	dah
dai	dai	tai	ㄉㄞ	dai	dair	dae	day
dan	dan	tan	ㄉㄢ	dan	darn	daan	dann
dang	dang	tang	ㄉㄤ	dang	darng	daang	danq
dao	dau	tao	ㄉㄠ	dau	daur	dao	daw
de	de	te	ㄉㄜ	de	der	dee	deh
dei	dei	tei	ㄉㄟ	dei	deir	deei	dey
deng	deng	teng	ㄉㄥ	deng	derng	deeng	denq
di	di	ti	ㄉㄧ	di	dyi	dii	dih
dian	dyan	tien	ㄉㄧㄢ	dian	dyan	dean	diann
diao	dyau	tiao	ㄉㄧㄠ	diau	dyau	deau	diaw
die	dye	tieh	ㄉㄧㄝ	die	dye	diee	dieh
ding	ding	ting	ㄉㄧㄥ	ding	dyng	diing	dinq
diu	dyou	tiu	ㄉㄧㄡ	diou	dyou	deou	diow
dong	dung	tung	ㄉㄨㄥ	dong	dorng	doong	donq
dou	dou	tou	ㄉㄡ	dou	dour	doou	dow
du	du	tu	ㄉㄨ	du	dwu	duu	duh
duan	dwan	tuan	ㄉㄨㄢ	duan	dwan	doan	duann
dui	dwei	tui	ㄉㄨㄟ	duei	dwei	doei	duey
dun	dwun	tun	ㄉㄨㄣ	duen	dwen	doen	duenn
duo	dwo	to	ㄉㄨㄛ	duo	dwo	duoo	duoh
e	e	e, o	ㄜ,ㄛ	e	er	ee	eh
ei	ei	ei	ㄟ	ei	eir	eei	ey
en	en	en	ㄣ	en	ern	een	enn
eng	eng	eng	ㄥ	eng	erng	eeng	enq
er	er	erh	ㄦ	el	erl	eel	ell
fa	fa	fa	ㄈㄚ	fa	far	faa	fah
fan	fan	fan	ㄈㄢ	fan	farn	faan	fann
fang	fang	fang	ㄈㄤ	fang	farng	faang	fanq
fei	fei	fei	ㄈㄟ	fei	feir	feei	fey
fen	fen	fen	ㄈㄣ	fen	fern	feen	fenn
feng	feng	feng	ㄈㄥ	feng	ferng	feeng	fenq
fo	fwo	fo	ㄈㄛ	fo	for	foo	foh
fou	fou	fou	ㄈㄡ	fou	four	foou	fow
fu	fu	fu	ㄈㄨ	fu	fwu	fuu	fuh
ga	ga	ka	ㄍㄚ	ga	gar	gaa	gah

PY	YALE	WG	ZYFH	ROMATZYH 1	2	3	4
gai	gai	kai	ㄍㄞ	gai	gair	gae	gay
gan	gan	kan	ㄍㄢ	gan	garn	gaan	gann
gang	gang	kang	ㄍㄤ	gang	garng	gaang	ganq
gao	gau	kao	ㄍㄠ	gau	gaur	gao	gaw
ge	ge	ke, ko	ㄍㄜ	ge	ger	gee	geh
gei	gei	kei	ㄍㄟ	gei	geir	geei	gey
gen	gen	ken	ㄍㄣ	gen	gern	geen	genn
geng	geng	keng	ㄍㄥ	geng	gerng	geeng	genq
gong	gung	kung	ㄍㄨㄥ	gong	gorng	goong	gonq
gou	gou	kou	ㄍㄡ	gou	gour	goou	gow
gu	gu	ku	ㄍㄨ	gu	gwu	guu	guh
gua	gwa	kua	ㄍㄨㄚ	gua	gwa	goa	guah
guai	gwai	kuai	ㄍㄨㄞ	guai	gwai	goai	guay
guan	gwan	kuan	ㄍㄨㄢ	guan	gwan	goan	guann
guang	gwang	kuang	ㄍㄨㄤ	guang	gwang	goang	guanq
gui	gwei	kuei	ㄍㄨㄟ	guei	gwei	goei	guey
gun	gwun	kun	ㄍㄨㄣ	guen	gwen	goen	guenn
guo	gwo	kuo	ㄍㄨㄛ	guo	gwo	guoo	guoh
ha	ha	ha	ㄏㄚ	ha	har	haa	hah
hai	hai	hai	ㄏㄞ	hai	hair	hae	hay
han	han	han	ㄏㄢ	han	harn	haan	hann
hang	hang	hang	ㄏㄤ	hang	harng	haang	hanq
hao	hau	hao	ㄏㄠ	hau	haur	hao	haw
he	he	he	ㄏㄜ	he	her	hee	heh
hei	hei	hei	ㄏㄟ	hei	heir	heei	hey
hen	hen	hen	ㄏㄣ	hen	hern	heen	henn
heng	heng	heng	ㄏㄥ	heng	herng	heeng	henq
hong	hung	hung	ㄏㄨㄥ	hong	horng	hoong	honq
hou	hou	hou	ㄏㄡ	hou	hour	hoou	how
hu	hu	hu	ㄏㄨ	hu	hwu	huu	huh
hua	hwa	hua	ㄏㄨㄚ	hua	hwa	hoa	huah
huai	hwai	huai	ㄏㄨㄞ	huai	hwai	hoai	huay
huan	hwan	huan	ㄏㄨㄢ	huan	hwan	hoan	huann
huang	hwang	huang	ㄏㄨㄤ	huang	hwang	hoang	huanq
hui	hwei	hui	ㄏㄨㄟ	huei	hwei	hoei	huey
hun	hwun	hun	ㄏㄨㄣ	huen	hwen	hoen	huenn
huo	hwo	huo	ㄏㄨㄛ	huo	hwo	huoo	huoh
ji	ji	chi	ㄐㄧ	ji	jyi	jii	jih
jia	jya	chia	ㄐㄧㄚ	jia	jya	jea	jiah
jian	jyan	chien	ㄐㄧㄢ	jian	jyan	jean	jiann
jiang	jyang	chiang	ㄐㄧㄤ	jiang	jyang	jeang	jianq
jiao	jyau	chiao	ㄐㄧㄠ	jiau	jyau	jeau	jiaw
jie	jye	chieh	ㄐㄧㄝ	jie	jye	jiee	jieh
jin	jin	chin	ㄐㄧㄣ	jin	jyn	jiin	jinn
jing	jing	ching	ㄐㄧㄥ	jing	jyng	jiing	jinq
jiong	jyung	chiung	ㄐㄨㄥ	jiong	jyong	jeong	jionq
jiu	jyou	chiu	ㄐㄧㄡ	jiou	jyou	jeou	jiow
ju	jyu	chu	ㄐㄩ	jiu	jyu	jeu	jiuh
juan	jywan	chüan	ㄐㄩㄢ	jiuan	jyuan	jeuan	jiuann

PY	YALE	WG	ZYFH	1	ROMATZYH 2	3	4
jue	jywe	chüeh	ㄐㄩㄝ	jiue	jyue	jeue	jiueh
jun	jyun	chun	ㄐㄩㄣ	jiun	jyun	jeun	jiunn
ka	ka	k'a	ㄎㄚ	ka	kar	kaa	kah
kai	kai	k'ai	ㄎㄞ	kai	kair	kae	kay
kan	kan	k'an	ㄎㄢ	kan	karn	kaan	kann
kang	kang	k'ang	ㄎㄤ	kang	kerng	kaang	kanq
kao	kau	k'ao	ㄎㄠ	kau	kaur	kao	kaw
ke	ke	k'e, k'o	ㄎㄜ	ke	ker	kee	keh
ken	ken	k'en	ㄎㄣ	ken	kern	keen	kenn
keng	keng	k'eng	ㄎㄥ	keng	kerng	keeng	kenq
kong	kung	k'ung	ㄎㄨㄥ	kong	korng	koong	kong
kou	kou	k'ou	ㄎㄡ	kou	kour	koou	kow
ku	ku	k'u	ㄎㄨ	ku	kwu	kuu	kuh
kua	kwa	k'ua	ㄎㄨㄚ	kua	kwa	koa	kuah
kuai	kwai	k'uai	ㄎㄨㄞ	kuai	kwai	koai	kuay
kuan	kwan	k'uan	ㄎㄨㄢ	kuan	kwan	koan	kuann
kuang	kwang	k'uang	ㄎㄨㄤ	kuang	kwang	koang	kuanq
kui	kwei	k'uei	ㄎㄨㄟ	kuei	kwei	koei	kuey
kun	kwun	k'un	ㄎㄨㄣ	kuen	kwen	koen	kuenn
kuo	kwo	k'uo	ㄎㄨㄛ	kuo	kwo	kuoo	kuoh
la	la	la	ㄌㄚ	lha	la	laa	lah
lai	lai	lai	ㄌㄞ	lhai	lai	lae	lay
lan	lan	lan	ㄌㄢ	lhan	lan	laan	lann
lang	lang	lang	ㄌㄤ	lhang	lang	laang	lanq
lao	lau	lao	ㄌㄠ	lhau	lau	lao	law
le	le	le	ㄌㄜ	lhe	le	lee	leh
lei	lei	lei	ㄌㄟ	lhei	lei	leei	ley
leng	leng	leng	ㄌㄥ	lheng	leng	leeng	lenq
li	li	li	ㄌㄧ	lhi	li	lii	lih
lia	lya	lia	ㄌㄧㄚ	lhia	lia	lea	liah
lian	lyan	lien	ㄌㄧㄢ	lhian	lian	lean	liann
liang	lyang	liang	ㄌㄧㄤ	lhiang	liang	leang	lianq
liao	lyau	liao	ㄌㄧㄠ	lhiau	liau	leau	liaw
lie	lye	lieh	ㄌㄧㄝ	lhie	lie	liee	lieh
lin	lin	lin	ㄌㄧㄣ	lhin	lin	liin	linn
ling	ling	ling	ㄌㄧㄥ	lhing	ling	liing	linq
liu	lyou	liu	ㄌㄧㄡ	lhiou	liou	leou	liow
long	lung	lung	ㄌㄨㄥ	lhong	long	loong	lonq
lou	lou	lou	ㄌㄡ	lhou	lou	loou	low
lu	lu	lu	ㄌㄨ	lhu	lu	luu	luh
luan	lwan	luan	ㄌㄨㄢ	lhuan	luan	loan	luann
lun	lwun	lun, lun	ㄌㄨㄣ	lhuen	luen	loen	luenn
luo	lwo	lo	ㄌㄨㄛ	lhou	luo	luoo	luoh
lü	lyu	lü	ㄌㄩ	lhiu	liu	leu	liuh
lüan	lywan	lüan	ㄌㄩㄢ	lhiuan	liuan	leuan	liuann
lüe	lywe	lüeh	ㄌㄩㄝ	lhue	liue	leue	liueh
lün	lyun	lün	ㄌㄩㄣ	lhiun	liun	leun	liunn
ma	ma	ma	ㄇㄚ	mha	ma	maa	mah
mai	mai	mai	ㄇㄞ	mhai	mai	mae	may

PY	YALE	WG	ZYFH	ROMATZYH 1	2	3	4
man	man	man	ㄇㄢ	mhan	man	maan	mann
mang	mang	mang	ㄇㄤ	mhang	mang	maang	manq
mao	mau	mao	ㄇㄠ	mhau	mau	mao	maw
mei	mei	mei	ㄇㄟ	mhei	mei	meei	mey
men	men	men	ㄇㄣ	mhen	men	meen	menn
meng	meng	meng	ㄇㄥ	mheng	men	meeng	menq
mi	mi	mi	ㄇㄧ	mhi	mi	mii	mih
mian	myan	mien	ㄇㄧㄢ	mhian	mian	mean	miann
miao	myau	miao	ㄇㄧㄠ	mhiau	miau	meau	miaw
mie	mye	mieh	ㄇㄧㄝ	mhie	mie	miee	mieh
min	min	min	ㄇㄧㄣ	mhin	min	miin	minn
ming	ming	ming	ㄇㄧㄥ	mhing	ming	miing	minq
miu	myou	miu	ㄇㄧㄡ	mhiou	miou	meou	miow
mo	mwo	mo	ㄇㄛ	mho	mo	moo	moh
mou	mou	mou	ㄇㄡ	mhou	mou	moou	mow
mu	mu	mu	ㄇㄨ	mhu	mu	muu	muh
na	na	na	ㄋㄚ	nha	na	naa	nah
nai	nai	nai	ㄋㄞ	nhai	nai	nae	nay
nan	nan	nan	ㄋㄢ	nhan	nan	naan	nann
nang	nang	nang	ㄋㄤ	nhang	nang	naang	nanq
nao	nau	nao	ㄋㄠ	nhau	nau	nao	naw
ne	ne	ne	ㄋㄜ	nhe	ne	nee	neh
nei	nei	nei	ㄋㄟ	nhei	nei	neei	ney
nen	nen	nen	ㄋㄣ	nhen	nen	neen	nenn
neng	neng	neng	ㄋㄥ	nheng	neng	neeng	nenq
ni	ni	ni	ㄋㄧ	nhi	ni	nii	nih
nian	nyan	nien	ㄋㄧㄢ	nhian	nian	nean	niann
niang	nyang	niang	ㄋㄧㄤ	nhiang	niang	neang	nianq
niao	nyau	niao	ㄋㄧㄠ	nhiau	niau	neau	niaw
nie	nye	nieh	ㄋㄧㄝ	nhie	nie	niee	nieh
nin	nin	nin	ㄋㄧㄣ	nhin	nin	niin	ninn
ning	ning	ning	ㄋㄧㄥ	nhing	ning	niing	ninq
niu	nyou	niu	ㄋㄧㄡ	nhiu	niou	neou	niow
nong	nung	nung	ㄋㄨㄥ	nhong	nong	noong	nonq
nou	nou	nou	ㄋㄡ	nhou	nou	noou	now
nu	nu	nu	ㄋㄨ	nhu	nu	nuu	nuh
nuan	nwan	nuan	ㄋㄨㄢ	nhuan	nuan	noan	nuann
nun	nwun	nun	ㄋㄨㄣ	nhuen	nuen	noen	nuenn
nuo	nwo	no	ㄋㄨㄛ	nhuo	nuo	nuoo	nuoh
nü	nyu	nü	ㄋㄩ	nhiu	niu	neu	niuh
nüe	nywe	nüeh	ㄋㄩㄝ	nhiue	niue	neue	niueh
ou	ou	ou	ㄡ	ou	our	oou	ow
pa	pa	p'a	ㄆㄚ	pa	par	paa	pah
pai	pai	p'ai	ㄆㄞ	pai	pair	pae	pay
pan	pan	p'an	ㄆㄢ	pan	parn	paan	pann
pang	pang	p'ang	ㄆㄤ	pang	parng	paang	panq
pao	pau	p'ao	ㄆㄠ	pau	paur	pao	paw
pei	pei	p'ei	ㄆㄟ	pei	peir	peei	pey
pen	pen	p'en	ㄆㄣ	pen	pern	peen	penn

PY	YALE	WG	ZYFH	ROMATZYH 1	2	3	4
peng	peng	p'eng	ㄆㄥ	peng	perng	peeng	penq
pi	pi	p'i	ㄆㄧ	pi	pyi	pii	pih
pian	pyan	p'ien	ㄆㄧㄣ	pian	pyan	pean	piann
piao	pyau	p'iao	ㄆㄧㄠ	piau	pyau	peau	piaw
pie	pye	p'ieh	ㄆㄧㄝ	pie	pye	piee	pieh
pin	pin	p'in	ㄆㄧㄣ	pin	pyn	piin	pinn
ping	ping	p'ing	ㄆㄧㄥ	ping	pyng	piing	pinq
po	pwo	p'o	ㄆㄛ	po	por	poo	poh
pou	pou	p'ou	ㄆㄡ	pou	pour	poou	pow
pu	pu	p'u	ㄆㄨ	pu	pwu	puu	puh
qi	chi	ch'i	ㄑㄧ	chi	chyi	chii	chih
qia	chya	ch'ia	ㄑㄧㄚ	chia	chya	chea	chiah
qian	chyan	ch'ien	ㄑㄧㄢ	chian	chyan	chean	chiann
qiang	chyang	ch'iang	ㄑㄧㄦ	chiang	chyang	cheang	chianq
qiao	chyau	ch'iao	ㄑㄧㄠ	chiau	chyau	cheau	chiaw
qie	chye	ch'ieh	ㄑㄧㄝ	chie	chye	chiee	chieh
qin	chin	ch'in	ㄑㄧㄣ	chin	chyn	chiin	chinn
qing	ching	ch'inh	ㄑㄧㄥ	ching	chyng	chiing	chinq
qiong	chyung	ch'iung	ㄑㄩㄥ	chiong	chyong	cheong	chionq
qiu	chyou	ch'iu	ㄑㄧㄡ	chiou	chyou	cheou	chiow
qu	chyu	ch'u	ㄑㄩ	chiu	chyu	cheu	chiuh
quan	chywan	ch'uan	ㄑㄩㄢ	chiuan	chyuan	cheuan	chiuann
que	chywe	ch'ueh	ㄑㄩㄝ	chiue	chyue	cheue	chiueh
qun	chyun	ch'un	ㄑㄩㄣ	chiun	chyun	cheun	chiunn
ran	ran	jan	ㄖㄢ	rhan	ran	raan	rann
rang	rang	jang	ㄖㄤ	rhang	rang	raang	ranq
rao	rau	jao	ㄖㄠ	rhau	rau	rao	raw
re	re	je	ㄖㄜ	rhe	re	ree	reh
ren	ren	jen	ㄖㄣ	rhen	ren	reen	renn
reng	reng	jeng	ㄖㄥ	rheng	reng	reeng	renq
ri	r	jih	ㄖ	rhy	ry	ryy	ryh
rong	rung	jung	ㄖㄨㄥ	rhong	rong	roong	ronq
rou	rou	jou	ㄖㄡ	rhou	rou	roou	row
ru	ru	ju	ㄖㄨ	rhu	ru	ruu	ruh
ruan	rwan	juan	ㄖㄨㄢ	rhuan	ruan	roan	ruann
rui	rwei	jui	ㄖㄨㄟ	rhuei	ruei	roei	ruey
run	rwun	jun	ㄖㄨㄣ	rhuen	ruen	roen	ruenn
ruo	rwo	jo	ㄖㄨㄛ	rhuo	ruo	ruoo	ruoh
sa	sa	sa	ㄙㄚ	sa	sar	saa	sah
sai	sai	sai	ㄙㄞ	sia	sair	sae	say
san	san	san	ㄙㄢ	san	sarn	saan	sann
sang	sang	sang	ㄙㄤ	sang	sarng	saang	sanq
sao	sau	sao	ㄙㄠ	sau	saur	sao	saw
se	se	se	ㄙㄜ	se	ser	see	seh
sen	sen	sen	ㄙㄣ	sen	sern	seen	senn
seng	seng	seng	ㄙㄥ	seng	serng	seeng	senq
sha	sha	sha	ㄕㄚ	sha	shar	shaa	shah
shai	shai	shai	ㄕㄞ	shai	shair	shae	shay
shan	shan	shan	ㄕㄢ	shan	sharn	shaan	shann

				ROMATZYH			
PY	YALE	WG	ZYFH	1	2	3	4
shang	shang	shang	ㄕㄤ	shang	sharng	shaang	shanq
shao	shau	shao	ㄕㄠ	shau	shuar	shao	shaw
she	she	she	ㄕㄜ	she	sher	shee	sheh
shei	shei	shei	ㄕㄟ	shei	sheir	sheei	shey
shen	shen	shen	ㄕㄣ	shen	shern	sheen	shenn
sheng	sheng	sheng	ㄕㄥ	sheng	sherng	sheeng	shenq
shi	shr	shih	ㄕ	shy	shyr	shyh	shyy
shou	shou	shou	ㄕㄡ	shou	shour	shoou	show
shu	shu	shu	ㄕㄨ	shu	shwu	shuu	shuh
shua	shwa	shua	ㄕㄨㄚ	shua	shwa	shoa	shuah
shuai	shwau	shuai	ㄕㄨㄞ	shuai	shwai	shoai	shuay
shuan	shwan	shuan	ㄕㄨㄢ	shuan	shwan	shoan	shuann
shuang	shwang	shuang	ㄕㄨㄤ	shuang	shwang	shoang	shuanq
shui	shwei	shui	ㄕㄨㄟ	shuei	shwei	shoei	shuey
shun	shwun	shun	ㄕㄨㄣ	shuen	shwen	shoen	shuenn
shuo	shwo	shuo	ㄕㄨㄛ	shuo	shwo	shuoo	shuoh
si	sz	szu, ssu	ㄙ	sy	syr	syy	syh
song	sung	sung	ㄙㄨㄥ	song	sorng	soong	sonq
sou	sou	sou	ㄙㄡ	sou	sour	soou	sow
su	su	su	ㄙㄨ	su	swu	suu	suh
suan	swan	suan	ㄙㄨㄢ	suan	swan	soan	suann
sui	swei	sui	ㄙㄨㄟ	suei	swei	soei	suey
sun	swun	sun	ㄙㄨㄣ	suen	swen	soen	suenn
suo	swo	so	ㄙㄨㄛ	suo	swo	suoo	suoh
ta	ta	t'a	ㄊㄚ	ta	tar	taa	tah
tai	tai	t'ai	ㄊㄞ	tai	tair	tae	tay
tan	tan	t'an	ㄊㄢ	tan	tarn	taan	tann
tang	tang	t'ang	ㄊㄤ	tang	tarng	taang	tanq
tao	tau	t'ao	ㄊㄠ	tau	taur	tao	taw
te	te	t'e	ㄊㄜ	te	ter	tee	teh
teng	teng	t'eng	ㄊㄥ	teng	terng	teeng	tenq
ti	ti	t'i	ㄊㄧ	ti	tyi	tii	tih
tian	tyan	t'ien	ㄊㄧㄢ	tian	tyan	tean	tiann
tiao	tyau	t'iao	ㄊㄧㄠ	tiau	tyau	teau	tiaw
tie	tye	t'ieh	ㄊㄧㄝ	tie	tye	tiee	tieh
ting	ting	t'ing	ㄊㄧㄥ	ting	tyng	tiing	tinq
tong	tung	t'ung	ㄊㄨㄥ	tong	torng	toong	tonq
tou	tou	t'ou	ㄊㄡ	tou	tour	toou	tow
tu	tu	t'u	ㄊㄨ	tu	twu	tuu	tuh
tuan	twan	t'uan	ㄊㄨㄢ	tuan	twan	toan	tuann
tui	twei	t'ui	ㄊㄨㄟ	tuei	twei	toei	tuey
tun	twun	t'un	ㄊㄨㄣ	tuen	twen	toen	tuenn
tuo	two	t'o	ㄊㄨㄛ	tuo	two	tuoo	tuoh
wa	wa	wa	ㄨㄚ	ua	wa	woa	wah
wai	wai	wai	ㄨㄞ	uai	wai	woai	way
wan	wan	wan	ㄨㄢ	uan	wan	woan	wann
wang	wang	wang	ㄨㄤ	uang	wang	woang	wanq
wei	wei	wei	ㄨㄟ	uei	wei	woei	wey
wen	wen	wen	ㄨㄣ	uen	wen	woen	wenn
weng	weng	weng	ㄨㄥ	ueng	weng	woeng	wenq

PY	YALE	WG	ZYFH	ROMATZYH 1	2	3	4
wo	wo	wo	ㄨㄛ	uo	wo	woo	woh
wu	wu	wu	ㄨ	u	wu	wuu	wuh
xi	syi	hsi	ㄒㄧ	shi	shyi	shii	shih
xia	sya	hsia	ㄒㄧㄚ	shia	shya	shea	shiah
xian	syan	hsien	ㄒㄧㄢ	shian	shyan	shean	shiann
xiang	syang	hsiang	ㄒㄧㄤ	shiang	shyang	sheang	shianq
xiao	syau	hsiao	ㄒㄧㄠ	shiau	shyau	sheau	shiaw
xie	sye	hsieh	ㄒㄧㄝ	shie	shye	shiee	shieh
xin	syin	hsin	ㄒㄧㄣ	shin	shyn	shiin	shinn
xing	sying	hsing	ㄒㄧㄥ	shing	shyng	shiing	shinq
xiong	syung	hsiung	ㄒㄩㄥ	shiong	shyong	sheong	shionq
xiu	syou	hsiu	ㄒㄧㄡ	shiou	shyou	sheou	shiow
xu	syu	hsü	ㄒㄩ	shiu	shyu	sheu	shiuh
xuan	sywan	hsuan	ㄒㄩㄢ	shiuan	shyuan	sheuan	shiuann
xue	sywe	hsüeh	ㄒㄩㄝ	shiue	shyue	sheue	shiueh
xun	syun	hsün	ㄒㄩㄣ	shiun	shyun	sheun	shiunn
ya	ya	ya	ㄧㄚ	ia	ya	yaa	yah
yai	yai	yai	ㄧㄞ	iai	yai	yae	yay
yan	yan	yen	ㄧㄢ	ian	yan	yean	yann
yang	yang	yang	ㄧㄤ	iang	yang	yeang	yanq
yao	yau	yao	ㄧㄠ	iau	yau	yeau	yaw
ye	ye	yeh	ㄧㄝ	ie	ye	yee	yeh
yi	yi	i	ㄧ	i	yi	ii	ih
yin	yin	yin	ㄧㄣ	in	yn	yiin	yinn
ying	ying	ying	ㄧㄥ	ing	yng	yiing	yinq
yong	yung	yung	ㄩㄥ	iong	yong	yeong	yonq
you	you	yu	ㄧㄡ	iou	you	yeou	yow
yu	yu	yu	ㄩ	iu	yu	yeu	yuh
yuan	ywan	yüan	ㄩㄢ	iuan	yuan	yeuan	yuann
yue	ywe	yüeh	ㄩㄝ	iue	yue	yeue	yueh
yun	yun	yün	ㄩㄣ	iun	yun	yeun	yunn
za	dza	tsa	ㄗㄚ	tza	tzai	tzaa	tzah
zai	dzai	tsai	ㄗㄞ	tzai	tzaii	tzae	tzay
zan	dzan	tsan	ㄗㄢ	tzan	tzarn	tzaan	tzann
zang	dzang	tsang	ㄗㄤ	tzang	tzarng	tzaang	tzanq
zao	dzau	tsao	ㄗㄠ	tzau	tzaui	tzao	tzaw
ze	dze	tse	ㄗㄜ	tze	tzer	tzee	tzeh
zei	dzei	tsei	ㄗㄟ	tzei	tzeir	tzeei	tzey
zen	dzen	tsen	ㄗㄣ	tzen	tzern	tzeen	tzenn
zeng	dzeng	tseng	ㄗㄥ	tzeng	tzerng	tzeeng	tzenq
zha	ja	cha	ㄓㄚ	ja	jar	jaa	jah
zhai	jai	chai	ㄓㄞ	jai	jair	jae	jay
zhan	jan	chan	ㄓㄢ	jan	jarn	jaan	jann
zhang	jang	chang	ㄓㄤ	jang	jarng	jaang	janq
zhao	jau	chao	ㄓㄠ	jau	jaur	jao	jaw
zhe	je	che	ㄓㄜ	je	jer	jee	jeh
zhei	jei	chei	ㄓㄟ	jei	jeir	jeei	jey
zhen	jen	chen	ㄓㄣ	jen	jern	jeen	jenn
zheng	jeng	cheng	ㄓㄥ	jeng	jerng	jeeng	jenq

PY	YALE	WG	ZYFH	1	ROMATZYH 2	3	4
zhi	jr	chih	ㄓ	jy	jyr	jyy	jyh
zhong	jung	chung	ㄓㄨㄥ	jong	jorng	joong	jonq
zhou	jou	chou	ㄓㄡ	jou	jour	joou	jow
zhu	ju	chu	ㄓㄨ	ju	jwu	juu	juh
zhua	jwa	chua	ㄓㄨㄚ	jua	jwa	joa	juah
zhuai	jwai	chuai	ㄓㄨㄞ	juai	jwai	joai	juay
zhuan	jwan	chuan	ㄓㄨㄢ	juan	jwan	joan	juann
zhuang	jwang	chuang	ㄓㄨㄤ	juang	jwang	joang	juanq
zhui	jwei	chui	ㄓㄨㄟ	juei	jwei	joei	juey
zhun	jwun	chun	ㄓㄨㄣ	juen	jwen	joen	juenn
zhuo	jwo	cho	ㄓㄨㄛ	juo	jwo	juoo	juoh
zi	dz	tzu	ㄗ	tzy	tzyr	tzyy	tzyh
zong	dzung	tsung	ㄗㄨㄥ	tzong	tzorng	tzoong	tzonq
zou	dzou	tsou	ㄗㄡ	tzou	tzour	tzoou	tzow
zu	dzu	tsu	ㄗㄨ	tzu	tzwu	tzuu	tzuh
zuan	dzwan	tsuan	ㄗㄨㄢ	tzuan	tzwan	tzoan	tzuann
zui	dzwei	tsui	ㄗㄨㄟ	tzuei	tzwei	tzoei	tzuey
zun	dzwun	tsun	ㄗㄨㄣ	tzuen	tzwen	tzoen	tzuenn
zuo	dzwo	tso	ㄗㄨㄛ	tzuo	tzwo	tzuoo	tzuoh